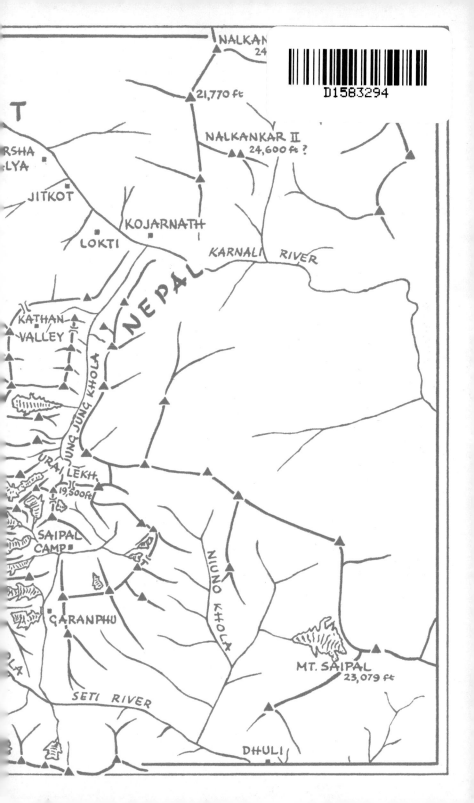

PRISONER IN RED TIBET

Prisoner in Red Tibet

SYDNEY WIGNALL
LEADER THE WELSH HIMALAYAN
EXPEDITION 1955

HUTCHINSON OF LONDON

HUTCHINSON & CO. (*Publishers*) LTD
178–202 Great Portland Street, London, W.1

London Melbourne Sydney
Auckland Bombay Toronto
Johannesburg New York

First published July 1957
Second impression August 1957

*Set in eleven point Fournier Old Face, one point
leaded, and printed in Great Britain
by The Anchor Press, Ltd.,
Tiptree, Essex*

DEDICATED TO

Gin-Din-Rhou, Abbot of Jitkot Lamasery, Tibet, and Chungnya, a young soldier of the Chinese Army.
Although they could not speak my language, by their friendship and understanding they helped me to maintain my faith in humanity during the bitterest moments of my despair.
Also to Jean, my wife, who, though she had only to sit and wait, had by far the harder part to play.

CONTENTS

7

CONTENTS

ILLUSTRATIONS

9

FOREWORD

The 1955 Welsh Himalayan Expedition to the West Nepal Himalaya (Api-Nampa-Saipal ranges) was not the product of a large organization, nor a national committee, nor was it financed by any trust or foundation. It was simply a private venture, sponsored by the Mountaineering Club of North Wales of which I was privileged to be secretary.

In April 1954 the club committee gave me a float of about £5, which was promptly converted into some very pretty Himalayan note-paper, and a few sheets of $2\frac{1}{2}d.$ stamps. That was the beginning.

From that moment on, our great problem was the raising of the necessary £2,400. We were rich in enthusiasm but woefully poor in material wealth. The members of the team were chosen; some because of their Alpine and other qualifications; others because they possessed a good sense of humour and were temperamentally suited to the conditions attendant on such an expedition. In the case of Harrop and myself, we suffered the great handicap of having no Alpine experience. Our climbing had been restricted to our home hills. But that did not deter us, for both Harrop and I had long held the opinion that a crack Alpine style and technique, however useful, was no substitute for sound common sense and a ready appreciation of an immediate difficulty. Some of the continental expeditions, both pre-war and post-war, that boasted the finest climbers their countries could produce, had also suffered the highest casualty rates. We had already decided that we were not going to be too ambitious. We had no reputations to lose.

When choosing our team, financial means were ignored, with the result that the maximum amount of hard cash the six members of the team could produce was less than £300, leaving us £2,100 short of our minimum target. I was forced to look elsewhere for finance and several trust funds were approached but without success. In the meantime, due to the kind co-operation of the Royal Geographical Society, three members of the expedition were trained in topographical survey. For this we are indebted to L. P. Kirwan, Director of the R.G.S., and Professor Stephenson, Instructor in Survey. The R.G.S. also supplied us with a photo-michroptic-theodolite, plane tables and aneroids. I then placed the survey programme in the hands of John Harrop, who is a B.Sc. Leeds University. He was, in fact, the only member of the party who had a university background. Our application for a permit to climb and explore in West Nepal was approved by the expeditions committee of the R.G.S. With this backing we approached our own Foreign Office, who gained for us the much-desired permit. With the financial problem unsolved we went to private industry for support and received the majority of our Himalayan equipment. Still and cine-cameras, foodstuffs, etc., either as an outright gift or at generous concession rates.

My last resort for financial support was, of course, the Press. So I approached a well-known provincial newspaper, the *Liverpool Daily Post*. It is, of course, common knowledge that many expeditions have been partly or wholly financed by newspapers. Most notable of all was the very commendable and public-spirited relationship between the Everest expeditions and *The Times*. There was, however, a possibility that one might fall into the wrong hands. A friendly conversation with the general manager and the managing director of the *Liverpool Daily Post* destroyed any fears I might have had. They were very interested in the first Welsh Himalayan Expedition; primarily because the *Post* enjoyed a very large circulation in North Wales, and because of its long association with Welsh affairs. Further to this, the *Liverpool Daily Post* was not interested in gaining a sensational story. They were interested in a plain straightforward narrative, and if the expedition was primarily concerned with geographical work then that was all to the good.

Thereafter we were sponsored by the *Liverpool Daily Post*, which was at that time celebrating its centenary year. It was an association for which we were extremely grateful and which we have never had any cause to regret.

When the *Post* learnt of our arrest by the Chinese, they made every effort to persuade officialdom to make immediate protests to the Chinese Government. The story goes—so I was told on my return—that the general manager picked up the telephone and said: 'Our boys are in prison in Tibet. Get me the Dalai Lama right away.' The fact that the switchboard operator in Lhasa might speak only Cantonese or Mandarin Chinese did not deter him, and the attempt to speak to Lhasa was only given up when it was discovered that Tibet was not on the 'phone. An effort was also made to talk to the Chinese Foreign Affairs Department in Peking, but Communist China would not accept the call. That we were released in two months, and were the first Europeans, it seems, to come out of Communist China in less than three years, is due in no small part to the efforts made by our own Foreign Office and the Governments of Nepal and India. To them we owe our gratitude, our freedom and perhaps our lives.

When, on December 28th, the Chinese announced that Harrop, Suwal and myself had been released, seventeen days earlier, on the northern approaches of the great Himalayan barrier, since when nothing had been heard of us, there was great anxiety for our safety. The *Liverpool Daily Post* even went to the lengths of trying to charter a helicopter to search for us amongst the high snow-filled valleys and passes of the Nepal-Tibet frontier region. A well-known Himalayan explorer was to accompany the pilot—if a pilot hare-brained enough could be found. The only safe way to send a helicopter into the West Nepal Himalaya would be to take it apart and send the pieces in on the backs of Dhoti porters. One of our main obstacles on the way back was the 19,500-feet Urai Lekh pass, crossed on December 16th. The average helicopter ceiling is about 19,000 feet. Fortunately for all concerned, a suitable helicopter could not be found.

The reader might, when reading the latter chapters dedicated to our 200-mile winter journey back from Tibet, be left with the impression that it was a serious, grim and very perilous undertaking. Maybe it was. But it didn't seem like that to Harrop and Suwal and myself at the time. There was not one situation, however difficult, that we did not make light of with some joke or other. I remember most vividly the moment on December 18th when we realized that the latter part of the track through the Seti gorge was impassable. We stopped by the edge of the river, knowing full well that we would have to go in and wade down between those awful canyon-like walls, not knowing if the fast-flowing river would be too deep for us, burdened as we were with our heavy loads. We didn't even know if we could get out at the other end. Harrop put his hand on my shoulder and bellowed in my ear, trying to make himself heard above the deafening roar of the river, 'Up the creek, and without a ruddy paddle.' He was grinning when he said it. It was getting dark and the air temperature was zero F.

I realize now that it was a sense of humour that kept us going.

Finally, my thanks are due to all those who helped to make the expedition possible. They are too many to mention by name, but they earned and receive our heartfelt gratitude.

SYDNEY WIGNALL

Chapter 1

BASE CAMP

THE weather forecast from Radio Delhi could not have been more discouraging. 'A depression over the United Provinces is moving towards the Api-Saipal region and winds of 30 to 40 knots at 10,000 feet and above can be expected.' Somebody at the other side of the mess tent cursed as I switched off the radio.

The date was October 16th, 1955—my birthday—and what a birthday! We had come to the mountains of West Nepal to climb and survey, and had spent most of the last three weeks camp-bound due to heavy, out-of-season snowfall. And now, two hours before, Harrop and Roberts, our two surveyors, had returned exhausted after a day plodding through thigh-deep snow, the photo-theodolite gone, lost under a gigantic avalanche. My two companions had escaped with their lives by a matter of seconds. Measuring out a base line when the avalanche fell, they had managed to get clear with only feet to spare.

It was dark now and I lit a candle in order to continue writing my diary. Henson was busy cooking dinner and, having finished, he yelled outside to the other members of the expedition to 'Come and get it!'

One by one they filed into our mess tent and sat down on packing-cases, knife and fork in hand. Of the original party of six, only five remained. In addition to myself there were John Harrop, a twenty-eight-year-old scientist from Bangor; George Dwyer, a professional mountaineering guide, who at forty-six was the oldest member of the party, and John Henson, also a professional guide, who had been climbing with Dwyer for over twenty years. They were both tough, hard-working and resolute. The last of the five was Geoffrey Roberts, a twenty-seven-year-old schoolteacher from my home town of Colwyn Bay, North Wales.

The absent friend was Humfrey Berkeley, whom I had sent back to the Nepalese town of Chainpur, nine days' march away, to hire the twenty porters needed to carry our equipment out of the Hima-layas to Pithoragarh, in the United Provinces of India. Berkeley had departed travelling light and accompanied by only one porter. Here, at base camp, we still had four permanent men: our sirdar Koila and three others—Ratti, Ungya and Giddy.

We ate our meal beneath umbrellas, to stave off the constant streams of water running through the holes in our tarpaulin roof. The mess tent, in fact, was not a tent at all. It was simply one of half a dozen roofless, circular stone shelters used by Tibetan salt traders who crossed the 19,500-feet Urai Lekh pass, six miles or so to the north. We had covered the shelter with a tarpaulin secured at the apex by a rope stretched across and tied to two upright sticks. The melting snow had discovered all the weaknesses in our covering and hardly a square foot of the interior remained dry. Harrop, Roberts and I slept in here, the others spending the night in three cotton/nylon, Everest-pattern Meade tents pitched outside.

The last to enter was our young Nepalese liaison officer, eighteen-year-old Damodar Narayan Suwal, from Khatmandu. Damodar, a college student, undertook the venturesome task of liaison officer to expeditions during his vacation. That same year, in the pre-monsoon season, he had accompanied the Kenya expedition in their attempt on Himal-Chuli in Central Nepal.

On the advice of many who had visited the Himalayas before, we decided on the post-monsoon period, which, although colder, usually guaranteed fine weather. In that we had been unlucky, and were right in the middle of what Radio Delhi described as the worst weather in recorded history. Every night we heard on the radio more and more of the dreadful damage and suffering that flooding had caused on the plains of India.

Up here at Saipal,[1] 14,000 feet above sea level, it snowed every day for more than three weeks, and now, after a month at base camp, we were almost completely snowed in. The porters' dome tent, having collapsed under the weight of snow, had been abandoned. We set these shivering, frightened fellows up in another stone shelter and covered it with the remains of the tent.

Our activities at Saipal had been further restricted by the absence, for nearly three weeks, of base-camp porters due to the desertion of our original three two days after our arrival. Terrified of being trapped on the northern side of the Seti gorge, they had fled without even asking for baksheesh—a rare, if not unique, occurrence. Forced to send Koila back to Chainpur for replacements, he returned nineteen days later with the men we now had with us. During those nineteen days we had been forced to do our own carrying in snow that was never less than knee deep and which sometimes reached up to the waist.

---

[1] Saipal camping ground in the upper reaches of the Seti valley is not to be confused with the 23,079-feet mountain of the same name.

Exhausting and heartbreaking work, it destroyed all hope of attempting to climb either 23,000-feet Saipal or 24,062-feet Nalkankar. The latter, reputed to be the highest mountain in West Nepal, we had not yet seen, due to our inability to place a camp on the northern side of the 19,500-feet Urai Lekh pass. Harrop and Roberts took advantage of the slightest break in the weather to plot the position of some peak or other, but most of the time the tops remained shrouded in a dark blanket of snow-laden cloud. The first avalanche to fall near our base camp had been exciting to watch. Now we took them for granted, not even looking out of the doorway when they rushed downhill, with the noise of a dozen express trains. Two of these avalanches fell regularly to the right and left of our base-camp shelter; the one to the north cutting the track and completely blocking the course of the Seti river, which took two days to carve a tunnel through the avalanche cone. The one that fell at the other side of the camp discharged at regular intervals, usually at eleven o'clock in the morning. We called it 'The Saipal Express'.

On October 17th the snow ceased and the clouds cleared away. Either Delhi had been wrong or the predicted bad weather had not yet reached us. On the 18th it still remained fine and I resolved on a final reconnaissance before the porters arrived from Chainpur to take us out. Plans were discussed, and I decided that Harrop and I, accompanied by Damodar and our four porters, should try to set up a camp in the Jung Jung Khola, at the other side of the Urai Lekh, in an effort to fill in the blank space on the Indian survey map corresponding to that area. Most important of all, we were eager to check the story that there was, in fact, a summit higher than Nalkankar.

On October 19th it was still fine and the snow around base camp had begun to consolidate due to the day and night process of thawing and freezing. To help on the earlier part of the first day's march, Henson, Dwyer and Roberts volunteered to carry part of the porters' loads over what we thought would be most difficult terrain, the soft snow between 14,000 and 16,000 feet. Although unaware of it at the time, the snow conditions higher up were, for some strange reason, worse than at base camp.

Dwyer and Roberts went ahead, blazing a trail, followed by the porters, with the other members of the expedition in the rear. As we gained height, we realized that our hopes of firm snow at high altitude were to be disappointed and at 3 p.m. the other members of the party bade us farewell, setting off downhill. I reckoned we would be back in a few days, and we resumed our march towards the distant Urai.

B

At 5 p.m. we packed in for the night, estimating that we had covered more than half the distance to the top of the pass.

A month before, to the very day, Harrop and I had crossed the Urai when the ground was clear of snow, only three days after setting up our camp at Saipal. At that time the eight-mile trip to the top of the pass could be completed in not more than five hours. Now we had taken a full day to cover about six miles, but we felt sure that we would reach the top of the pass on the morrow and would camp well down on the other side. On the previous occasion, we had only descended the northern side of the pass by about 500 feet and had, to our disappointment, seen no sign of Nalkankar.

We pitched our two tents and cooked a meal of pemmican and meat blocks for ourselves and the four porters. They lacked enthusiasm for our concentrated high-altitude rations, preferring their tasteless and stodgy chupatties.

The weather holding the next morning, we resolved to cross the pass and get well down below the snowline before nightfall. Camping above the snowline meant melting snow for all cooking, and continuing to cook for seven people on Primus stoves would quickly exhaust our paraffin supplies.

Our sirdar Koila told us that a great many Tibetans used this route during the season and that we should be able to make excellent yak-dung fires once we reached the snow-free valley of the Jung Jung river. A party of Tibetans was at that moment camped only four miles or so south of our base-camp site. They had set up their trade post at Garanphu, waiting for the Dhotials from the nearest Nepalese village of Dhuli to bring tsampa flour to trade for the Tibetan rock salt. These Tibetans had told us that they had never experienced anything like the weather we had had at this time of the year, and that if it continued they and their herds of yaks and sheep would have to stay in Nepal until the spring of the following year.

We set out at daylight, Harrop, Damodar and I carrying part of the porters' loads to ease their work over the exhausting thigh-deep snow. The going was worse than on the previous day, and we sank some three feet at every step. After half an hour in front, I handed over to Harrop, thereafter changing by mutual consent whenever the one in front had had enough. Never in my life have I known such strenuous going, and the fact that we were carrying about 45 lb. each greatly increased the strain.

At midday I stopped and looked back. From the previous camp site a line of deep holes formed a continuous trench, and I thought longingly of a bulldozer. I shared out boiled sweets amongst the porters and encouraged them by enlarging upon the *baksheesh* that would be theirs once the job was done. They smiled and plodded wearily on. At five o'clock we had all had enough and dumped our loads in the snow. We had been on the march for more than eight hours and had covered less than half a mile! It didn't seem credible. I wondered whether we ought to give up and go back the following day, but the sight of the summit of the Urai Lekh only a mile and a half away spurred me on. We could at least climb to the top and have a look down the other side, and if the going didn't improve we would give up and return to Saipal.

As soon as the tents were pitched we ushered our four porters into their tent, pushing their sleeping-bags after them. Above the snowline we had to do everything for them, for they were like terrified children. They ate some tsampa flour mixed with tea while we dined off pemmican and meat blocks. It froze hard in the night and was bitterly cold. In the porters' tent little Ungya started crying and Koila, stalwart at all times, quickly shut him up. Then they started to sing in chorus. The sound of their voices on the still night air had a reassuring effect on all of us. I suggested that, at first light, we would have a scratch breakfast and while Harrop and Damadar packed the loads, I would start out ahead, travelling some 15 lb. lighter than the day before, and blaze a trail to the top of the pass. The sight of a reasonably firm path stretching well ahead might have a good effect on the morale of our porters.

In the morning I discovered that I had left all my camera equipment out all night, but, to my surprise, none of the shutters of the still cameras had been affected by the cold, although our 16-mm. cine-camera ran very slowly. The night temperature had been sub zero and at 7 a.m. it was only five degrees higher.

I began the wearisome task of breaking the trail, trying to make as much progress as possible before the sun began to soften the crisp surface of the snow. I had covered less than a hundred yards when I broke through the crust. It was thoroughly demoralizing. Two steps on the surface then a foot would break through and I would plunge in thigh deep. In my efforts to extricate myself, the other leg would go through and I would try to crawl out on my stomach. Sometimes the snow held, but often it collapsed under me, and underneath my blue windproofs my clothing was soaked with sweat.

After an hour I found the snow, though soft, less deep than before and I made better time. There was firm ground beneath my feet and the snow was less than knee deep. As there was no sign of anyone following, I sat down to rest. Then I recognized Harrop's figure, clad in the same blue cotton nylon outfit as myself. He was waving to me and I could faintly hear him shouting, asking me to return. The porters had gone on strike.

I cannot adequately describe my feelings of that moment. All my trail-blazing was for naught. Picking up my ice-axe, I started off downhill and, by taking advantage of my own tracks, reached camp in about fifteen minutes. Koila was sitting alone, while the other three porters were already on their way downhill about a hundred yards away. After much shouting and arguing they consented to return and we held a lengthy enquiry. But nothing would persuade them to go on under such hostile conditions, and after an hour of futile argument we gave up. Just as I was about to announce that we would return to Saipal, Harrop turned to the smallest porter, Ungya, and asked him why he refused to stay. To our surprise he replied that he had no wish to let us down and that he would stay if the others would do the same. This caused the other two to curse him roundly, and we then discovered that Ungya had instigated the plot and had talked the others into striking. Ratti and Giddy declared that if Ungya could stick it then they could. Picking up their loads, they set off for the pass, vowing never to be influenced by the little man again. Ungya, it was evident, was thoroughly frightened and had no wish to make the trip back to base camp alone. We had no more porter trouble after that.

At midday we stood on the summit of the pass, looking down its northern side into the snow-filled upper reaches of the Jung Jung Khola. The right-hand side of the valley was walled in by a twelve-mile-long barrier of limestone peaks, all covered with thick snow. There was hardly a break anywhere in this austere curtain of precipitous rock faces. On the left, some small valleys ran down into the Khola. One of these was the exit of the northern branch of the 'hidden valley'. We had discovered this valley on September 18th—Harrop's birthday—when we climbed a high snow col immediately to the west of the Urai Lekh, eagerly expecting to look down at any moment into the Tinkar valley, which drains away west into the Sacred Kali river and which marks the boundary between Nepal and India. But, to our surprise, we saw nothing of the Tinkar area. Instead, we had looked down a 3,000-feet vertical ice-covered face into the westernmost branch of the Seti valley, only a short distance from where our base camp was situated. The northern end of this 'hidden valley' terminated in a glacier, which rose up to a narrow col, and through the gap we could see yet another branch valley, this time draining to the north-west into the Jung Jung Khola. We were separated from the Tinkar valley by a barrier of snow-clad peaks and glacier-laden valleys flow-ing south and north. Once again the map was entirely inaccurate.

Our base-camp site at Saipal was surrounded by snow peaks ranging from 19,000 to 22,000 feet high, only one of which we could identify on the map, its name being Kapkot. Later, from a pass Dwyer and I had found to the east of our camp we had looked down into the Niuno Khola and identified 23,000-feet Mt. Saipal, its position being much closer to our base camp than the map would suggest.

For finding one's way around, a chart of the estuary of the river Conway would be just as useful as the quarter-inch Indian survey sheets of that part of West Nepal.

The most puzzling items were the positions shown on the map for the Tinkar and Urai passes and the Jung Jung Khola, for now, as we looked down the northern side of the Urai pass on October 21st, we saw not the Tibetan plateau, as shown on the map, but the Jung Jung Khola, which again according to the map should have started to the west, the Tinkar pass marking its head. One thing was certain— the Jung Jung Khola was situated more to the east than the map position suggested, and the Tinkar pass was many miles away to the west, separated from us by about sixteen miles of high mountain barrier. Another thing was sure—the Jung Jung Khola emptied into the Karnali river in Tibet immediately opposite the town of Kojarnath and did not point towards Taklakot. Even without a theodolite we could still take compass bearings and photographs, and I reflected that on this final reconnaissance we would in all probability discover more about the landscape of the border area of Nepal and Tibet than we had during our entire month's stay in the Seti valley. The urge to find out what lies at the 'other side of the hill' is one that anyone endowed with even a modicum of adventurous spirit cannot resist. The ex-ploration that we had set out to do might, when completed, be con-sidered so insignificant as to lie in some scientific body's pigeon-hole forever undisturbed, but to Harrop and me it meant a great deal. I for one would never be able to afford to visit the Himalaya again— therefore I was determined that the first Welsh Himalayan expedition should produce something of lasting value, even if only a few alterations to the map.[1]

[1] See map—endpaper.

Chapter 2

INTO THE JUNG JUNG KHOLA

W HEN the porters had rested, we started off down the northern side of the Urai Lekh. As this side receives the full force of the cold winds that sweep down from the Tibetan plateau, the snow at this point was iron hard. The steep track down which Harrop and I had ambled a month before was now a vertiginous slope, and we were forced to spend weary hours cutting steps for the porters. Harrop took the lead, cutting steps that suited his length of stride, while I followed hacking out intermediate footholds for the porters. For the last fifty feet or so we all glissaded, our four Dhoties enjoying the thrill immensely.

Once away from the shadowed confines of the head of the pass we suffered abominably in the sun-softened snow that stretched ahead for several miles. Harrop, Damodar and I forged ahead, halting, at 4 p.m., in the shadow near a low stone wall that had been built by traders. I put on an extra sweater and a down-filled jacket, but it made little difference. An icy wind cut through like a knife as we waited for the porters to arrive with the tents. We stamped around in the snow for half an hour and were numb with cold when our men finally arrived. Handicapped by frozen fingers, we struggled with tent guys, and, because we had to melt snow for the purpose, cooking proved a tedious business. It was 7 p.m. when we crawled into our sleeping-bags.

The next morning we limited breakfast to tea, intending to cook a better meal once we got beyond the snow. We set off at 7 a.m., to discover, to our surprise and dismay, that the snow here was almost as bad as on the other side of the Lekh. This was due to the fact that we had to traverse a section of completely flat valley bottom where, for some three-quarters of a mile, the snow lay in drifts. Harrop and I took it in turns to lead, reaching the far side of the flat stretch only when we were absolutely fatigued.

Here the valley narrowed and turned slightly north-east through a narrow neck, then it widened again and to our delight we saw running water. Koila broke the ice at the side of the stream and filled a billycan. Then we all retired to a house-size boulder and set up the Primus for another brew of tea. The short distance we had covered had taken nearly three hours. By some mistake we had come this far carrying three extra enamel plates and a spring balance that were completely superfluous. Digging a hole in the snow, we buried them at the side of the boulder, intending to retrieve them a few days later. Then we set off again, wearily plodding through deep snow until we passed two lakes.[1] On our left soared majestic ice-covered peaks, which, Harrop commented drily, must be a mirage, as, according to the map, we should have been standing on a bleak, stone-covered plateau, with an uninterrupted view of Tibetan villages and the Karnali river to the north. At 3 p.m. the snow began to thin out and patches of bare ground appeared. The wearying part of our journey lay behind us. Henceforth the going would be much easier.

We turned a corner to find the ground completely snow free, and Koila pointed to a low circle of stones lying about fifty feet below the track.

'Tharedunga, Sahib,' he cried.

Tharedunga was indeed marked on the map, and the Tinkar Lipu pass was shown running down to it from the west. Westwards there was, in fact, a valley opposite, filled with the moraine debris of long-since-extinct glaciers. Its far wall rose sheer and vertical for a couple of thousand feet, and there was no pass into the Tinkar valley there. A great glistening snow peak, very similar in shape to Everest, bounded one wall of this valley and this we named 'Tharedunga Ata'. There was an exit leading due north, but it could only lead, not into Nepal, but out on to the Tibetan plateau. The Tinkar pass was nowhere near the place marked on the map. In fact, as we discovered later, it is situated several miles away to the west and does not run into the Jung Jung Khola at all. A few yards farther on we came to a flat camping ground and set up camp for the night. It was still early and there was marching time left, but we were completely spent after the severe snow conditions of the morning.

Here we were able to conserve our precious paraffin supplies, our porters cooking dinner on a brushwood and yak-dung fire. The next day's march, our last, would also be a short one, and we hoped to set up camp at a place called Kalapani, from where we intended to make one or two general reconnaissances to map out the mountain valley systems that were spread around us. We had not yet caught so much as a glimpse of Nalkankar, and were beginning to wonder if it did, in fact, exist.

Our final march on October 23rd took us past a huge 3,000-feet-high limestone cliff closely resembling the Marmolata in the Dolomites. Its red and orange buttresses and chimneys soared above us

---

[1] Neither of which is marked on the Indian Survey Map.

and we walked along mentally selecting possible climbing routes. It was not a healthy place in which to loiter as the newly shattered rock debris on the track testified.

After an hour's pleasant meandering along a fine straight path we dropped down to the river's edge and came to a small but finely made bridge. Ahead the track curved upwards across a scree slope and Koila pointed to a spot where a tree grew at the bottom of a tall cliff, high on the hillside.

'There is Kalapani, Sahib. There we make a final camp.'

Koila had for many years used this route to trade with the Tibetans in the Taklakot area and was well acquainted with the local terrain. The Jung Jung river, he pointed out, now flowed into an impenetrable gorge, emerging again some five miles away where it flowed into the Karnali river, immediately opposite Kojarnath. The only escape from the Jung Jung Khola lay over the Kathan pass, several hundred feet above and to the west of our new camp site. Beyond the pass lay the valley of Kathan and the first of the Tibetan villages.

Europeans travelling farther north than this camp site risked running into the Chinese Communist troops stationed at Taklakot, of whom there were supposed to be about 200—a most erroneous estimate of the actual number, as we were to discover.[1]

At 11 a.m. we reached Kalapani and spent half an hour clearing away sufficient stones to pitch our tents. At our backs rose the great sheer cliff, while, in front, the ground fell away steeply until it made the final plunge to the bed of the river several hundred feet below. There was any amount of dried yak dung about and we soon had a fine fire going. The journey from Saipal had taken us five days—five days to cover a bare seventeen miles. Under normal conditions the Tibetans cover the journey from Kathan village to Saipal in two days. I was concerned about the food situation. If the weather conditions for the return trip showed no improvement we possessed only sufficient food, European and native, to reach Saipal base camp if we started back that same day.

We had managed on about 2,000 calories a day from Saipal to Kalapani, and for such arduous journeying we needed double that amount. I asked Koila if he was prepared to stay here for a few days and risk getting back to Saipal on short commons. This time the decision lay with him and his three porter friends, for in a matter of

---

[1] There are approximately 4,000 Chinese regular troops in the Taklakot area—and more garrisoned to the north-east and at Gartok—the residence of the Governor of West Tibet.

such importance we had no right to force any decision upon them. Koila, head on knees, thought hard for several moments. Having no wish to hurry him, we resumed our conversation concerning the whereabouts of Nalkankar, which we should have been able to see from our position.

After a short conversation with Ratti, Koila said: 'Four miles away, Sahib, at the other side of the pass, is the village of Kathan. I have traded there and know the head of the house, old Phrupa, very well. If I go there with Ratti we can buy about 50 lb. of atta or tsampa. Then our problem will be solved.'

Seeking further assurance, I asked Damodar's advice. As Nepalese liaison officer, the say should be his, and we asked if there was danger of our men getting into trouble.

'On the contrary,' Damodar replied. 'There is an agreement between my government and the Peking Government to the effect that Nepalese nationals have free access into Tibet for trade, and for pilgrimage to Lake Manasarowar and to Kailas.'

Reassured, I handed Koila a bundle of rupee notes and, at noon, he and Ratti set off up the track that led to the top of the Kathan pass, promising to return the following afternoon. They were to return all right, but not the following afternoon, and by no means as they anticipated.

We spent the rest of the day sorting out our photographic equipment for the morrow's reconnaissance, and I polished up the most treasured item of all, the 36-mm. telephoto lens for my Edixa reflex-camera. If Nalkankar had a higher and unknown summit, with that lens I should practically sit on the top of it.

Sleep proved difficult as the tent was pitched on a slope and, being on the outside, I suffered the combined pressure of both Damodar and Harrop against me all night.

On the 24th Harrop and I left camp early and toiled to the top of the pass to look for a good viewpoint. With us came the tiny, bow-legged Ungya carrying our 16-mm. turret lens cine-camera and all my telephoto lenses.

It was a dreadful track, scored with sharp angular stones which shot from beneath the feet when trodden on. Harrop and I quickly deserted the recognized path and scrambled up some smooth slabs that rose alongside. Higher up the angle eased and we traversed a pleasant little hollow filled with tiny prickly whinberries. The rock track gave place to pleasant grass slopes interspersed with patches of bare soil. To the left rose a great rock peak, its upper reaches sheathed in ice. This was part of the barrier that stretched back to the Urai Lekh. On the right or northern side of our pass rose a light-brown limestone peak and, as it offered a good viewpoint, we headed for it.

A steep scramble over relatively easy terrain brought us to the rock face, easy to climb and covered with wonderful jug-handle type holds. Harrop, the first up, uttered an exclamation of surprise as he looked over the top. Standing beside him, I looked north, out across the Tibetan plateau. As a viewpoint it lacked nothing. All that we had come to see was there. Down on the left was the valley of Kathan and on the far slopes we saw the four seemingly miniature houses that made up the village. The landscape ahead was dominated by the majestic massif of Gurla Mandhata, 25,350 feet, its great south precipice looking most forbidding. But other easier and less awesome ridges ran down towards Taklakot, parallel with the shores of the sacred lake of Manasarowar, concealed from us by a high escarpment.

Taklakot was somewhere in the foreground, but there was nothing to distinguish the place from the monotonous brown of the plain. Taklakot is the administrative centre of the province of Purang, itself part of the greater province of Ngari Korsum, the capital of which is Gartok, from 90 to 100 miles to the north. Before the advent of the Chinese Communists, the Tibetans had been ruled by the Garpon at Gartok, recognized as the highest dignitary in the area. Like all Tibetan towns, Taklakot had its Dzongpen, an official equivalent to that of a county sheriff or magistrate, who was at all times under the authority of the Garpon. What changes the Chinese had made we did not know, but our darkness in this matter, as in many others, was soon to be enlightened.

Purang's main claim to fame is, of course, the lake of Manasarowar, sacred to all Hindus. It was natural when Europeans first heard mention of this wonderful place that some adventurous spirits sought to travel to it. The first, William Moorcroft, reached the lake in 1812. In 1846 came Colonel Henry Strachey, whose description of the lake still ranks as a classic of its kind. In 1897 A. H. Savage Landor[1] entered both West Nepal and Tibet illegally and after many adventures was captured by the Tibetan authorities, taken to Taklakot and tortured, escaping over the Indian border to the south after a brief imprisonment.

In 1905 C. A. Sherring,[2] a British Government agent, made an official visit to both Taklakot and Gartok by way of the Lipu Lekh

---

[1] *Tibet and Nepal*, by A. H. Savage Landor (1905).
[2] *Western Tibet and the British Borderland*, by C. A. Sherring (1906).

pass. He was accompanied by the well-known Himalayan explorer, Dr. T. G. Longstaff,[1] who, while Sherring attended to his official duties, took with him the two Swiss guides, the brothers Brocherell, and made a lightweight attack on 25,355-feet Gurla Mandhata. The trio achieved the notable feat of ascending nearly 4,500 feet in a day, but an avalanche caused them to make a speedy descent to the Gurla glacier, 3,000 feet below. They finally abandoned their attempt on the west face at a height of about 23,500 feet. In the same year, a young British officer, now General Gausson, visited Taklakot and was attacked by brigands at the foot of the hill where the Dzongpen's fort is situated. Left for dead, he and his porters were cared for by local villagers and were soon able to resume their journey to Manasarowar.

In 1936 the Swiss scientists, Heim and Gannser,[2] entered the Tinkar valley of Nepal and carried out a theodolite survey of the surrounding mountain peaks. While camped in the valley, Gannser crossed the Tinkar Lipu pass and entered Tibet. By-passing some disused buildings which his porters called Tharcdunga, he journeyed to Jitkot Monastery and had tea with the Lamas, who proved to be extremely friendly. It seems that there are, in fact, two places named Tharedunga and that the Indian surveyors, without travelling over either the Tinkar or Urai passes, assumed that there was only one and placed it, according to the native lore of the upper Seti valley, in the Jung Jung Khola. This would explain why the Tinkar pass is shown as issuing out into the Jung Jung Khola, which, in fact, is not the case. Heim and Gannser were later arrested by Nepalese officials and sent back over the Kali river into India. The only blot on Heim and Gannser's work from a mountaineer's point of view was that they mistook Api for Nampa and called Nampa the Chisel peak. We can forgive them for that.

In the same year Herbert Tichy,[3] a twenty-three-year-old Austrian student, crossed the Lipu Lekh into Tibet disguised as a dumb Indian religious mendicant intent on visiting the sacred lake. While staying at Taklakot Monastery for a few days he narrowly escaped detection. Later he made an attempt on Gurla Mandhata accompanied by only one Sherpa and was forced to give up the attempt at about the same height as Longstaff. He then set off to make the circuit of the holy mountain Kailas, and so good was his disguise that he was befriended

[1] *This My Voyage*, by T. G. Longstaff.
[2] *Throne of the Gods*, by Heim and Gannser.
[3] *Tibetan Adventure*, by Herbert Tichy.

by a Tibetan official who invited him to join his party. Tichy, greatly daring, accepted the offer, and his true identity was never discovered.

Not until 1944 did Europeans pass that way again, and this time the travellers were bent, not on exploration, but on escape from British India. Heinrich Harrer[1] and Peter Aufschneiter, members of the Nanga Parbat reconnaissance of 1939, had been interned at the outbreak of World War II. In 1944, escaping from a prisoner-of-war camp at Dehra Dun, they crossed the frontier into Tibet intent on making their way to Lhasa, achieving their goal after many adventures and a very arduous journey. Although Harrer and Aufschneiter did not visit Taklakot proper, they passed along the shores of Lake Manasarowar on their way east.

With so much to engage the world's attention, the land of mystery, Tibet, was forgotten. But it came to mind sharply with the Communist invasion of 1950 and the knowledge that the Chinese had taken possession. The following year Harrer emerged to tell his moving and enthralling story of his life in Tibet and the enduring friendship that had sprung up between himself and the young Dalai Lama. I still regard Harrer's story as my favourite travel book.

In 1953 W. H. Murray and J. Tyson entered the Tinkar valley intent on reconnoitring Mt. Api, 23,400 feet high. They also tried to find a pass connecting the Tinkar with the Seti valley, but failing to find a feasible route across the intervening mountain barrier, they turned north in search of another route by which they could complete their intended circumnavigation of the whole of the Api and Nampa ranges of West Nepal.

They crossed the Tinkar Lipu pass, skirted the mountain slopes to the east, entered the Jung Jung Khola and crossed the Urai Lekh into the Seti valley. They saw no sign of habitation, but, at night on one of their final marches, they saw a horseman ride by and heard a dog barking. Although they did not know it at the time, they were passing Kathan village, the track passing within a hundred yards of the four houses.

'If you want Nalkankar,' Harrop said, 'there it is.'

I looked to the north-east and there, in truth, it was. There were far more peaks than the map suggested, and the one marked at 24,062 feet was certainly not the highest. The highest was nearer to us and its height could not be far short of 25,000 feet. I wound up the clockwork motor on the cine-camera and took a long series of runs of the main skyline. Then I fitted up the 36-cm. telephoto lens

[1] *Seven Years in Tibet*, by Heinrich Harrer.

and took a 180-degree panorama with my Edixa reflex-camera, Harrop in the meantime jotting down compass bearings.

The limestone peak commanded the final part of the Jung Jung Khola, invisible from our camp site at Kalapani. Straight ahead, about five miles away, framed in the sides of the gorge, was the Tibetan town of Kojarnath, distinguished by its trinity of great red monasteries. Harrop took another round of pictures with his own camera and I focussed my telephoto lens on the village of Kathan. Someone was discernible in a small field near the largest house; a Tibetan driving a few yaks. The track from the Kathan pass ran steeply down the Tibetan side, levelling off by the banks of a small river. There was a bridge, and then the track vanished into a shallow gully, to reappear on a small plateau, threading a few small fields until it reached the houses.

The brown and purple hillside behind the houses was cut by long straight horizontal lines, denoting the leets dug to funnel the glacier water of the snow peaks down to the handkerchief-size fields.

We sat until late afternoon waiting for Koila and Ratti, but we waited in vain. Disheartened, we returned to our camp, anxious lest they had suffered an accident or fallen foul of the Chinese. The other porters voiced the opinion that the Tibetans at Kathan might not have had the quantity of flour we required, in which case Koila and Ratti would have to wait while the Tibetans sent a man to another village.

Back at camp we sorted out some fossils Harrop had collected near the summit of the pass. We were happily ignorant of the fact that those harmless-looking pieces of stone were to cause us a great deal of trouble and heartache in the very near future. It is on such insignificant, chance-found objects that a man's freedom—even his life—can be sentenced away.

Chapter 3

ENTER THE PEOPLES' LIBERATION ARMY

I SPENT most of that night being squeezed against the side of the tent by Harrop and Damodar, and for me morning came none too soon. Little by little the sunlight crept across the valley and stole along the cliff face above until it bathed our tiny Meade tent in its resplendent glow.

Already fully dressed, I struggled through the tunnel entrance and donned a pair of boots. Ungya and Giddy were still asleep and I roused them to go and fetch some water. Our fireplace was at the foot of a tiny tree growing by the cliff face and I busied myself with a few twigs and a heap of dried yak dung. Using our air mattress inflater as a bellows, I soon had a good fire going and made a large brew of tea.

My thoughts strayed to the relative luxury of our base camp at Saipal, where to hand were soup, dehydrated meat, potatoes, cabbage, dehydrated gooseberries or apples and evaporated milk. In comparison with our monotonous diet of pemmican and chupatties they fared sumptuously. How I hated chupatties! But I consoled myself with the thought that there would be little more of this sort of thing. There had been no snow since we left base camp and, with a little luck, the snow conditions around the Urai Lekh would be so improved as to allow us to make the return trip.

Damodar pushed his face through the tent entrance and asked what day it was. Some mental reckoning was necessary before I could tell him that it was October 25th. I expressed my anxiety about the non-arrival of Koila and Ratti, but Damodar was unconcerned.

'What would happen,' I asked, 'if a Chinese patrol visited Kathan while they were there?'

'Our men are Nepalese,' Damodar replied confidently. 'They have every right to trade freely with Tibet. That has been agreed with Peking.'

'I know. But what will happen if the Chinese discover that our men are with a Europen party? We're in the region of an undemarcated frontier.'

'We are in the mountains at a height of 16,000 feet,' Damodar reminded me, 'and the Chinese have never been known to go up into the hills. Besides, do not the British and Chinese Governments preserve good diplomatic relationships?'

This was true, and Damodar's confidence seemed quite justified. But Koila and Ratti had been absent for two days, and I could discover no adequate reason for their delayed return.

After breakfast I sat outside the door of the tent writing up my diary. Harrop was using up the last of our native flour in an effort to make oatmeal cakes, and Damodar was helping him to the extent of eating every other one, after plastering it with the contents of our three remaining tins of jam. Ungya and Giddy were gathering dried yak dung to make another fire on which to cook their chupatties. Every so often Ungya would walk a few paces away from the cliff face and look up the track to see if there was any sign of Koila and Ratti. Seeing nothing, he would return to his fire to slap out more chupatties. He was very glum when Koila wasn't there to mother him.

The track, visible from where I sat, was a rock-strewn pathway zigzagging uphill until lost to sight round a bend. I was busy writing when I heard the sound of stones being dislodged beyond the bend. I looked up. Someone was coming down, but he had not yet turned the corner. I waited, but saw nothing. Returning to my diary, I was disturbed by Ungya who came and sat beside me, looking apprehensive. There was still no one on the track. Or was there?

Extracting a pair of binoculars from my rucksack, I focussed them on the highest part of the track, to detect small brown figures hopping from boulder to boulder down the track. I counted one—two—three. All told there were five of them.

As they drew nearer my heart began to pound and my mouth felt dry. There was no mistaking them now. Clad in khaki quilted cotton uniforms, some wore ordinary army boots, others very smart-looking rubber and canvas basket-ball boots. As they descended there was a constant clatter of stones, punctuated by the sound of metal striking metal as their Tommy guns and magazine bandoliers jangled together on shoulder-straps.

They even carried canvas holders containing stick or 'potato masher' grenades.

Although John and Damodar were now aware that all was not well, their view was obstructed by the small tree growing out of the rock face.

'Who is it?' Harrop asked.

'Only the Peoples' Liberation Army,' I replied.

Damodar, his mouth full of oatcake, was unable to speak.

'They've chosen a bad time to call,' Harrop said, not even looking up. 'We haven't enough of these things to go round as it is, let alone feed visitors.'

I felt helpless. It was impossible to make a run for it. We could only sit it out, hoping—even then, I felt, vainly—for the best. Perhaps it was only a routine check up; perhaps they merely wished to confirm our presence was as innocent as, in fact, it was. All the same, it was an unexpected and unwelcome development, for we had it on the authority of the Governor of Baitadi that this spot was inside Nepal.

My thoughts were interrupted by the arrival of the Chinese.

The first one, bearing a Russian-style Tommy gun, ran straight past us, halted some twenty feet beyond our tents, squared up and cocked his gun. He regarded us blandly over the levelled barrel. Number two also ran past, to drop into a gully leading down to the river bank. He, too, aimed his gun. Number three climbed some broken rocks on to a ledge projecting from the cliff face above and sat, legs dangling, his Tommy gun aimed at my head.

These men, or youths—for none looked older than twenty-two— were well trained, adopting quickly a routine which had been worked out beforehand. Escape routes were cut off and we were well and truly in the bag.

The last two came down the track at an easier pace. Both were armed with automatic pistols and appeared to be of higher rank than the rest. The taller of the two took charge, smiled and held out his hand. Feeling that a friendly attitude was essential under such circumstances, I shook hands with him. He started to speak in Chinese and then in Tibetan, but I signified that we could speak neither language.

He looked less Chinese than the rest of them and, as Chinese go and by European standards, he wasn't bad looking. He overtopped my six feet by a good couple of inches. His plain khaki drill denim tunic and trousers contrasted with the padded uniforms of the others, which brought to mind pictures of the Chinese troops who had taken part in the Korean War.

His assistant, a weedy little youth, fidgeted around, nervously handling an automatic pistol that looked almost as big as himself. He wore pebble-lensed glasses and his little eyes were magnified out of all proportion to their true size.

Our linguistic efforts were interrupted by a group of Tibetans who had evidently been toiling in the wake of the Chinese. There was the usual rag-bag of sheepskin-clad, felt-booted, unwashed individuals followed by two who, because of their bearing and the cut of their clothes, stood out from the rest.

As they started conversing with the tall Chinaman, their compatriots proceeded to take our kit apart and go through it. The sight of these filthy individuals upending a kitbag containing hundreds of pounds' worth of cameras and telephoto lenses was too much for Harrop and me. As I yanked one Tibetan away from our food-box, another dived into the tunnel entrance of our Meade tent. I pulled him out by his felt boots, only to be tripped up by another of his compatriots who was making for Harrop's rucksack. Damodar, wise in Tibetan ways, decided that it was all in the hands of the gods and took the opportunity to make short work of the few remaining oatcakes.

When it was all over and the Tibetans, by weight of numbers, had won the day, our possessions were strewn all over the track. Our nomadic intruders then sat about in little groups examining everything item by item. The binoculars interested them the most and they fought for turns to look through the wrong end. What they saw must have impressed them, for they squealed with delight like children.

A word of command from the older of the two better-dressed Tibetans brought these depredations to an end. The hilarity ceased and the 'unwashed' withdrew, leaving us to tidy up the mess.

I had a good look at this old boy. His cloak was made of good quality, purple, Indian cloth, trimmed with silver and gold thread with a high fur collar. Around his waist was a belt of linked silver plates, from which hung an eighteen-inch silver dagger, its handle studded with semi-precious stones. His high felt hat was trimmed with fox fur and his leather riding-boots were far superior to the usual rope-soled sandals worn by the peasantry.

He came over to me and tried to converse, so I interrupted Damodar's gastronomical marathon and asked him to interpret for us.

The old gentleman (he appeared to be about sixty years old) spoke both Hindi and Nepali, and introduced himself as Gin-Din-Rhou, High Lama of Jitkot Lamasery. His friend, he said, was the headman of Taklakot.

One glance at the headman convinced me that I did not like him. He was dressed entirely in black from his hat to his boots, and his filthy face matched his apparel.

'When your two porters entered Kathan,' the old Lama said, 'the elder of the family living at the house of Phrupa kept your porters prisoners and sent a rider to Taklakot to inform the Chinese.'

From this I deduced that the local Tibetans could not be considered friendly to us and that they were loyal to the Chinese. But, as later events were to prove, I was wrong in this assumption. The Tibetans at Kathan were compelled to inform the Chinese. Tibetans are nomads and notorious gossips, and news spreads like wildfire. The Chinese would have learnt of our presence in the Jung Jung Khola within a matter of days, and the occupants of Kathan village would have found themselves in serious trouble had they failed to report our presence with the maximum speed.

'Ask the old boy what the Chinese intend to do,' Harrop said.

Damodar obliged and Gin-Din-Rhou had a long conversation with the tall Chinaman. Gin-Din-Rhou eventually replied, via Damodar.

'First let me explain who these Chinese are,' he said. 'The tall one is not an army officer, but the highest of all the Chinese in Takla-kot. He says that he wishes you well and would willingly allow you to go about your business, but he fears that his superior, the Chinese provincial governor at Gartok, might be annoyed if you were not brought in for questioning. Also he says that he must search you and your equipment, and he humbly apologizes for any inconvenience you might suffer.'

It was put so nicely that it was impossible to take offence. Through Damodar I asked the old man how long we would be detained, receiving the reply that we would be allowed to return perhaps within two or three days.

To test the sincerity of the Chinese I told him that we came from a country where friends did not point guns at one another. He smiled, exposing a beautiful set of sparkling white teeth, bowed courteously and snapped an order to his escort. Tommy guns were lowered and the pebble-lensed, weedy youth regretfully lowered his pistol.

The Lama Gin-Din-Rhou said, 'To save you embarrassment, the Chinese official suggests you show him whatever you have in your pockets, thus absolving him of the responsibility of searching your persons.'

We complied with this request little realizing what an immense favour the tall Chinese thought he was doing us. To the Chinese the greatest tragedy of all is to lose face, and the tall one, having apparently taken a liking to us, had decided to avoid humiliating us in front of the soldiers and Tibetans.

Our cameras, films, maps and other items were packed into a kit-bag and carried off in the direction of the Kathan pass, escorted by two soldiers. We struck camp, packed our rucksacks, and were doing so when we saw our two porters, Koila and Ratti, dejectedly descending the pass. Koila was in tears. As sirdar of our porters he considered he regarded himself as responsible for the two sahibs, and now he felt that he had been instrumental in bringing about our arrest by the Chinese.

I told Damodar to tell him that he was not to worry as it was not his fault. I was still under the naive impression that we were going to have a friendly lunch with the officers at Taklakot, to be quickly released with a cheery farewell. I was soon to be disillusioned.

I was compelled to reassess the position when Koila told us that he and Ratti had been beaten on the head and shoulders with Tommy-gun butts to make them tell where our camp site was.

I could hardly believe my ears, but one look at Koila's tear-filled eyes and I knew he was telling the truth.

We shouldered our rucksacks, picked up our ice-axes and started for the top of the Kathan pass.

Chapter 4

PHRUPA'S HOUSE

WE soon spaced out on the track. Harrop and I in front, Damodar somewhere behind and the porters bringing up the rear. I noticed that the old Lama and the headman of Taklakot stayed close to us all the time, perhaps because the Chinese had made them responsible for our behaviour.

After resting at the top of the pass, we descended the Tibetan side and were intrigued by the numerous cave dwellings dotted all over a cliff face a few hundred yards from Kathan village. Erosion over many years had scoured away the conglomerate cliff structure and the entrances of the caves were now many feet above ground level. There were no ladders and the caves appeared to have fallen into disuse.

The Tibetan side of the pass remains in shadow the greater part of the day and in consequence was covered with hard, consolidated snow. The two Tibetans scampered down this like a couple of seasoned mountaineers, the old man being much the faster of the two. At the bottom we reached the small bridge where the Tibetans had two ponies tethered. Gin-Din-Rhou and the headman mounted them, signifying that we were to follow on foot. I stopped for a drink of water and, looking up, noticed that this small river drained the whole of the Kathan valley, running east into the Jung Jung Khola through a narrow gorge. There was no way through, the only exit being over the Kathan pass. That meant that to get out of the valley we would have to surmount another low pass. Being unable to see one, I wondered where it was situated.

The headman and Gin-Din-Rhou dawdled along in front, never getting more than about twenty feet ahead. They seemed apprehensive that we might make a break for it at any moment. This was an impractical course, for, without food, porters, tents and stoves, we had little chance of making the journey back to Saipal. Escape was also made well-nigh impossible by the Chinese Tommy gunners who were in front and behind us.

The tall Chinese was the local Dzongpen, his rank being political and not military, which explained why the Lama had said that he was not an officer though he enjoyed a high position. The Dzongpens of Taklakot area have always been Tibetans—until recently. The

Chinese, however, have changed that, and the office, which has been traditionally Tibetan for centuries, is now held by a Chinese. Our Dzongpen, who spoke Tibetan like a native, hailed from a Chinese province that borders on the eastern Tibetan region of Kham, which, no doubt, explains why he got the job.

I very much doubt that he ordered Koila and Ratti to be beaten. We later discovered that his authority over the army was absolutely nil. Our guards were under the orders of the Chinese C.O. at Takla-kot, referred to by the Nepalese and Tibetans as 'The Cheenee Bara Rajah Sahib'. They do not appear to have any equivalent to 'O.C. troops, Taklakot'. Neither Harrop nor I had any wish to meet this illustrious figure in the flesh, for the little we knew of him classed him as a cold-blooded murderer. On our way into the hills we had met an Indian official whose duty it was to collect information leaking from Tibet. He had told us a fully authenticated story about the 'Cheenee Bara Rajah Sahib'. One of the young soldiers in the garrison had been agitating for leave. As a result he was executed in front of the entire garrison, being made to kneel in the middle of the parade area, the C.O. himself killing him with a pistol bullet in the base of the skull.

We passed through a shallow gully where the ground was covered with great moraine boulders of enormous size, some the size of a two-storey house. Then the track climbed out on to the tiny fields we had seen through binoculars the day before. We hopped over the water-courses, eventually arriving at a Chorten (Buddhist shrine) and a Mani wall, all the boulders composing the wall being stained red. The phrase 'Om Mani Padme Hum' was engraved on every one of the hundreds of stones. We took care to pass the wall on the left side to avoid offending the religious principles of the old Lama, and he smiled graciously in acknowledgment.

The village was now in sight and in a very few minutes we reached the first of the houses. Kathan hardly ranks as a village, being limited to only four houses, of which three are occupied. The fourth, next door to that of Phrupa, the headman, is used as a storehouse. All three dwellings are occupied by members of the same family, and in Phrupa's household alone there were twenty-two occupants; among them, surprisingly, Phrupa's mother and father, for Phrupa himself could not have been less than sixty years old. With him, too, were his sons, their wives and children.

The house was square and flat-roofed, with large, tightly bound bundles of brushwood stacked along the top of the perimeter wall, the place being built on the lines of a fortress; all windows looking only into the central courtyard. The boma of brushwood was designed to catch the snow which, in melting, ran down the twigs to drip on to the ground outside. Without this protecting layer of twigs, the melting snow would soon have penetrated the mud brick walls, causing them to crumble quickly. Buildings in Tibet left unused and unattended rapidly deteriorate.

There was a small yard at the front of the house and this, surrounded by a low wall, was crowded with tiny Tibetan ponies and Chinese army mules, most of them saddled against an early departure. The sun was vanishing behind the mountains to the west and the house itself fast took on the mantle of darkness.

Threading our way through the animals, we crossed the yard, ducking our heads to enter the small passageway connected with the main courtyard of the house. We didn't duck low enough, however, and John's laugh, when I banged my head on a low beam, was replaced by curses as he did the same. Doorways in Tibet are seldom more than five feet high, and generally are much lower. I never mastered the habit of marching around in a perpetual crouching position, and my frequent collisions with various pieces of Tibetan architecture were an endless source of amusement to the natives.

Once in the courtyard we were met by the Dzongpen, who, in perfect English, invited us to 'Please, sit'. But, as our efforts to engage him in conversation revealed, these two words comprised his entire English vocabulary.

As I pulled back the sleeve of my Anorak to look at the time, the Dzongpen came over to inspect my watch. Showing me his watch, he pointed out that the local Chinese time was half an hour in advance of that shown on our timepieces. His watch, I noticed, was a good-quality Swiss Rolex Oyster the same as mine. By signs I managed to convey to him that my watch was an automatic one which needed no winding. Having pointed to his own winder he said, 'Roleckas'; and then:

'*Chai, Yappa Do?*'[1] ('Tea, yes?')

We nodded assent and he departed through a distant doorway to arrange for a welcome brew of tea.

In the absence of seats we squatted on the mud floor with our backs to the outer wall. I dropped my rucksack on to a wooden box covered with rags, only to be reviled by half a dozen Tibetans who were peering at us in the half-light through an open doorway. One of them entered the yard and screamed down a rectangular hole in the

[1] *Yappa do*—Tibetan for 'Yes'.

middle of the floor. Not until then did we notice this shaft leading down into the bowels of Phrupa's residence, and from it emerged a crowd of filthy old hags. The oldest and dirtiest looked like 'Gagoul' of King Solomon's mines fame, being blind in one eye and hardly able to walk. She crawled over the edge of the black, shadowy hole on hands and knees, her unkempt hair hanging in long greasy strands. What little of her face appeared from behind this unpleasant screen was lined and pock-marked. I have never seen such a face before. She could have been a hundred years old.

In a land where the expectancy of life is thirty-five or so, age is bought dearly, and the ravages of smallpox and syphilis are apparent on the faces of many of the old people. Few, indeed, grow old gracefully in Tibet.

The old hag reached the box, pushed my rucksack to one side, and dug around amongst the filthy rags piled on top of something which now showed signs of life. I moved closer to have a look, immediately being nauseated by the most appalling stench. The old woman lifted a baby out of the box which was as filthy as she was. She offered the child to me and I fell over Harrop's feet in my effort to get out of the way.

At that moment Damodar appeared with our four porters. He viewed the scene with amusement, and when I asked him to explain that I was not available for baby sitting, he betrayed me by telling the Tibetans that I would be honoured to mind the baby for an hour or so.

I backed around the yard, declining as gracefully as I could, and my salvation appeared in the form of old Phrupa himself, bearing an iron kettle full of Tibetan yak-butter tea.

We had not met this old demon before, and from what we had heard he was something of a character. He, too, was blind in one eye, and his good eye glared malevolently at us. I salaamed and he grunted an acknowledgment. He placed the kettle on the ground and produced small wooden cups from the folds of his voluminous sheepskin cloak.

The tea was Chinese brick tea with yak butter, spice and ginger added. Being thirsty, we drank the first cup fairly eagerly, but after the second John remarked: 'It must be the cause of the high death rate. A couple of pints of this muck and we will all go blind.'

The taste, certainly unique, was like split-pea soup laced with rancid fat. The flavour of tea itself was virtually non-existent.

Phrupa's entire family came out to watch the tea-drinking and there was a great scramble for the lead foil coverings when we dined off three of our concentrated meat blocks.

Dinner was interrupted by the Chinese who appeared like shadows out of the darkness. Phrupa, knowing they could not speak Nepali, took advantage to tell Damodar that he and his family wished us well and hoped we would be able to return within a few days, not as prisoners, but as guests.

Thanking him for his hospitality, we were ushered along the low dark passage again and found ourselves amongst a group of Chinese and Tibetans packing our loads on to mules and ponies. They intended to carry only the essentials for the three of us for that one night, Koila and the other three porters having been detailed to follow on foot the next day with the remainder of our kit.

I had never before ridden a horse, and the pony I was offered had neither stirrups nor reins. Even more ominous was the absence of a saddle, and, after much arguing, I was supplied with a Tibetan pack-saddle. One look at the thing was enough to cause me to cry out for mercy. For it was made of two wooden crosses joined together by bars of square-sectioned timber running fore and aft, set with the sharp edge of the wood uppermost. On this I was supposed to sit for a night ride of only heaven knew how many miles. But my protests were of no avail. The Tibetans led the pony to a low wall, got me to climb first on to the wall and then on to the pony.

The sharp edges of the wood nearly cut me in two. But my complaints, uttered with great vociferation, were cut short by Phrupa handing me what served as the pony's reins. This was no more than a piece of string leading to the left-hand side of its halter. A tentative pull on the string and my mount shot away from the wall, executed a couple of left-hand circles and ran head on into the Dzongpen's mule.

That gentleman showed his displeasure by giving my steed a flick with his riding-crop which sent it galloping off into the night. Bereft of whatever faith I ever had in the leading string, I relinquished it and grabbed the pony's mane with both hands. Lack of stirrups did not help matters and I began to slide to the left.

Crisis overtook me when my horse charged head-on at a Mani wall that was obviously certain to prove his Waterloo. But, at the very last moment, he came to an abrupt halt, leaving me to continue my journey alone. This carried me to the top of the Mani wall, on which I landed flat on my face and from which I bounced to the other side, landing on my head and shoulders.

Having made sure no bones were broken, I rose somewhat un-

steadily expecting a sympathetic hearing. Instead, I found the entire
population doubled up in merriment. Without more ado I was lifted
on to the Mani wall and then on to the pony's back. By now he had
quietened down and accepted my presence as an inescapable and
unfortunate burden.

Meanwhile, Damodar was engaged in a long argument with
Phrupa. The ponies, it appeared, belonged to the Tibetans, and we
would have to pay 2rs. (about 3s.) for the hire of them when
we reached our destination. Damodar was most indignant about this,
for, as our official liaison officer, he felt it his bounden duty to obtain
the best possible bargain on each and every occasion. The idea of
being kidnapped and then made to pay for the transport to prison was
too much for his correct and businesslike mind. Harrop and I, seeing
the humour in it, said we would pay the 3s., but thought we ought
to become permanent owners of the horses. The Tibetans roared with
laughter, told the Dzongpen and he, evidently having no sense of
humour, solemnly replied that it was not permitted for foreigners to
buy articles for export out of Tibet.

He was persuaded to laugh, however, when Harrop, measuring
his fourteen stone against his pocket-size pony, asked, 'Do I ride the
thing or am I supposed to carry it?' With that, he put his arms round
it and managed to raise the front half of the terrified beast about a
foot from the ground.

From the heart of the mounted throng appeared the figure of
Lama Gin-Din-Rhou. He rode past me to the head of the cortège and,
stopping by a Chorten or shrine set in the middle of the Mani wall
that had just ended my first gallop, muttered a prayer. His voice rose
and fell. As he finished and spurred his horse on, each of the Tibetans
on reaching the Chorten followed his pious example.

A whinnying from the yard was answered by my pony, and a tiny
foal, no more than four feet high, trotted into sight, nuzzling my
mount which was obviously its mother.

A word of command from the Dzongpen and we moved off, Gin-
Din-Rhou and the Taklakot headman first, we prisoners next, then
the Chinese and, finally, a group of Tibetans.

Thus began my first horse ride.

Chapter 5

NIGHT RIDE TO JITKOT

IT was now so dark that we had little idea of the outline of the countryside. We knew hardly more than that we were travelling uphill very slowly. The horses and mules snorted, fought for breath and stopped every few yards to rest. The going was so steep that I had difficulty in countering a tendency to slide backwards over my horse's tail.

At about the end of an hour we reached the top of a small pass and, in the last rays of the sun reflected from a snow-covered hillside below, we looked on to the Tibetan plateau. Before us stretched the wide valley of the Karnali river and somewhere ahead, hidden in the shadows, lay our ultimate destination, Taklakot. The horizon was fringed with the distant snow-covered peaks of the Trans-Himalaya, the centre foreground being dominated by the majestic massif of the much nearer 25,350-feet Gurla Mandhata, which towered above Taklakot itself.

The summit, capped in a pale yellow light, contrasted with the deep purple of the sky. It appeared to be suspended in mid-air, completely detached from the ocean swell of the plain lying in sombre garb below.

My contemplations were rudely interrupted by the Taklakot headman, who whipped the rump of my pony, causing it to gallop headlong down the snow-covered hillside below. Rapidly I overtook every other member of the party. I saw the bend in the track bordering a drop of some thirty feet, but, lacking the requisite horse control, I shot off at the corner and proceeded downhill like a ball, my head between my knees.

My journey ended abruptly in a deep snowdrift, out of which I staggered with some difficulty. The Tibetans helped me to remount, and had just succeeded when the saddle slipped off. This provoked an argument lasting ten minutes as to whose fault it was.

A ride of some fifty yards brought me to Harrop, who was sitting in the snow cursing Chinese and Tibetans with a fine lack of discrimination. His horse, it appeared, kept falling down bodily, always to the left.

Two hours' riding made Harrop, Damodar and me painfully aware of the primitive pack-saddles. Damodar relieved his agony by lying flat on the animal with both arms round its neck. Surprisingly he managed the whole journey in this position without once falling off.

Throughout my tormenting journey I was consoled by the little foal, which came over to look at me enquiringly every time I fell off. I hit the ground four times in all, and the last time, as we were beyond the snowline, I struck hard gravel.

Mounting for what proved to be the last time, I set off in pursuit of the others, who had now gained a lead. Managing to stay on while crossing a level escarpment, I urged my mount into a trot. One by one I overhauled the rest of the cortège to the accompaniment of a rousing cheer from the Tibetans as I rode by.

Only one man remained ahead, and I could not overtake him, try as I would. This was Gin-Din-Rhou, who muttered the prayer 'Om Mani Padme Hum' as he rode. He goaded his horse into a gallop and my pony, sensing that the end of the journey was near, followed suit. The night was cold and windless, and all that could be heard was the clatter of horses' hoofs on the still air.

I looked apprehensively ahead. We were riding amongst ruins, the ruins of what must once have been a fortress of huge dimensions.

Slowly the dim outline of a high-walled building appeared. Flat-topped, and with slightly sloping sides, it looked far from inviting in the dim light. As we approached, heavy double doors silently opened; beyond them nothing but blackness.

My pony trotted briskly forward in a manner suggesting that he had been here before and knew just where he was going. Sensing that we were back in the land of low beams, I took the precaution of lying flat along my horse's neck.

Although I could hear the scuffling of feet in the darkness, I could see neither faces nor figures. Still in complete blackness, hands gripped me about the middle and I was lifted bodily from my pony. The rest of the party crowded in through the doorway and we were pushed backwards and forwards in the ebb and flow of the ever-increasing company of men and animals.

At last a flickering light moved towards us. As it came nearer I saw that we were standing in the middle of a courtyard, at the centre of which was a flagpole, only visible in its lower reaches. The lamp was held by an old crone who pushed the thing into my face to have a closer look at me.

The Tibetans use the primitive ghee (butter) lamp, a bowl-shaped piece of hammered iron with a wick floating in the melted yak butter. In the shadows around us we could now make out a group of about twenty monks, all hatless and their heads clean-shaven. In the yellow, wavering light of the lamp our surroundings were eerie and mysterious. I felt that we were standing in a place impervious to time, where nothing had changed for centuries. Here was preserved a way of life that was old when our ancestors, clad in skins, chased woolly mammoths over the Welsh hills.

They crowded round, fingering our windproof clothing and ruck-sacks, their investigations ending only when Gin-Din-Rhou ordered them to bed the ponies down for the night. By now our escort had shrunk to manageable proportions, and of the Chinese only the Dzongpen and his midget-sized, pebble-lensed comrade remained.

I was only just beginning to realize that we were not in a fort or barracks, but in a Lamasery. This was quickly confirmed by the old Lama. We were not in Taklakot, but in Jitkot, and in a Gompa (Tibetan for monastery). Gin-Din-Rhou was the head of the establishment and spiritual eader of the people of an area that reached as far as Kojarnath in the south and the outskirts of Taklakot, eight miles to the north.

At this stage we were less concerned with examining our surroundings than with finding out what was in store for us. The Dzongpen was in earnest conversation with the old Lama, and when it was finished the old man turned to us.

'The Dzongpen,' he said, 'rides for twenty-three miles tonight to see his commanding officer. He will show him your equipment and tell him your story, and probably you will be released within a few days. In the meantime, if you promise not to escape, the Chinese soldiers will be withdrawn.'

The advantages of such an agreement were obvious. If we were to remain in Tibet for only a few days we could spend the time studying monastic life far better without the supervision of armed guards.

Harrop and I felt that the immediate outlook was not as dismal as it had first appeared. We were to have an unequalled opportunity to study Tibetan life at first hand, and in an area that had long been neglected.

Our pact was made. We gave the assurance that we would make no attempt to escape and, before making his departure, the Dzongpen shook hands with all three of us. At the door he turned to offer further apology for causing us inconvenience, and I thought he would have made an ideal travel agent.

Mounting his mule and accompanied by his bespectacled comrade, he rode out into the darkness. With the immediate future settled, I had opportunity to realize that I was not only very, very tired, but also exceedingly saddle-sore. We were all suffering from the same discomfort and had the greatest difficulty in following Gin-Din-Rhou across the yard to a small doorway situated at the top of a short flight of steps.

Three small prayer-wheels were fixed to the wall at about chest height and as the Tibetans entered the building each gave one or all three of the wheels a spin. Once inside the door we lost contact with the lamp-carrying crone and found ourselves again in complete darkness. We had to be led by the hand, but even this did not save us from our usual fate of having our skulls in sharp and painful contact with the low beams.

Chapter 6

LIFE IN A LAMASERY—I

THE stairways between the floors consisted of tree-trunks set at an angle with notches carved for hands and feet. Fumbling our way along in the darkness, we were eventually shown into a room. We dropped our rucksacks on the floor and for the first time that day we were left to our own devices.

By the light of Damodar's rubber flashlight we examined our new quarters. The room measured about 16 feet by 12 feet. The floor and walls were of dried mud and the ceiling, supported by a carved centre crossbeam, was a mixture of stones and mud resting on roughly cut slim willow branches.

Squatting on the bare floor, we tried to foresee what the future held for us. Damodar wasn't particularly worried about the prospects. He was confident that when the Chinese saw his letter of authority, issued by the Nepal Foreign Office, they would understand the situation and give us every assistance to return to our base camp at Saipal before the winter snows made a crossing of the 19,500-feet Urai Lagna pass impossible.

In addition, Damodar felt that he was on the threshold of achieving his life ambition. For, if the Chinese would give the necessary permission, he would make a pilgrimage to the sacred lake of Manasarowar.

None of us expressed any doubt then that the Chinese authorities would be anything but friendly and co-operative. But at the back of my mind was the terrible thought that we might be wrong and that the Chinese Communists might suspect us of being 'Imperialist spies'. If events took that turn, there might be a trial by a 'Peoples' Court', followed by an unreckonable term of imprisonment in some filthy dungeon in Chungking.

I reflected on the parole we had given to the Dzongpen. If the Chinese kept clear of the Lamasery and our porters showed up on the morrow, we might perhaps make our escape the following night. That would mean leaving our valuable cameras in the hands of the Chinese, but that was a trifle compared with the prospect of ten years in a Chinese prison cell. We decided to leave the matter until the following day and turned in. I was asleep the moment I closed my eyes.

I was awakened at 8 a.m. the following day by the most dreadful cacophony. Beating drums, clashing cymbals, interspersed with the occasional deep booming note of a horn. Added to this was a human voice that rose in a spine-chilling shriek and then descended to a note that was barely distinguishable from the sound of the horn. This singing transfixed us all. We sat up in our sleeping-bags, struck dumb by its penetration. It continued for some fifteen minutes, then ceased as suddenly as it had begun.

The sound of the drums, cymbals and horn had been eerie enough, but the singing was right out of this world. The spell was broken by Harrop, as always, for his sense of humour was equal to all occasions.

'If he starts again, give him sixpence and tell him to go and sing in the next Gompa.'

We were exceedingly hungry, for we had not had a proper meal since breakfast the previous day, and Damodar valiantly offered to brave the mysterious Lamaistic world in an effort to find food.

Light now reached our room, for it boasted a Chinese-style window of lattice-wood strips covered with a thin white paper. By Tibetan standards it was a big window, measuring almost the length of one side of the room. In the far corner opposite the door were a couple of rifles, examination of them showing they were of little value, being Tibetan muzzle-loaders of a very antique pattern. From the butt to the muzzle they were six feet long, and to this was added the double-pronged fork rest peculiar to Tibetan rifles.

My examination of the weapons was brought to an end by the appearance of the horn and singing prodigy, who had come down to the kitchen for his 'elevenses'. From the doorway he saw me handling the artillery and decided to take the guns out of temptation's way.

He came in and rudely pushed me aside, shouting for help as he did so. Within seconds the room was full of monks. Old Gin-Din-Rhou pushed his way to the front, but being in the middle of chanting his morning prayer was unable to take part in the ensuing debate. Damodar was brought from the nearby kitchen and told to explain to us that we must not touch anything in the Lamasery.

Everything was removed from the room. Poking about under an old sheepskin, the monks disclosed some fine silver-decorated wooden saddles, some leather boots and a fur hat. These were carried out in the van of the rifles.

Seeing a rather blackened-looking slab of dried meat hanging from

the roof, I succeeded in buying it from Gin-Din-Rhou for the sum of
3rs. (about 4s. 6d.). The financial negotiations were conducted by
nods or shakes of the head, for throughout the old man pursued his
monosyllabic prayer which he repeated over and over again without
appearing ever to stop for breath.

As his voice rose and fell he went almost blue in the face in his
efforts to do justice to his religion and carry through the business
transaction at the same time. Never once did he so much as pause and,
the agreement reached, he pocketed the three rupees and departed,
still chanting his prayers.

Alone once more in our bed-sitter, I decided to help Damodar
with the breakfast preparations and we set off for the monastery
kitchen to buy tsampa with which we hoped to make some passable
porridge.

Outside our room was a small courtyard with three exits. One
into the old Lama's room situated next door to ours, one into the
kitchen and the other, a much larger door, led out on to the roof of
the monastery. Standing in the centre of this courtyard was Gin-Din-
Rhou, about whom minor officials fussed, organizing the day's routine
of prayers and tax-collecting.

An old woman emerged from the kitchen bearing a bowl of hot
water which was set down on a small decorated table just outside the
door of Gin-Din-Rhou's room. Squatting down, the old man proceeded to wash his hands and face, a proceeding which amazed me; for
everything I had read about Tibetans had served to convince me that
under no circumstances do Tibetans wash.

I asked Damodar to enquire about this remarkable occurrence,
and, on hearing of my curiosity, Gin-Din-Rhou turned towards me,
his face dripping with water. There was a look of injured dignity on
his otherwise benign countenance. Damodar said that the old Lama
would, under the circumstances, forgive my obvious ignorance of
Tibetan life and customs. Evidently washing was not unknown, but
in all our stay in Tibet we never saw any of the other natives resort
to water to clean themselves, and the old Lama did not use soap.

His ablutions completed, a small mat was brought out and placed
in the centre of the courtyard, and on this Gin-Din-Rhou seated himself
cross-legged. Next a small porcelain cup with a heavy, silver, hand-
worked cover was placed at his right, some scrolls of paper at his
left, and pen and a bottle of ink were set down. Still muttering his
prayers, he started the day's business.

I tried to open up a conversation with him, but he smilingly waved me away. When he was in the middle of one of his prayers, which might last as long as an hour, he would allow nothing to interrupt him.

My attention was diverted from Gin-Din-Rhou by what seemed to be the noise of a small diesel engine running in the kitchen. There was a steady pulsating 'chug-chug-chug' and, greatly intrigued, I went inside to investigate.

I might have entered hell's kitchen itself. I found myself in a black cavern of a room with one window the size of a pocket-handkerchief. This provided a very inadequate light, and a tiny hole in the roof served as a chimney. The whole place was wreathed in acrid smoke. I could hear Damodar somewhere ahead, coughing violently enough to dislodge his lungs. I placed a hand on the wall and it came away covered thickly with soot. Long sooty cobwebs festooned the place and I kept wiping them off my face.

After a few moments my eyes became accustomed to the semi-darkness and I saw that the source of the engine sounds was a Tibetan tea-making cylinder operated by the Lama's official tea-maker. He was standing at the side of the combined fireplace and oven, a mud-brick affair shaped like a large office desk. A tunnel penetrated the oven from one end to the other and into it an old woman pushed handfuls of brushwood and dried dung. On top of the oven, large copper and brass pots stood covering circular holes through the edges of which licked an occasional tongue of flame. It was certainly an efficient fireplace, everything put inside roaring into flame immediately.

Its major drawback was its lack of chimney. The room was filled with volumes of smoke that issued from every opening and cranny in this Tibetan-style 'Aga' cooker.

Damodar introduced me to the tea-maker, who claimed—rightly, I believe—that he was the hardest-worked man in the monastery. At least thirty years old, he had been an official tea-maker since the age of eight. This remarkable claim proved, as we discovered later, to be no exaggeration. Tea-drinking is more than a habit with the Tibetans. It is an obsession. Rotary Clubs, Women's Institutes, cinemas, theatres, radio and TV are non-existent. So what else is there to do but sit around the tea-urn exchanging gossip with anyone willing to trade the latest bit of scandal from Gyantse, Gartok or Lhasa?

The tea-making machine was in action without pause from morning to night, and the tea-server was everlastingly carrying out kettles of tea for Gin-Din-Rhou and his associates. The tea is first boiled in one of the kitchen pots which may hold anything up to two gallons.

Afterwards it is poured into the wooden tea-mixing cylinder, yak butter, salt and spices generally being added. The mixing is done with the aid of a plunger or piston, a wooden rod with a circular disc attached to the bottom. The disc has holes drilled in it and with this primitive but effective instrument the mixture is blended.

A bout of long-winded haggling resulted in Damodar buying a small bowl of tsampa, flour made from native roasted grain. The price was steep, being ten times what we had been charged in Nepal.

Overriding the objections of the old woman stoking the fire, we borrowed the cooking-pot and soon had a steaming bowl of porridge ready. Enamel plates were extracted from rucksacks, and Harrop, Damodar and I squatted to eat in the middle of the courtyard. Old Gin-Din-Rhou and his associates were greatly amused that we should take the trouble to cook the tsampa. Tibetans eat it uncooked, simply mixing water and flour in a small bowl until a hard ball or sausage of dough results. During our stay we never saw the Tibetans eat meat, their diet being limited to tsampa and tea.

During breakfast I asked how it came about that we were able to buy meat from people sworn by their religion never to take life, whether that of a human, an animal or even an insect.

'We are Buddhists,' the tea-server told me, grinning slyly. 'We do not take life.'[1]

He admitted that he and the Lamas seldom ate meat. When they could afford it, however, they hired an outsider who did not share their religious scruples, and he killed a sheep or yak which he sold to the Lamasery.

Gin-Din-Rhou, learning of my question, smiled and assured me that we had nothing to fear from the meat we had bought. The animal had not died of a disease, at least not a serious one, and was not much more than a year old. Reassured, I announced that we would boil the meat and have it for dinner that night. If we died of poisoning, the Lamas would have to answer to the 'Cheenee Bara Rajah Sahib' at Taklakot.

After breakfast, Harrop and I made a tour of the building. It was much larger than we had realized and was honeycombed with a maze of passages and small rooms. One room held a store of prayer-flags; thousands of gaily coloured bits of bunting hanging from ropes stretched from one side of the room to the other.

Quite by accident we walked into the holy of holies, strictly for-

---

[1] I still cannot reconcile this with the fact that dried mutton is part of the Tibetan nomads' staple diet.

Jitkot Monastery

bidden territory as far as we were concerned. Pushing aside a tattered curtain from a doorway, I walked through the opening. In front of me, on a dais, stood four six-feet-high brass statues of Buddha. The floor was carpeted and bowls of incense lay smoking at the Buddhas' feet. The room had two tiny windows through which streamed thin shafts of light to illumine the faces of the images. Small flowers like marigolds were strewn about the altar, and there was an offering of tsampa dough on a plate before the largest figure.

The solemn atmosphere certainly discouraged levity on my part, but not so on Harrop's. Hearing the sound of a monk shuffling along the passage outside, we froze into immobility. Happily he passed the door and entered another room.

'Let's get out of here,' I said to Harrop. 'If the old man finds out where we've been he'll burst a blood-vessel.'

Satisfied that we were not observed, I slipped out through the curtain, Harrop behind me. Looking back at the largest Buddha, he grinned and said, 'No offence, Cock.'

I am sure, had it been possible, the sunlit Mona Lisa-like features of the Buddha would have broken into a smile. No one can be offended by Harrop, not even the gods.

It was now mid-afternoon and the sun shone from a cloudless blue sky. We walked on to the main roof and sat down. Near us a little girl was combing her long black hair with a bunch of twigs.

each one sharpened to a point, the whole of them being tied together in a bundle.

Here, at Jitkot Lamasery, I had the finest view of my life. To the north towered the mighty 25,350-feet Gurla Mandhata. From the foot of its south precipice stretched a series of ridges right across the skyline, making a magnificent panorama of purple and brown rock peaks that culminated in the Nalkankar massif on the Nepal border.

About eight miles away we could see the great monastery of Taklakot perched on top of a conglomerate cliff. Below it could be seen the white-painted Tibetan houses and cave dwellings. Immediately below our monastery and beside the banks of the Karnali river was the village of Jitkot, built, like our monastery, amongst the ruins of an ancient Chinese fortress. The derelict walls of the fort were used, where feasible, to form part of a house.

The largest and most comprehensive ruin of all was situated on top of a hill, which, according to Harrop, was man made. Irrigation channels provided water for the fields, the smallest of which was about ten feet square, the largest being no more than some fifty yards by twenty. Beside the river was the only greenery visible. Everywhere else, as far as eye could see, was nothing but a brown, rubbly, lifeless plateau.

Harrop commented that while Tibetans had migrated into Central and Eastern Nepal they had ignored this region in the west. Why they should struggle to eke out such a bare existence when they might have lived much more comfortably in the richer agricultural land of the Seti valley it was impossible to say. The Tibetans of the Taklakot area depend for their living on trade with the Nepalese. Crossing the passes into West Nepal and seeing the greater fertility of the land and profuse timber, they must compare it with the treeless, stony ground from which they derive such a precarious existence.

As we discovered later, the truth is that, with the advent of the Chinese Communist Army and their Draconion taxation, the population of Taklakot area is decreasing rapidly. In ever-increasing numbers the Tibetans are leaving for ever the land of their birth and making a living begging in the United Provinces of India. This is the answer to the Chinese propaganda which claims that the lot of the Tibetans is now improved.

Koila and our porters appeared at 3 p.m., having been on the march since dawn. Koila, worried about the Chinese, feared that John and I would not see the outside world again for ten years. Our assertion that we would be on our way back into Nepal in a few days, and certainly long before the winter snows set in, did little to reassure him, and he disappeared down a ladder leading into the dark, mysterious heart of the building. The Tibetans would not allow Koila and the three porters to use the monastery kitchen and they were compelled to find a substitute. Wreaths of blue smoke emerging from the stairway all day long made it plain that they were not going short of their ration of chupatties.

The exit from the roof used by Koila was surrounded by crude window-boxes made of dried mud. These were filled with soil, and the lovely crop of marigold-like flowers growing in them received almost hourly attention from the monks, who shuffled in and out with small copper bowls of water which they poured on to the parched soil.

Jitkot Monastery having no supply of its own, all water is carried from a stream issuing from the hillside about 300 feet below. The woman who tended the fire in the kitchen had, too, the unenviable task of keeping the cooking-pots filled. She was probably thankful that, apart from Gin-Din-Rhou, none of the inmates washed. In addition to twenty monks, there were about fifteen small boys in residence. In training for holy orders, they were dressed exactly like the men, even to the extent of having their heads shaved. They all wore long-sleeved cloaks and highly coloured felt boots, and their faces were so much alike they might have been members of the same family.

These boys were friendly and inquisitive, and amused themselves by repeatedly ransacking our equipment. It says much for their honesty that nothing was ever stolen.

While Harrop sunbathed on the main roof, I returned to the courtyard to see if I could gain information from the High Lama. He was seated cross-legged on the floor, tax-collecting, an assistant seated at his left. I was invited to sit at his right to watch as the local villagers came in to pay their dues. They salaamed as they entered and, upon being informed that I was a guest of honour, they favoured me with the same courtesy.

As Damodar was in our room sorting out his belongings, the Lamas shouted in to him in Hindi or Nepalese whenever I was required to take part in the conversation. He shouted to me in English and transmitted my remarks to the assembly of tax-gatherers and tax-payers. The money changing hands amounted to but very few rupees, and was probably intended for the upkeep of the monastery. No opportunity was lost to make it known in the most definite terms that everyone resented the new Chinese taxes which weighed grievously on the population.

While the tax-gathering was in progress, yak butter tea was served in the usual wooden cups. The tea-making cylinder could be heard pursuing its endless task in the dark recess of the kitchen. The tea-server scurried in and out bearing kettle after kettle of tea, and as fast as I emptied my cup it was filled again. I had heard that Tibetans can drink as many as sixty of these cups a day. It was by no means as palatable as some Himalayan travellers make out, and I soon decided that I had had more than enough.

I kept asking questions about the daily routine and running of the monastery, and learnt that Jitkot Monastery had its own fields and employed a staff of forty men and women who worked continuously on the primitive agriculture. As few of the fields are large enough to permit the use of the yak-drawn plough, the hoe is employed, as it has been for countless centuries. The pay of the monastery employees was about 10rs. a month, or approximately 15s.

I was also told that the horn which we had heard blown that morning was made from a huge sea-shell, probably a conch-shell. When I enquired how such a shell had found its way into Tibet, Gin-Din-Rhou said that it came from the sea and was very holy. It had always been in use at the monastery and no one could say how old it was.

Meanwhile, my cup was refilled and, not wishing to offend my hosts, I drank the contents. Again my cup was refilled—for the tenth time! Damodar, who had come out and seated himself on the door-step of our room, watched my marathon tea-drinking with a grin of amusement. For he knew a fact of which I was ignorant: that it is considered good manners in Tibet to walk away leaving a full cup untouched. He could have told me this, but preferred to sit and enjoy my discomfiture as I drank each cup determined not to show what I assumed would have been a grave discourtesy.

As I reached my thirteenth and then fourteenth cup, the monks looked at me with a puzzled air. My embarrassment mounted and to such a degree that Damodar burst into uncontrollable laughter. At fifteen cups I had reached my maximum capacity. Nature called and, expressing my apologies, I made a hasty departure.

When I left, my cup was refilled, and Damodar told the monks of the misunderstanding which had caused me to consume so much of their tea. The joke was greatly appreciated, and I heard their guffaws from the other side of the wall.

The sanitary arrangements in this Tibetan Lamasery had to be seen to be believed. The procedure for building a latrine was simple. They bricked up the doors and windows of one of the top-floor rooms and then made a circular hole in the roof. In this instance the room was nearly filled with human excreta. I looked down through the hole and shuddered. What happened when the room had reached its maximum capacity I did not dare imagine. Would they brick up the windows and doors of another room and start the procedure all over again? If so, then we have perhaps the real reason for the current housing shortage in Tibet.

When I returned to our room I found it occupied by a couple of very smelly individuals. I remarked upon their obnoxious odours and Damodar unfortunately translated my feelings to them. Both pushed past me with highly indignant expressions on their faces. The incident had its sequel five minutes later when a monk came in bearing an iron shovel containing a heap of dried herbs which he ignited with a match. They gave off a not unattractive musky odour, and the pale blue smoke quickly pervaded the room. The old herb burner pointed to the side of his nose and then at Harrop and me. He inferred that we smelled. Then almost the entire populace came and looked in through the door. They stood grinning at my obvious embarrassment. At last I could no longer ignore the joke and all three of us burst into fits of uncontrollable laughter. Late in the afternoon we cooked our meat over the kitchen fire. At 6 p.m. we turned in.

Chapter 7

LIFE IN A LAMASERY—II

OCTOBER 27TH was heralded for us by the hideous din of the cymbal, horn and singing from the roof, the mixture being as before. Gin-Din-Rhou entered our room as soon as he had finished prayers to inform us that he had taken a great liking to us and that he regarded us as his brothers. As evidence of his friendship he intended to ride to Taklakot to see the Chinese officers and plead with them for our release.

I asked him if he could make the six-day ride to Gartok to see the Chinese Governor, but he regretfully shook his head.

'We are not permitted,' he explained, 'to leave the Taklakot area for any other part of Tibet without the written permission of the Chinese, and that is only given to those who can prove that they have what the Chinese call "a purpose".'

So much for the so-called 'Liberation of Tibet' and the Tibetans' new-found 'freedom' under the aegis of Chinese Communism.

The old man left, not having broken his fast. He galloped off through the doorway, waving us adieu with his riding-crop as he went down the track to Taklakot. Harrop and I, assuming that none of the other monks had authority to tell us what to do, took advantage of Gin-Din-Rhou's absence to do a little exploring outside the monastery.

Harrop set off to explore the interiors of several Chortens whose flag-bedecked roofs were only fifty yards from the front gate of the monastery. I decided to explore some old cave dwellings situated below the track to Taklakot, about four hundred yards to the north.

I went forth dressed in a filthy old blue sweater and windproof trousers, my feet encased in a monstrous pair of Everest-pattern kapok-padded high-altitude boots. When I passed a group of Tibetans on the ground floor they giggled at my curious footwear.

The monastery is built on high ground at the edge of an escarpment which, emerging from the foothills of the Nepal/Tibet watershed, runs from Jitkot to Taklakot at an average height of about 200 feet above the level of the Karnali. The track to Taklakot runs along the top of the escarpment for a quarter of a mile or so and then drops down across the rubble-studded cliff face until it reaches the valley bottom proper. From there it meanders by the banks of the Karnali river, passing through the tiny fields and one or two villages.

Skirting Harrop's Mani walls, I saw him climb in through the small and very highly placed doorway of the largest of the Chortens. Luckily he wasn't noticed. Had he been seen in his exploration, there would have been a hue and cry from the devout inhabitants, who were far more numerous than we had supposed. About twenty yards away a small child of four or five years was herding yaks along. He or she (the sex could not be determined by appearance) whacked the ungainly, slow-moving creatures with a stout stick and occasionally threw stones at their thick skulls. The yaks showed no sign of resentment or fright, and ambled along at their usual pace. Some travellers have claimed that the yak travels at an average speed of about two miles an hour. This, I think, is an exaggeration. All that can be said of the yaks I saw in Tibet was that, occasionally, they moved their feet.

On the northern side of the monastery, concealed among the old fortress ruins, I came upon a house. Outside the front door were lined up a couple of dozen finely made, but as yet unfired, earthenware pots which had obviously been made on a wheel. Some were shaped like large teapots with finely worked handles and spouts. Others were simple water-carrying vessels similar to the amphorae of Asia Minor, their capacity varying from about a pint to four gallons.

Apart from the plaiting of ropes and the making of rope-soled, felt-uppered boots, I had seen few local examples of Tibetan craftsmanship. Wishing to know more, I put my head through the open doorway into the yard. Two men were there: one in his early twenties, the other anything from fifty to a hundred years old. At our base camp in Saipal, in West Nepal, we had met many Tibetan traders, and our efforts to determine their ages produced the most amusing answers. An old man who looked about a hundred said he had lost count when he was twenty, but thought that by now he might well be twenty-five or even thirty. Another who was fifty if he was a day said that his age was six.

The old potter of Jitkot suffered from the ravages of syphilis, which seems to be so widespread in that part of Tibet. He was blind in one eye, had little sight in the other, and walked stiff-legged as if his knees lacked joints.

The young man beckoned me into the yard, and pointed to the roof where yak dung was drying. A woman was gathering it into a wicker basket and passing it down into the arms of the old man. The young man, his father behind him carrying the basket of dung, went out through the doorway and I followed them across some open ground to the top of a small hill.

There another score or more of vessels lay ready for firing. I looked round for a kiln, but nothing remotely resembling such a structure could be seen. As I watched, the Tibetans built a circle of stones to the height of about a foot. The pots were placed inside, an inch or so separating them, then twigs were scattered in the spaces and yak dung piled on top. Twigs were also dropped into the pots, followed by yak dung. With flint and tinder the fuel was lighted. At one side of the circle the old man worked a pair of leather bellows while his son, taking deep breaths, gave vent to formidable blasts of air that put the bellows to shame.

In little time the fire was well away, and I was surprised at the intensity of the heat. Never bursting into flame, as wood must have done, the dung gave a concentrated glow. It is said that glass can be melted easily on a yak-dung fire. As the fire grew, the fuel in the pots was ignited and the two Tibetans started to pile on the yak dung. I became so interested that I found myself helping with this fuelling and blowing with all my might to help it into flame. My puny efforts were not very rewarding and the young Tibetan stopped his efforts to sit down and laugh at me. The old man could not appreciate the fun for, at ten feet, he was unable to see me.

I was aroused from my arts and crafts efforts by a voice bellowing from the roof of the monastery. It was the loud-voiced individual who invaded our sleep each morning. He had seen me from his little room on the roof, having gone up there to shatter the peace of valley and mountains with an afternoon interlude of cymbal and drums, accompanied by his weird-sounding vociferations. I decided that, if I was to pursue my exploration, I had better make myself scarce before he roused the monks to sally forth and bring me in by force.

Wishing the two potters a hasty good day, I galloped off along the Taklakot track to the point where it starts to go downhill. Here the entire cliff face was honeycombed with cave dwellings, the first one displaying a semi-modern built-up front of mud bricks, the door being padlocked. I decided that the padlock indicated the cave contained something worth seeing, and I prowled around seeking means of access.

The built-up front of the cave projected from the cliff for some three feet and had a small flat roof of about six feet by three, which backed on to the cliff proper. I climbed on to the roof and found a stone weighing about a hundredweight covering a trap-door. While moving it I felt the roof give under the combined weight of the stone and myself. It held, however, and, with the opening clear, I slid down through a gap of no more than eighteen inches by twelve. The outer edges were smothered in soot and I got well and truly plastered with the stuff.

It was dark inside, the only light being admitted by the tiny hole through which I had dropped and which obviously served the purpose of a chimney. As my eyes became accustomed to the dim interior I beheld a breathtaking sight. The cave was full of images of the Buddha, varying in size from a few inches in height to about a foot. There were, indeed, hundreds of them. There were other objects too, which outnumbered the Buddhas. These were religious ornaments or charms moulded in a kind of coarse plaster. There was a large sack of the raw material in the far corner of the cave. The charms varied considerably, some depicting one god, others as many as six. There were also small objects like miniature towers, about two inches tall and looking like pawns on a chessboard. There was no sign of metal or clay moulds, although the figures and charms were obviously moulded. I was venturing into the darkest and farthest reaches of the cave when I heard the sound of loose stones sliding down the steep track outside. Someone was coming.

If the cave was to have a visitor then it was no place for an un-invited Englishman. I reached up and grabbed hold of the sides of the trap-door. As I did so the footsteps stopped at the outer door. I started to pull myself up, exit proving much more difficult than entry. A key turned in the lock; hands fumbled to remove the padlock of the hasp. Pocketing a souvenir, I wriggled up with great difficulty through the small aperture and lay on the roof. Turning on my side I managed to pull the flat stone over the hole just as the door opened.

To my horror the heavy stone rose. Fortunately it lifted only a couple of inches, and a pair of brown hands, palms against the under-side of the stone, came into view. The stone was moved to one side, and I waited with bated breath, expecting a head to appear. But no. The occupant simply wanted a little light to illuminate his workshop.

The door was shut, so I lowered myself to the ground. I had barely reached it when the door was rudely kicked open and the idol-maker emerged. He was a gruff, rude-looking individual who did not appear to take kindly to visitors. My gaze moved down his sheepskin coat to his footwear, and, unable to restrain myself, I burst out laughing. In place of the usual gaily coloured felt boots he was wearing an old pair of British Army boots, and his legs were clad in a pair of very sporty-looking cotton socks of obvious Indian origin, worked in the most bilious and brilliant colour scheme I had ever seen. To add an utterly ridiculous note, his red, yellow and blue-banded, calf-length socks were held up by a pair of bright green suspenders, fastened round his bare legs just below the knee.

My laughter ended abruptly when he picked up a handy-sized rock, and, not wishing to have it crack against my head, I beat a hasty retreat up the track.

Deciding that I had seen enough cave dwellings for one day, I headed back to the monastery. On the way I passed the potters and hailed them, receiving a friendly salaam in reply. Damodar was waiting for me at the front door. Harrop and I had been missed, and John had been rounded up some time before. Luckily he had finished his examination of the Chortens and was brought in merely for vagrancy.

The tea-maker met us half-way across the ground-floor yard near the stables and upbraided me for going out and Damodar for allowing me to do so. In fairness to the Tibetans they would have been in trouble with the Chinese had they learnt we had been able to go out at all and contact the local inhabitants. He grumbled to himself all the way across the yard. I had distracted him from his vital task of working the tea-pump. He spun all three of the prayer-wheels situated outside the door as he went into the building. There were some monks watching, so Damodar and I gave the wheels an extra spin as we passed, hoping to placate the Tibetans if not their gods.

Harrop was in the kitchen trying to boil some water for a brew of our own tea. The woman who stoked the fire was shrieking at him, and Damodar arrived in time to save the day. Leaving dinner preparations to Damodar, Harrop and I went outside to sit on the roof. The sound-effects man was needlessly rehearsing in his little room and we could hardly hear ourselves speak. As we had seen no Chinese soldiers for two days we were beginning to feel optimistic about the chances of an early release.

I showed Harrop the little plaster ornament I had taken from the cave as a souvenir, and which consisted of six figures. To my surprise he pulled half a dozen similar ones from his pocket. He then surprised me more by lifting the front of his jersey to reveal against his chest a thick wad of paper. The sheets were all about nine inches by six and were covered with beautifully handwritten Sanskrit. Harrop said that the Chortens were full of them, so much so that he hardly had room to move in the Chorten into which he had ventured. Plaster models were stacked against one wall as if dumped by the sack-load. The paper scrolls were piled against the other wall to a depth of several feet.

At that time I still had a diary which had entries dating from October 19th, when the three of us and our four porters left base camp in Nepal. That night I started to make my usual entry and found that my pen had run dry. When I went next door and asked Gin-Din-Rhou's right-hand man for some ink he handed me what appeared to be a stick of carbon. Taking it back to our room, I asked Harrop and Damodar if they knew what it was.

'Chinese ink powder,' said Damodar. 'Stick it in hot water and it will become ink.'

'Ruin your ruddy pen,' warned Harrop, but I decided to give it a try.

Harrop, however, was right. The pen became blocked with a thick sludge and diary writing had to be continued with a pencil. Making notes about everything we had seen and heard, I came to the question of the marigolds growing in the window-boxes on the roof.

'Where do they get the flowers from?' I asked Harrop, who was wriggling into his sleeping-bag.

'They probably pop down to Woolworth's at Taklakot and buy a sixpenny packet of seeds.'

My question unanswered, I too turned in. I dozed off thinking about Gin-Din-Rhou and wondering whether he would be successful in his overtures to the Chinese. What about my wife and son, who would know nothing about my predicament? What about the others at base camp? In a few days' time twenty porters would arrive at Saipal from Chainpur ready to carry the expedition equipment for the eighteen to twenty days' march back to the border of India. I was blissfully unaware that the decision that we should not be there had already been made by the 'freedom-loving' Communists in Taklakot.

Chapter 8

THE JOURNEY TO PRISON

THE morning of October 28th saw all our hopes betrayed. Gin-Din-Rhou arrived back from Taklakot before we were out of bed, bringing the depressing news that the Chinese had ordered that we were to be taken to Taklakot and placed under close arrest. We were to move off that very morning.

Disdaining to wait for the escort of Chinese soldiers, we decided to go in on our own to show them that we didn't give a damn for their army and its stupid ideas about security. Damodar reminded us that the Dzongpen had now broken his word, or his superiors had broken it for him, and, therefore, we were no longer under any obligation to honour our parole.

Could the three of us and four heavily laden porters make a break for it now? It seemed unlikely. We would have to make the seven or eight miles to Kathan village on foot, whereas the Chinese would be able to pursue us on horseback. Beyond Kathan we were still liable to arrest or a bullet in the back until we reached the sanctuary of the snowline, beyond which the Chinese would not dare to venture.

Reluctantly we decided that escape at this stage was impossible. In any case, why should we run away? The Chinese would interpret that as guilt on our part and claim that we were, in fact, foreign spies. And there was still a chance that they would prove to be intelligent and reasonable people who would release us after a brief questioning. For that matter, if they were in radio contact with Lhasa or Peking, they would be able to approach the British Government, who would quickly vouch for the fact that we were, indeed, harmless explorers and not spies.

I still possessed a coloured silk scarf Damodar had given to me at base camp and decided to present it to Gin-Din-Rhou as a farewell gift. When he had completed his morning meditations, I approached him, offering the scarf spread over my outstretched hands. Damodar made a little speech and the old man was completely overwhelmed. He responded by giving me a small butter lamp and a wooden riding-crop.

He said that if we ever visited Jitkot again he would gladly welcome us as his guests and would allow us to move about freely to study the life of the people and examine the ancient ruins in which we had shown such interest. He qualified the offer by adding that, of course, we should need the permission of the Chinese, or, better still, perhaps we would come when the Chinese had gone. We expressed our gratitude to him for his hospitality and for his concern about our well-being. With that the tea-maker was instructed to pump up a special brew; we drank a toast to our hosts and to the Tibetan people in general, and then the old man sat down to eat his morning meal of tsampa.

Not feeling like eating, we had no breakfast. Koila was told the sad news, and he and the three porters broke down in tears. They told Damodar that they were not crying because of their own misfortunes, but because they were sure that the two white sahibs would never again see beyond the borders of the new China.

'Only last year,' Koila said, 'the Rajah of Bajang was making a pilgrimage to Manasarowar and Kailas when he and his retinue were arrested by the Chinese and kept here at the monastery for two days. Later they were allowed to go only as far as the lake, under escort all the way, and were made to return immediately afterwards.'

The Rajah was subjected to this inconvenience simply because he happened to be dressed in European clothes, which automatically branded him as a foreign spy.

John wanted to know what the Chinese were so anxious to hide here in the Taklakot area, where they were supposed to have only some two hundred soldiers, and where there was nothing to guard but rubble and semi-desert. Nepal and India, he pointed out, were pacifist nations threatening no one. Then why all the secrecy and such rigid security measures? Why, too, the interference with pilgrims? We were tempted to believe that we had stumbled on to something important and that we had arrived on the scene at a most inopportune moment.

If the Chinese had something to hide, then our chances of getting out were bound to be disquietingly slender.

At that moment a strange figure appeared in the shape of an Indian national. A cheerful young fellow in his middle twenties, he was dressed in the usual tight-fitting cotton trousers and an old tweed sports coat.

Gin-Din-Rhou vouched for him, explaining that he was a trader from Almora, who also had a shop in Pithoragarh. His business was selling cheap Indian cotton cloth to the Tibetans, and he had arrived only that day from over the Lipu Lekh pass.

He complained to us of the treatment meted out to the traders at Taklakot. Although the Chinese depended upon India for about ninety per cent of the foodstuffs required to feed their garrison, they were making things increasingly difficult for traders. He also told us that the Chinese were building new fortifications with materials that were brought from India, all the roof timbers and beams, all the furniture and other items being transported over the Lipu Lekh pass.

We remarked that there was little for India and West Nepal to fear from the Chinese at Taklakot if that garrison was dependent on these two countries for food and raw materials. It seemed a sensible conjecture at the time, but future events proved it to be false. The Chinese have no intention of remaining dependent on India for supplies for their Taklakot garrison, but, being unscrupulous opportunists, have taken advantage of the friendly attitude of India and Nepal to fill a temporary gap. How were the Chinese to feed and supply a large army?

That we were soon to find out. That was Taklakot's big number one secret and was the reason for our arrest.

I wrote a letter to Mr. Benson Greenwold, a Christian missionary at Pithoragarh who had kindly acted as our mail depot while we were in the hills. All our letters to and from home were addressed to Mr. Greenwold, who sent them on to us by native porters, or back into the Indian plain by the postal service which, due to a dispute with the local bus company, has its mail carried the ninety miles to the railhead at Tanakpur by an official mail runner.

When the Indian trader realized that we wanted him to deliver a letter to India he looked frightened and said that, if we didn't mind, he would rather not do so. After a great deal of arguing, with Harrop and me reminding him that we were all three members of the British Commonwealth, he agreed to deliver our note. By this means we hoped to notify the outside world of our imprisonment.

The trader said that business would detain him in the Taklakot area for about seventeen days and that he would also be dealing with the Chinese barracks at Taklakot. Which explained his reluctance to take our letter, as he was afraid he might be searched, for, he claimed, the Chinese regularly searched the Indian traders. One had recently been arrested because he had a book with a map printed on the cover. The map was not even remotely related to the Taklakot area, but that was of no significance to the Chinese officers who had probably never seen any publication other than the official party propaganda issued by Peking. Another Indian trader, who had smuggled a camera in and taken a picture of the monastery and village of Taklakot, had been held under the most frightful conditions and had almost starved to death during his nine months' imprisonment.

An Indian university professor on a pilgrimage to Manasarowar had also been arrested and searched, and his camera had been confiscated. He was carrying only such simple drawing instruments as a protractor and a pair of compasses. But these were declared instruments of espionage and he was fortunate to return to India without suffering anything worse than a few days' imprisonment. Plainly, the Chinese trusted nobody.

With these items of news to do nothing to allay our anxiety, the Indian trader left the monastery. The letter to Mr. Greenwold was never delivered. No doubt, having weighed our future against his own, the Indian had decided that the possibility of being discovered with my letter and the penalties it might incur were too great for him to ignore them. It is safe to assume that he destroyed it before there was danger of it landing him in trouble.

At 11 a.m. we packed our kit and left the monastery on foot accompanied by Gin-Din-Rhou riding his horse. In my pocket I carried letters addressed to Jack Henson at our base camp. It was my intention to smuggle these into the hands of any Tibetan trader we might meet on our way to Taklakot, hoping that the offer of an adequate reward would tempt him to make the journey over the passes to Saipal. The chances of getting a letter out once we reached the Chinese H.Q. were virtually non-existent.

Our luck was in. No sooner were we clear of the monastery than we encountered some Tibetans coming our way driving a herd of sheep. The sheep carried the usual double saddle-bags containing salt for trade with either Nepal or India. We recognized the leader of the party right away, having bought a sheep from him at our base camp in Nepal some six weeks before. At that time he and his companions were on their way back to Tibet with a load of tsampa purchased from the Nepalese villagers.

Gin-Din-Rhou was a few yards ahead and we were nearing a Mani wall. In accordance with his religious scruples the old Lama rode along the left side of it, while we slipped along the wrong side, Damodar taking opportunity to offer the letters to the Tibetan. He intended to go over the Urai Lekh to Saipal again provided the heavy monsoon snow had consolidated. He asked a price in rupees, and I wrote a p.s. on the outside of the letter to the effect that the bearer was to be paid the agreed sum on arrival.

E

Gin-Din-Rhou had not noticed what was going on, and we quickly caught up with him. But all our efforts were to prove of no avail, for the letters were never delivered. We know now that no Tibetans entered Nepal over the Urai Lekh from the time we left base camp until the time the expedition departed on its way back to India. But fate squared her account later that same day when the Chinese themselves put into our hands the means of getting a message home.

The track dropped towards the river bank and we passed the cave dwellings I had visited the day before. The path wound its way through the small irrigated fields and, occasionally, there was a little grass. There was little evidence of crops, and Harrop claimed that most of the fields were neglected and were reverting to semi-desert. Nowhere between Jitkot and Taklakot did we encounter the least sign of mechanized farming.

In India we had heard a great deal about the improvements that the Chinese had brought to West Tibet, particularly with regard to the use of tractors and fertilizers. It was all the utmost nonsense; propaganda to delude the outside world into believing that the Chinese had taken over Tibet for the good of the Tibetans. No machines had been brought to West Tibet to aid the peasants in their struggle to increase the fertility of their obdurate soil.

On the way to Taklakot we passed through the village of Marsha Kalya, shown on the Indian Survey Map as Lokpo. We sat down on the northern outskirts for a breather, and the villagers soon gathered round us to have a look at the strangers. They answered our questions in a surprisingly open manner, stating that there had been no improvements under the Chinese. Taxes had risen; freedom of movement had been curtailed. It was the same story that we had heard of before When they were asked if they liked the Chinese Communists they gave the stock, highly revealing reply, 'The Chinese are our masters.'

'They are all afraid,' said Harrop, 'that Big Brother might be watching, or at least listening-in.'

Gin-Din-Rhou, watering his horse by a stream, called out to us, and Damodar interpreted.

'He says that when we meet the Chinese we must not speak to the Tibetan people, as to do so would create difficulty for them. The Chinese would think the villagers were in our employ.'

The old man certainly knew what the score was with the Chinese, but he was too circumspect to voice any outright criticism.

Meanwhile our captors came into view. They had come expecting to convoy us all the way from Jitkot, and were, no doubt, surprised that we should come along on our own without the threat of armed force. There were the by now familiar figures clad in quilted cotton khaki uniform, hats with black sheepskin earflaps and the usual brown or bright blue tennis shoes. As usual, they were well armed, every man carrying a Tommy gun, four spare magazines clipped to the belt and four stick grenades slung from the shoulder in a canvas holder.

With them was the Dzongpen, but he was no longer the friendly, agreeable fellow of a few days before. When we tried to strike up a conversation with him, to remind him that he had promised our release within four days, he retained a sullen silence. Our arguments were dismissed with a wave of the hand and we were told to keep close to the soldiers. The headman of Taklakot was also with them and, unlike the Dzongpen, he had much to say. Talking volubly to Gin-Din-Rhou and then to the Dzongpen, he pointed at us with a far from friendly look on his filthy face.

The troops having formed up around us, we started off again. As we trudged along the narrow stony track the sinister, squat figure of the headman dominated the entire party. Eager to ingratiate himself with the Chinese, he kept pushing his horse into us to hurry us along. When I threatened to brain him with my ice-axe, he appealed to the escort and thereafter I was urged on with the barrel of a Tommy gun.

Once—whether by accident or design I did not enquire—Damodar managed to poke the headman's horse in the rear with the point of his ice-axe. The horse jumped, nearly unseating its rider, who swung round and cursed us with obscene Tibetan phrases which were soon to become all too familiar to us. They were employed endlessly by some of our Chinese guards.

The company of the Chinese and the Taklakot headman marred a walk which, otherwise, had everything to commend it. It was a beautiful sunny day with a bright blue sky ornamented with a few odd wisps of cloud. The air was pleasant to the nostrils, save when the too-near presence of the headman gave to it the odour of a foul drain.

The weather in Tibet in autumn and winter compares favourably with a really good summer on the south coast of France. Finding it too hot for sweaters, we peeled them off while our guards shepherded us along. I still wore my old tweed fishing hat which the Chinese found amusing. Harrop sported a pair of old grey flannel trousers with a hole in either knee. His big blue sweater had a hole a foot square in the chest. The holes in the trousers were the results of fair wear and tear, but the hole in his sweater was the work of mice back in our base camp in Nepal.

Surprisingly the Chinese always wore the same outfit in every kind of weather, and on hot days they must have boiled inside their padded uniforms.

We shared a bar of chocolate as we walked, and when it was finished I screwed up the wrapper and tossed it away. A young Chinese soldier dashed after it, imagining perhaps that we were trying to dispose of incriminating evidence. He handed it to the Dzongpen, who examined it carefully before putting it into the breast pocket of his tunic.

The track now ran parallel to a small village and for reasons I could not fathom the Dzongpen, Gin-Din-Rhou and the headman dismounted and called to some Tibetans who took the horses and mules away. Thereafter they continued on foot.

We had not yet reached the end of our journey, having at least a mile to go before arriving at our new quarters. Our porters with their heavy loads now lagged well behind, but the Chinese paid them only scant attention. The track ran down to a small bridge which spanned a river not marked on the map; a tributary of the Karnali. The great ridge overlooking Taklakot lay dead ahead and the huge monastery with its rambling structure could be seen perched at the highest point.

It was considerably larger than Gin-Din-Rhou's Gompa, but not as symmetrical in shape. It gave the impression that the original building had been much smaller and that odd rooms and outer walls had been added as need dictated throughout its long history. A highly picturesque place, its colours were totally different from those of the monasteries of Jitkot and Kojarnath. In addition to the usual monastic red, there were walls painted in white and yellow—a fine subject for a colour film.

The colours of the monastery contrasted strangely with those of the scattered homesteads. The latter were coloured with a kind of whitewash, the usual stacks of brushwood lining the outer edges of the walls and roofs. Occasionally we passed a house that sported a little clump of parched-looking poplar trees outside.

We crossed the bridge to see a huge encampment of tents ahead. There must have been a hundred of them at least, but, contrary to expectations, they did not house a regiment of Chinese troops. They made up a trading bazaar populated by Bhotia traders from India. Tibetans from the local villages came here to trade their salt and buy articles ranging from cheap Indian shoes to bowler hats. A Tibetan clad in sheepskin and wearing a bowler hat adorned with a large pink silk bow is a sight for weary eyes. The Tibetans like strange headgear, and the more bizarre it is, the higher the price they are willing to pay for it.

Soap was sold here, but the Tibetans would have none of it. It was bought only by the Chinese soldiers.

The Dzongpen was determined that we should have no chance of meeting any Indians who might carry the news of our arrest to the outside world. We turned sharp right and skirted the bottom of the ridge. In spite of this, I thought that the Chinese idea of security measures was completely inadequate. The Tibetans, who are notorious gossips, would be bound to talk about us to the Indians. For that matter there was the Indian trader at the monastery at Jitkot, whom the Chinese obviously knew nothing about.

It was evident by now that we were not to be quartered at Taklakot Gompa, for we had already passed the track that led up to it.

The cliff face we were skirting was honeycombed with cave dwellings. There were hundreds of them dotting the vertical two-hundred-feet wall of conglomerate. Some of these dwellings were quite elaborate in design, the fronts being bricked up, entrance being gained via a well-fitted wooden door. Some had small courtyards in which animals were tethered. The higher ones, however, were the most interesting, having terraced verandahs built out of the rock face. These verandahs were made of slender tree branches and had handrails running around the outer edge, and from them hung hundreds of brightly coloured prayer-flags. In some instances half a dozen caves were joined by a single verandah, the sole means of entrance and exit being a forty-feet ladder made of poplar branches. The number of these dwellings compared with houses convinced me that the majority of the inhabitants of Taklakot are still cave-dwellers.

Smoke issued from most of the entrances, and there was a great deal of activity, people constantly coming and going, scurrying up and down the ladders. Most of the heavy load-carrying was done by women.

'Just think,' said Harrop, 'we're going to eat Chinese for a while at no charge.'

A few months earlier, when on a visit to the Royal Geographical Society in London, I had taken Harrop to a Chinese restaurant where he had had his first experience of Chinese cooking. His enjoyment of the chicken chop suey had been marred by a too large helping of chilli sauce which had brought tears to his eyes.

'Bags of chop suey, eh,' he said, 'and no ruddy chillies!'

I brightened a little at the prospect, for I had become utterly weary of tsampa and chupatties.

'Do you think we shall have dinner with the officers?' I asked.

'Bound to.' Harrop was blessed with an exuberant confidence. 'They can't be so uncivilized as not to invite two strangers into their mess.'

In this optimistic and unsuspecting frame of mind we visualized the various tempting and exotic menus for which we would ask.

The area was dotted with the ruins of ancient mud-brick forts, and I expressed to Harrop the hope that the Chinese might allow us to examine, measure and photograph them. How naive we were! These ruins were similar in appearance to the ones excavated by Sir Aurel Stein in the Taklamakan desert in Central Asia in the early part of the present century.

It is possible that these forts once formed part of the trade life-line that stretched from Peking to India, being built to protect the caravans that, two thousand years ago, carried the precious silks and spices of old Cathay on their long journey across Asia. The number of European travellers in this area could be counted on the fingers of one hand, and it is possible that these ancient ruins dated back to either the Song Dynasty of A.D. 960 to A.D. 1280, or to the Tan Dynasty of A.D. 617 to A.D. 907. They might, indeed, have been built during the Han Dynasty of 206 B.C. to A.D. 220. Of one thing we were sure: they had never been investigated by any European.

Reaching a point where the river lapped against the cliff face, we overcame the impasse by ascending a steep track to the top of the ridge.

Suddenly my deliberations were violently interrupted. A blow from behind jarred me in the middle of my back. It was our old friend the headman giving a little demonstration of his power when protected by six men armed with machine-guns.

In a fit of rage I grabbed him by the coat with my left hand and hit out with my right. In his efforts to avoid the blow he stepped back over the edge of the track and tumbled some twenty feet, executing a couple of cartwheels as he did so.

Tension relaxed when the two young Chinese soldiers bringing up the rear burst into laughter. They shouted some rude remarks at the headman and then laughed even louder. But when they heard me join in, the boyish good humour vanished from their faces. One of their staunch supporters had lost face and at the hands of a 'foreign devil' at that. They grimly motioned me to proceed up the track.

As the track reached its highest point, I looked to my right across the Karnali river. The river bank opposite rose into a vertical cliff that at times was overhanging. There was ample evidence of its decay in the huge blocks of conglomerate that lay at its foot. Beyond were two large buildings. One, painted red, was a residence of monks or Lamas, but the other building, obviously of recent construction, was painted a dull, flat grey. Both had only one storey, but each covered a much larger area than the average Tibetan house. The sides of the grey building were about fifty yards in length and the walls were about fifteen feet high, and it was obvious that this was an army barracks built by the Chinese. The red building had been commandeered from the Lamas and was now used as officers' quarters. Here resided the C.O. of Taklakot, the cold-blooded butcher who, only a few months earlier, had shot one of his men.

Behind the two buildings was a hill several hundred feet high and building work was in progress on the top of it. The walls of a much larger barracks were in the final stages of completion, and scores of khaki-clad figures scurried in and out. They never walked anywhere, everything being done at the double.

A winding track led to the top of the hill, and this was covered by a ceaseless procession of human figures and animals. Yaks carried huge balks of timber, and mules fitted with pack frames carried boxes of equipment or loads of four-gallon tins of water. Long lines of Tibetan women trudged slowly and wearily uphill, each one bearing a basket on her back supported by a head-band. The baskets were filled with stones, and each woman must have been carrying at least a hundred pounds.

A queue of women with empty baskets ran nimbly downhill, skilfully circumventing the clumsy slow-moving yaks which seemed to take up all the available space. Down by the river bank a platoon of soldiers was filling the four-gallon cans with water and loading them on to the mules, four cans to each mule. The production line was active all the time and never once became still during the ensuing seven weeks of our imprisonment.

The three buildings at the other side of the river were to assume a great significance for us. The red-painted one was the H.Q. of the interrogating committee and 'Peoples' Court'. The new building on the top of the hill was to become, not only a barracks, but also a short-wave radio station by which the Chinese kept in daily contact with

Lhasa and Peking. Although we did not know it at the time, the Dzongpen had made a serious *faux pas* by taking us along a track that gave us a full view of the building operations. It is significant that, on our release, we were taken away on mules and made to ford the Karnali river twice to prevent us climbing this high-level track which gave us such a fine view of the new Chinese military fortifications.

After skirting the top of the hill for some two hundred yards the track descended again and we walked along within a few yards of the river's edge. The dwellings to be seen were now few in number, and we came to the last one. Beyond it the bank declined gradually towards the river and to a large bridge which connected our side of the river with the one that was crawling with Chinese.

The last building was to be our new home. At precisely 3 p.m. the double doors leading into the courtyard opened and we stepped through. Apart from interrogations we were not to set foot outside the building again for nearly seven weeks.

Chapter 9

PRISON LIFE

'It doesn't look like a luxury hotel, does it?'

I had to agree with Harrop. Our new quarters were depressing in the extreme, and we consoled ourselves with the hope that they were merely temporary. We were left standing in the middle of the yard, our armed escort vanishing through a doorway. Gin-Din-Rhou, the Dzongpen and the Taklakot headman, after a short conversation, followed the soldiers indoors. Left to our own devices, we decided to have a look round.

The courtyard was in two parts, one higher than the other and connected by a small flight of steps. The higher part of the yard was surrounded by living quarters comprising four rooms. The lower part had a wall running round it equipped with a firing step so that the guards could survey the outside at will. On the right-hand side of the yard door by which we had entered was a primitive kitchen which was nothing more than two walls with a tattered tarpaulin thrown over the top. The fireplace was the usual Tibetan one made of dried mud. Three large urns were boiling away on top of it.

At the opposite end of the yard was the lavatory, consisting of a walled enclosure with two holes in the floor which gave access to a pit under the foundations. At the rear of the yard stood the main building, equipped with two windows. The small one had iron strips fastened across it, while the other, a much larger one, was paned with glass— the first glass window we had seen in Tibet. This was the guard-room, while the room with the barred window was to be our communal cell.

On either side of the yard were two tiny cells, neither of them in the least inviting. What light penetrated the small window holes showed the interior to be mud-floored and mud-walled and inches deep in dust. The building, once a Tibetan house, was now used as the official Chinese prison. Two small dead trees occupied either end of the roof and a string of tattered prayer-flags hung dismally in between.

We dumped our rucksacks on the floor and sat on the bottom of the courtyard steps. We were beginning to feel hungry and our appetites were further strengthened by the odour of boiling mutton

73

from the kitchen. Every so often I looked at the glass window, which was evidently intended as an observation point. The Dzongpen was talking to someone whom I could not see.

I got the impression that we were being watched by more than one pair of eyes. I turned to Harrop and was discussing the situation with him when I was startled to hear a strange voice behind me addressing Damodar in Hindi.

Turning, I was surprised to see an Indian-looking individual emerging from the guardroom. Friendly looking, his smile was made more noticeable by two prominent gold teeth. His hair was well greased and brushed back and he wore clothes that stamped him as of higher caste than the coolies we had met on our march into Nepal. Most impressive were his boots, a beautiful pair of knee-high riding-boots of excellent quality leather. They were unusual in that they had a slit down the back where they were laced up.

He walked over to Damodar and sat beside him. He spoke Nepali as well as Hindi, and to our surprise he greeted us with outstretched hand instead of the usual salaam with palms held together. His coat was of well-tailored gaberdine cloth and light blue flannels were tucked into his leather riding-boots. His right hand, which held mine in a firm handshake, was covered with gold rings, some of them set with stones.

He told us that he was a trader from Kalimpong, having a house and shop there, and that he visited Taklakot once a year in pursuit of his trade as a cloth merchant. While in the tent bazaar at Taklakot he had heard of our predicament and feeling that one member of the Commonwealth should help another he had come along to give what assistance he could.

When I asked if he was afraid of the Chinese, he replied that there was no cause to fear them. The Chinese were his best customers, buying a great deal of cloth from him.

His confident manner quickly reassured us. He promised to have a chat with the Dzongpen and the C.O. of the garrison and matters would be put right very quickly. Our plight, he told us confidently, was due to nothing more than a misunderstanding. The Chinese were naturally suspicious of our intentions, but an honest statement of our reasons for being in that part of the Himalayas would clear matters up.

He asked who we were, the name of our expedition, how long we had been in West Nepal, how many were in the entire party, and several other questions. But his question as to who sent us created

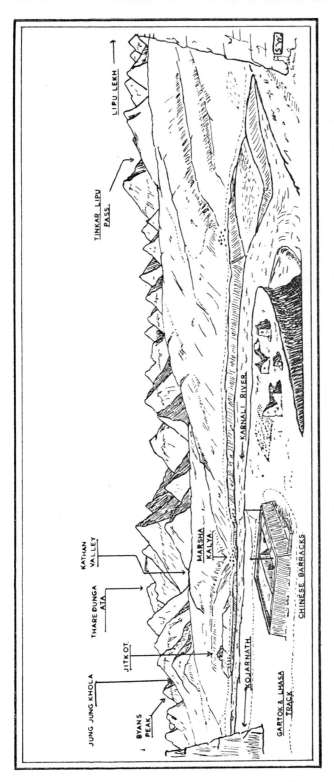

Author's sketch of the Nepal-Tibet Himalaya skyline (Zaskar Range) from his cell window at Taklakot military prison

difficulty. He seemed unable to believe that we were there simply because we wished to visit the Himalayas and climb mountains.

Coming a little closer, he whispered, 'If you tell me the real reason why you are here I shall be in a better position to help you.'

That was enough. Both Harrop and I smelt a rat, a Chinese-inspired rat. We broke off the conversation and the Indian called back to the guardroom, but not in Hindi or Nepalese. This time he spoke in Chinese, and he spoke the language fluently.

The Dzongpen came out, followed by the entire retinue of armed guards. We were lined up against the wall and told that we were to be searched. We clasped our hands behind our heads while the Dzongpen ran his hands through our pockets, once again apologizing for the inconvenience we were suffering. He was rudely pushed aside by the Indian, who went over us much more thoroughly. He missed not a thing. We even had to remove our boots for him to examine them for concealed messages.

The search was in progress when Koila and the other three porters arrived, and the Chinese soldiers went through our kit item by item. Bars of chocolate, meat blocks and pemmican were opened, the contents being thrown back into our food-box with expressions of disgust and disappointment. They wanted us to be spies and they could find no evidence to support their suspicions.

The Dzongpen wished to end the search, but the Indian engaged him in a heated argument and finished up by searching us a second time. By now Harrop and I were beginning to lose our tempers, and the whole business was becoming deadly serious.

What was it they expected to find? Whatever it was, all our equipment was carried away and deposited in the tiny cell next door to the guardroom. As the food-box was going in company with the rest Harrop shouted: 'They're not getting away with that. God knows what the food will be like here.'

All three of us raised hell, and, after a long argument, the food-box and one billycan were restored to us and we were told to put them in what they called our 'room'. In no other part of the world would it have received such a dignified term.

We were allowed to keep a few items of personal clothing, our Li-Lo air mattresses, torches and sleeping-bags. My diary and a Penguin publication of *The Century of Poetry from Pope to Keats* were confiscated, Harrop's protests concerning the poetry being of no avail. The book might contain a code or cypher and away to the political intelligence bureau it had to go.

The diary was no great loss, as it contained nothing more than an account of events since leaving base camp on October 19th. There was nothing in it that could be employed against us, and nothing that could not be remembered should it not be returned to me.

We were motioned indoors and carried our sleeping-bags into our communal cell. Damodar dropped his in the middle of the floor and clouds of dust rose to choke us. We soon learnt that it was unwise to stamp about in our new home. The dust on the floor was at least two inches deep and, in spite of all our precautions, it succeeded in getting into everything we possessed. The dust was the room's only furniture, and there was no heating. The food-box we placed in the middle of the floor as a table, piling our sleeping-bags on top of it until we had the air mattresses inflated and laid on the floor.

I bent down and looked through the iron-strapped window, to see the first of the regular shift of guards just coming on duty. He emerged from the guardroom slinging his Tommy gun over his shoulder. Walking to our window, he motioned me away from it with the barrel of his gun.

Because he was tall we christened him 'Lofty', and we soon had appropriate nicknames for all of them. 'Fatty', 'Monkey Face', 'Chubby', 'Chungnya', 'Schickelgruber' and 'Marlo', the last being an abbreviation of the swear word with which he prefaced every sentence.

Guard duties never lasting longer than two hours, we saw different faces at frequent intervals. Not for a moment were we without supervision, and the guards stood outside the window twenty-four hours a day. At 5 p.m., when we had about settled into our new home, dinner was brought in. The guard who brought it was cook for that day and the two ensuing days. The cook was changed every three days, without any reference to skill or experience in such an important sphere. As luck had it, only one knew how to cook, the one who brought us our first meal. We asked him his name. He responded by pointing to his nose—a trick of the Chinese when referring to themselves—and said something that sounded like 'Chungnya'. In fact, we got it wrong. The word is not pronounced like that, and what he really said was that he was Chinese. The name stuck, however, and whenever we wanted him we shouted 'Chungnya' and he came running.

He was twenty-two years old and very likeable, as was his bosom friend Chubby. The rest of them were far from pleasant and at times were downright disagreeable.

The food on that first day was good, but the quality was not to last. Thereafter it deteriorated day by day until, in the end, it was unfit to eat.

Dinner consisted of curried mutton and rice. We had barely begun to eat it when there was a commotion outside. We leapt up, to see Koila put his face to the bars.

'The Chinese are sending us away,' he cried. 'We shall never see you again.'

Pushing past the guard in the doorway, we ran into the yard in time to see our faithful Dhoties being pushed through the yard door. Our cell guard ran over to give a hand in thrusting Koila out for he was putting up quite a struggle. I seized the opportunity to ru,sh back to the cell and scribble a note on a scrap of paper, addressing it to Jack Henson at our base camp in Saipal. I stated briefly that we were in the hands of the Chinese and that he must get word to the U.K. High Commission in Delhi without delay.

I returned to the yard to find Koila gone. He was walking down the track with the other three Dhoties, but when I called to him he ran back. I got one leg through the yard door, but was seized by the guards. Koila, tears streaming down his face, threw his arms round my neck.

As the Chinese tore us apart I managed to stuff the folded piece of paper into his hand. With that he was gone. As they went I told Damodar to shout after them and tell them they had served us well; that we appreciated their loyalty, and that they could keep the sleeping-bags, windproof clothing and boots we had issued to them.

I sighed with relief as I was being dragged back to the cell. Very soon the outside world would know of our plight. If it was humanly possible to get back over the mountain barrier under the prevailing monsoon conditions, then Koila was the man to do it. Nevertheless, he and his friends faced a formidable task. The Chinese had not allowed us to give them either food or money, and they had neither tents nor stoves with which to cross a 19,500-feet pass, well above the snowline at that time of the year.

The note was essential to get things moving without loss of time. For while the other members of the expedition would realize something was wrong when Koila returned without us, none of our party could speak Hindi or Nepali, nor would an interpreter be available until they reached the Nepalese school at Chainpur, eight or nine days' march from base camp. The note would make everything clear within seconds.

That the Dhoties did win through under the most hostile conditions, arriving at Saipal camp in the final stages of physical exhaustion, does them the greatest credit. Harrop, Damodar and I have every reason to be grateful to our faithful porters.

We finished our meal, refusing a second helping because our appetites had vanished under a weighty depression. Harrop voiced all our thoughts when he said:

'Sending back our porters is hardly the action of a friendly people. It looks as though they intend to keep us here for some time.'

'Maybe they are going to send us to Lhasa,' said Damodar. 'Or, worse still, Chungking.'

It was such a dismal possibility that it stifled further conversation. We turned in.

Chapter 10

ENTER SCHICKELGRUBER

Sleep on that first night in prison was fitful and troubled. I had to get up once to make a journey to the lavatory, the guard at the door accompanying me to my destination and back, his Tommy gun levelled at me all the time.

After that I slept a little, my dozing being interrupted by a torch being shone on my face through the window every five minutes or so. Our objections to the torchlight only succeeded in arousing the guard's anger and he annoyed us all the more.

For me, morning could not come too quickly, and it was heralded by the sunlight projecting the pattern of the barred window on the wall by the foot of Harrop's bag. As it was bitterly cold we simply sat up in our sleeping-bags waiting to see what would happen next.

At 8.30 a.m. the young fellow who had delivered the evening meal came in bearing a bowl of hot water. No soap was provided, and our efforts to explain that we could hardly wash without it merely caused the guard to shake his head.

Sorting amongst my possessions I had the good fortune to come upon a tiny piece of soap. A very small cube, its real purpose was to rub on to the lenses of snow goggles to prevent them misting over. Harrop and I had a wash, but Damodar decided to follow the example of the Tibetans and revert to nature.

Breakfast arrived at 9.30, a thin stew of very small turnips which the Chinese called 'chigada', in which were the bones from the previous night's dinner. There was plain rice for a filler, so we made up for the lack of quality with bulk food.

The air temperature outside now beginning to become bearable, Harrop went into the yard to greet the sun. Small pools of ice covered the yard floor where the Chinese had thrown the slops from their tea the night before. Personal cleanliness and hygiene seemed to be absent from their nature. We could hear them clearing their throats and spitting in their own quarters and even in the kitchen. This was a very objectionable universal habit, in which all seven of the guards indulged throughout the day. They did not suspend this unpleasant activity even during their meals, very often putting me off my food.

Breakfast was being served to the guards, and Harrop called

Damodar and me out to see the 'animals being fed', as he put it. Six of the guards sat cross-legged in the form of a circle in the centre of the yard floor, the sentry on duty remaining at his post. Each man had a small bowl containing rice, and before them in the middle of their circle was a huge brass pot filled with turnip and meat stew. We noticed that the guards had a more generous supply of meat with their meals than was given to ourselves.

Each man dug into the communal pot with a pair of chopsticks and fished out a piece of meat. Anything not to his taste he spat out on to the floor. When the chopsticks failed to perform their function, a grimy hand was thrust into the pot and then it seemed a competition took place to see who could wash his hands in the gravy first. My curiosity as to how they picked up the rice with the chopsticks was satisfied when the guards placed the lip of a small bowl in their mouths and then pushed the contents in with the aid of the chopsticks.

This was accompanied by the most awful noise, like water vanishing down a bath plug. We started to laugh and tried to imitate their animal-like gurglings, but our parody of their actions had no effect on their bland faces. They simply went on eating bowl after bowl of rice followed by enormous quantities of meat.

We were motioned to the kitchen to obtain our morning mug of tea. One of the soldiers interrupted his gargantuan meal to follow us inside the canvas-covered enclosure. Lifting the lid from one of the pots boiling on the top of the fire, he revealed the 'tea'.

The raw product of this Chinese tea comes in the form of a brick and is equally hard, the slab being about a foot square and two inches thick. The guards had to break it up with an axe, lumps of brick tea flying all over the yard as they did so. About half a pound having been placed in a bag, the bag is immersed in the water. Whether the water was hot or cold seemed of no importance. The tea did not infuse immediately as does the Indian tea to which we are accustomed, but had to boil for some time before it started to colour the water.

The tea stewed day and night and the contents of the bag were changed only once a week. The longer it stewed the more darkly it stained the water, but the taste remained always the same—mild and insipid. As the tea was consumed, the urn was topped up with ever more cold water and by the end of the week the brew was simply hot water, having neither taste nor colour.

Our guards had a small supply of sugar which looked for all the world like rock salt, supplied by the Indian traders who camped in the shadow of the great monastery nearby. Sugar did not figure as part of

F

the Chinese rations, and the troops had to purchase it at their own expense, along with soap, toothpaste, hair creams and cheap perfumes.

We were surprised to discover that these men used perfume. Quite unselfconsciously they came out of their quarters rubbing the foul-smelling stuff over their faces as if it were an after-shave lotion.

We devised a rationing system of our own, conserving the pemmican and meat blocks should the food become either unacceptable in quality or inadequate in quantity, at the same time enjoying a little of our precious sugar and condensed milk in the tea.

Breakfast over, the remains of the bowl of meat were tossed over the wall. Our plates were taken into the kitchen for washing-up, a scene which I devoutly wished I had never witnessed. The greasy dishes swam about in lukewarm water to be eventually dried with a cloth that was soot-black with dirt. If the diet didn't bring us down with disease, then I felt sure that the microbes would. Several times during the washing-up, Lofty paused to clear his throat and spit on the floor. A little monkey-faced character sat by the fireplace cutting up meat and bones for the evening stew, every so often thrusting a chunk of raw mutton into his mouth and eating it with obvious relish.

Harrop was quick to discover what we could and could not do. Looking over the yard wall was strictly forbidden. Approaching the yard door or even looking through it when it was open was sufficient to bring a stern reproof from the guard who stood on the roof during daylight hours. Exercise outside the yard, too, was forbidden, which provoked from us a long letter of protest to the officers, in which we drew attention to our unpleasant living conditions, lack of heating and the general state of the food. We included a request to be allowed a daily walk along the river bank accompanied by a guard. This letter, like every one that we wrote, was ignored. The officers never so much as deigned to visit our cell.

This was a curious state of affairs, and it seemed that none of the Taklakot officers had the authority to carry out an interrogation, and that they were awaiting the arrival of superiors, possibly from Gartok. In the meantime we could only wait, anxiously wondering how long the waiting would last.

At 5 p.m. we were ushered indoors at machine-gun point and the long night began. Once the sun went down it was too cold to stay out of bed, and it was too cold to get up before 9 a.m. Thus when we turned in at 5 p.m., which we often did, we were compelled to spend no less than sixteen hours in bed.

Putting on our down-filled jackets and windproofs, we walked about the cell. It soon became dark and, as we had no means of illumination, into bed we had to go. I tucked myself in, secreting Harrop's torch inside my sleeping-bag. Then, deep down inside my bag and out of sight of the suspicious eyes of our captors, I wrote my diary.

For two days the diary was written in this manner, but on the third day one of the guards came in and subjected me to a search. The pieces of evidence were confiscated and my diary-writing was suspended for the time being.

The guard who confiscated the diary signified by mime and sign language that he was riding off that day to see the officers who were either at or on their way from Gartok. This guard looked most un-Chinese and reminded us of a friend back home, Flight-Lieutenant 'Rocky' Sims, a member of the R.A.F. expedition to the Indian Himalayas that same year. So striking was the resemblance that both Harrop and I commented on it simultaneously.

'Looks like Sims,' I said.

'Yes,' said Harrop, 'but he's a bit smarter than Sims.'

'True, but his boots could do with a bit of a polish.'

From then on we called this character 'Flight-Lieutenant J. R. Sims'. He left that day, and was never again posted back to our prison, but we saw him pass our cell on occasion, while carrying out his new duties as courier. A fine horseman, who handled his mount like Buffalo Bill, he used to give us a yell as he went by.

'The Lone Star Ranger rides tonight,' we would shout. 'Hi-ho, Silver!' It was then that we noticed he wore a pair of leather riding-boots, laced up at the back, the same as the self-styled Indian trader who had searched us on October 28th.

The following morning a new, and by no means pleasant, face appeared in the yard. We were sitting down eating a meal of boiled turnips, minus any meat, when two of our regular guards, Chubby and Marlo, came in through the yard door bearing a load of bedding. Behind them came a man who was to be the bane of our existence. He was appointed sergeant in charge of our guards, probably for the purpose of stiffening up discipline before the officers arrived.

An ugly character with a mean, bad-tempered air, he looked more Japanese than Chinese, and we soon christened him 'Schickelgruber'.

His bedding was taken into the guardroom and he stood looking at us. We looked at him—hard.

'Here's a character to be watched,' said Harrop.

He had barely spoken when the ugly little brute screamed an

order. The guard on duty ran over and handed his Tommy gun to Schickelgruber.

Holding it in one hand, he waved it back and forth from one to the other of us. We had stopped eating and waited, watching his left hand which kept opening and closing. He muttered under his breath, his voice rising and falling. Gradually it became louder and his eyes started to bulge. I had never before seen a Chinaman lose his temper and it was anything but a pretty sight.

The louder he shouted the more his eyes seemed to thrust out until they appeared to stand out like pegs. I felt more and more uneasy until the colour of his face changed from its normal sallow complexion to a deep purple.

The rest of the guards came into the yard, their preparations for breakfast disturbed by their new N.C.O.'s coarse voice. The situation exploded when he levelled his gun and screamed at the guards, who started to usher us into our cell. We started to kick up a fuss at being sent indoors so early in the morning, but without avail.

I wrote a strong letter to the officers and shouted for Chungnya through the window. He took the note and went across the river to the officers' quarters. I never received a reply.

That night I resolved that I would somehow manage to keep a diary, which all three of us regarded as essential. But where was I to hide the entries where the guards would not discover them? In addition, an entry damaging to the Chinese might result in a worsen- of our conditions if the notes should fall into their hands.

I was turning over in my sleeping-bag when I found the answer to the problem. I felt the ground beneath me. The air mattress had developed a slow leak, so I leaned over to blow a little air into the inflator tube. There was the solution.

I would roll the daily entries up into a slim tube and slide them down inside the pillow of the air bed. If I kept the bed constantly inflated, the Chinese would never tumble to my trick. I wrote out a brief description of the day's events on a piece of chocolate wrapper and, with the aid of a broken chopstick Damodar had stolen from the kitchen to use as a teaspoon, I pushed the roll of paper inside the bed.

After that I used toilet paper (while it lasted), Ovosport wrappers, Chinese paper cigarette packets which we picked up from the yard, and Kendal Mint Cake wrappers. A record of everything that took place and the questions and answers during my five periods of 'thought reform' at the hands of the 'Peoples' Court' were duly pushed into the pillow. The immediate problem had been solved, but there was the chance that the air bed might be deflated and the bulging contents discovered when the time came for our release. I could only wait and see.

Harrop decided that a calendar was needed to keep a check on the date and days of the week. The top twelve inches of the wall of our cell was painted white and blue, as though the previous tenants had undertaken some simple decorating. Harrop used the white-painted sections, which were about six inches by nine, to write the date and day of the week, adding pertinent and insulting remarks about the intellect and habits of the Chinese Communists. In large bold type I wrote: 'Harrop, Suwal and Wignall of the Welsh Himalayan Expedition. Kidnapped by the Chinese Communists on the 25th of Oct. 1955, and imprisoned in this cell from Oct. 28th until . . . ?'

The final date could only be filled in by the Chinese.

The days dragged slowly by. Harrop, writing the November days one by one on the wall, remarked that there were not many shopping days to Christmas, and what did we intend to buy for the 'Cheenee Bara Rajah Sahib' if we were still in clink on Christmas Day? The final decision was a copy of *How To Win Friends and Influence People*, with a *Shot of Deadly Nightshade* in his morning porridge as a close second.

I had promised my wife that we would be back home in England a fortnight before Christmas. Now we were faced with the prospect of spending one, and perhaps several, Christmases in a Chinese prison, a thought too stark to be entertained.

'Let's see what the Chinese officers are like,' said Harrop. 'If they don't act reasonable, we'll all go over the wall.' With that we were all in agreement. The Chinese had the place well guarded, but the thought of several years in a cell was sufficient to make us decide that, should there be no hope of an early release, then we had to escape.

That night my sleep was disturbed by something crawling over my face. The guard happened to shine his torch through the bars just as I awoke, and I found myself looking into the face of a very under-nourished-looking rat perched on the lip of my sleeping-bag. He beat a hasty retreat across the room and vanished behind Damodar's head. Afterwards I could hear this rodent chewing something, but for all Damodar cared it might have been his left ear, for nothing ever disturbed him once he had fallen asleep.

Unlike Harrop and me, who accused each other of snoring in the most atrocious manner, Damodar moaned and cried in his sleep. When we chaffed him about it he asked if it kept us awake, and when we said no he replied that our snoring kept him awake all night. This was unlikely, for we had the greatest difficulty in getting him out of bed in a morning. Nothing short of a well-aimed rubber flashlight succeeded in waking him, and even then he only stirred at the sight of food.

After that the rats and occasional small pug-nosed fat little mice became more bold and appeared in the daytime. Once we heard one chewing something hard in a corner of the room, and Harrop commented that it was probably chewing an old chupatty. This was meant to be a humorous remark, but, to our surprise, when we investigated we found that it was indeed half a very ancient and crisp chupatty that the rat had been chewing. The Tibetans claimed that they never ate chupatties, and the Chinese would not touch them. Could it be that one of the Indian nationals had been a prisoner in our cell? That was one of the many questions that remained unanswered.

On November 3rd Harrop decided to try and get some of our equipment from the guardroom, and he tackled Chungnya about it. We were allowed to follow two of the guards into the small bare room where our kit was kept and after a great deal of argument we managed to carry away our last packet of toilet paper, a pair of scissors, two spare flashlamp batteries and some pills.

Schickelgruber was away at the time, and had he been there I am sure he would have denied us access to our kit. Later in the day, Chungnya brought in two tiny Tibetan stools for use as tables. We piled our few precious possessions on them and thanked him for his kindness.

I soon began to feel the effects of dysentery, which I had contracted in Meshed in Eastern Persia several months before and which had never left me. The pills we had taken from our bags were Sulphaguanadine tablets and were carried expressly to cure my illness.

I sat in the middle of the yard and pulled out the bottle of pills from my pocket. The little monkey-faced guard had just entered the yard with Schickelgruber and they saw me putting one of the pills into my mouth. Instantly they dashed over and Monkey Face snatched the bottle, handing it triumphantly to Schickelgruber. I started to protest, and Harrop and Damodar, hearing the commotion, ran out of the cell. It all ended with several of the guards seeking out their Tommy guns and herding us back into our cell. It was only noon, but we were locked in for the day. The final indignity was to have to make several trips to the lavatory hole during the afternoon, accompanied by an armed guard who, throughout, held the barrel of his Tommy gun about three inches from my ear.

We sent a further letter of protest to the officers, and from our cell window saw it delivered to the grey barracks on the other side of the river. Harrop eventually discovered why our letters were being ignored. 'Perhaps they haven't anyone in Taklakot who can speak English,' he said. 'If so, they'll probably bring someone in who can read our letters.'

In fact, he was perfectly right. The only man in West Tibet able to speak or read English was the assistant to the provincial Governor, and this gentleman was very soon to make his appearance. Perhaps all the letters were handed over for translation, but if so it made no difference. None of our complaints or requests was ever acknowledged.

On November 4th, feeling no better, I remarked that I could not face the boiled turnips that morning. So Harrop and Damodar kindly offered to take our billycan into the yard and make a separate brew of tea, the Indian tea we had brought from England.

They disappeared through the cell door and, a few minutes later, I heard an argument in progress in the kitchen. Damodar came back and placed his face against the window bars.

'Marlo is on duty and won't let us have any boiling water. We will make a separate fire of our own in the yard.'

With that he went back to Harrop who had suspended the can from a stick jammed into a cleft in the mud-brick wall. He soon had a small fire going underneath it, and I was anticipating the luxury of a cup of tea when a fearful hubbub broke out in the yard. Still feeling shaky and feverish, I crept to the window to see Marlo looking at the water-filled can and shrieking his head off. This hullabaloo brought out the rest of the guards and Harrop pointed to the cell and tried to explain that I was sick. It had no effect on our captors, least of all on Schickelgruber, who started to push Damodar about.

Harrop demanded that he should lay off Damodar, and the sergeant turned and kicked the can across the yard. He then picked up a heavy stick about five feet long and aimed it at Damodar, who leapt nimbly out of the way of it. Harrop's physical intervention was restricted by two of the guards, who grabbed him by either arm. Both the Chinese were small and light, and Harrop, who is over six feet tall and weighs fourteen stone in his stocking feet, managed to work his way across the yard, carrying the Chinese with him.

The armed guard whom we called Fatty now joined in the fray and started to push Damodar about with the barrel of his Tommy gun. Infuriated by this senseless example of intolerance, I shouted insulting remarks through the window. This only brought out more Chinese and very soon six of them were engaged in the mêlée in the yard. I called to Damodar to make for the door before he got hurt, and he did so, fighting every inch of the way. When Harrop arrived in the doorway he had five of them hanging on to him.

They were determined to get him back indoors and, just for the hell of it, he refused to go in. It was obvious that Harrop, either disregarding or not realizing his danger, was thoroughly enjoying himself. Orders were no doubt that we were not to suffer physical harm until after the interrogation. Even so, Fatty cocked his Tommy gun and kept it trained on Harrop throughout the struggle.

It was an encouraging spectacle seeing one Englishman take on five Chinese at once. Fatty is not included in the count, for he merely kept pointing his gun and screaming with rage. Harrop had Marlo by the face, holding him firmly by the jaw with one hand. Monkey Face held on to Harrop's other arm, swinging on it like a small child.

Schickelgruber had Harrop by the neck, but Harrop, as if accidentally, moved back so that Schickelgruber was jammed between Harrop's muscular bulk and the doorway, which was now crammed with struggling human beings.

At last satisfied, Harrop slammed Marlo's head against the opposite wall of the passage. Shaking the rest of the guards from his shoulders like a man shaking raindrops from a coat, he strolled back into the room as if nothing had happened.

'Busy morning, eh?' he remarked casually.

With that the door was slammed and locked for the second day in succession.

Having the whole day before us with nothing to do, we sat and talked about our somewhat gloomy future prospects. I lay down to try to sleep after a while and Harrop busied himself searching for the fleas which made his life a torment. They must have been well camouflaged, for search as he might he could find none in his sleeping-bag. Gradually the trouble spread and after a few days we were bitten by all manner of things in the night.

Chapter 11

THE OFFICERS ARRIVE

FEELING feverish, the perspiration pouring down my face, I crawled back into bed. I was refused pills or medical attention and even denied a cup of tea. I began to fear that, in the absence of treatment, my condition might deteriorate to such a degree that I would be unfit for the march back to India when our day of release or escape came. I felt thoroughly depressed; so much so, in fact, that I could not remember feeling so dispirited before.

My depression was lightened a little by the running commentary from Damodar as he kept watch through the window. 'Marlo is holding his head in both hands. Perhaps John Sahib has broken his skull. Perhaps little bastard yellow is going to die.'

Despite my condition, I had to laugh. Damodar was always mixing up his sentences, amusing us when looking for something by saying, 'Where my socks are?' or 'Where my flashlight is?'

Marlo, however, was suffering from nothing worse than a headache, for Harrop's treatment had been much too gentle to break his skull. The Chinaman went indoors bemoaning his fate, and Chubby took over kitchen duties for the rest of the day. Shortly afterwards all the guards except Marlo gathered in the yard for a general discussion about the prisoners. They sat cross-legged in a circle and occasionally pointed to the cell to emphasize some point they were trying to make.

'They are sending Chungnya in,' said Damodar. 'Shall we do him as he comes through the door?'

The phrase 'do him' was one Damodar had picked up during his weeks with the expedition.

Harrop and I decided that we needed at least one friend while held under such foul conditions, and so we greeted Chungnya as if nothing had happened. By now he was able to pronounce our names in such a way that we knew to whom he was referring. Damodar he managed easily, but John he pronounced as 'Jung' and Syd as 'Chid'.

Sitting at the edge of my bed, he said nothing for a few seconds, then he grinned and pointed to Harrop, saying: '*Jung, ha, ha, ha. Yappa do.*' He meant that when in a good humour Harrop was considered to be all right by the Chinese. Then Chungnya clenched his hands, adopted an angry expression, and said, '*Jung, yappa mindo*,'[1] meaning that Harrop in a bad mood was to be considered a no-good character. The sign language thereafter became very involved, and we tried to put over our side of the case. At last he realized that I was ill, and he acknowledged our repeated requests for the Dzongpen with the word '*Lalasso*', which the Chinese use when they mean yes.

He had barely left the room when Schickelgruber appeared in the yard accompanied by a tall soldier who was greeted by some of the guards with a sloppy salute. His clothing differed not at all from that of the common soldier, for he wore the padded suit, fur-trimmed Davy Crocket hat and usual tennis shoes. Nevertheless, he was clearly superior in rank to Schickelgruber, who was obviously explaining the events of the morning.

His exaggerated mime was most amusing as he described how he kicked the deadly tea-can out of Harrop's hand and how he and his five friends, unaided, had succeeded in forcing two prisoners back into their cell. The man, apparently impressed, gave Schickelgruber an encouraging pat on the shoulder and left. There was no holding the poisonous N.C.O. after that, and he strutted round the yard like a rooster.

Marlo emerged from the guardroom holding his head and looking very sorry for himself. He pointed over the wall at the receding figure of the officer, apparently asking for some decoration to compensate him for his injuries. He and Schickelgruber finished up swearing at each other, their profanity consisting mainly of Tibetan words that we now understood.

Harrop grinned at me from his vantage point beside Damodar at the window. 'Looks,' he said, 'as though Marlo is going to start a counter-revolution.'

'Only because he has got a big head,' said Damodar, causing us all to laugh.

Schickelgruber suspended his altercation with Marlo to reprimand someone coming out of the guardroom. This was Chungnya, who ignored him and came into our cell, carrying an eiderdown quilt from his own bed. It was decorated with a beautifully coloured green silk panel with a fearsome-looking dragon rampant in the centre. I was already excessively hot in my sleeping-bag, but he ignored my protests and tucked the eiderdown all round me.

About half an hour later he appeared again, this time with a small bowl of very thin noodles on top of which was a poached egg. I could

[1] Tibetan for 'No'.

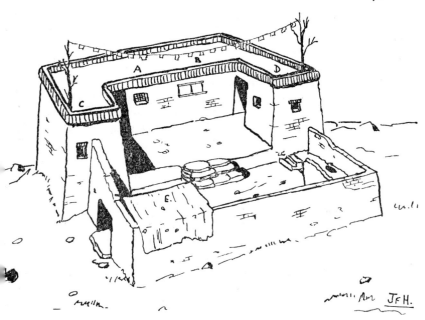

The prison at Taklakot in which Wignall
Harrop and Suwal were imprisoned
(a) Communal cell.   (b) Guardroom.   (c) Damodar's cell.
(d) Author's cell.   (e) Prison kitchen under tarpaulin.

hardly believe my eyes. We had seen one or two scraggy-looking
hens running about outside, but we had never thought to see an egg
in our prison. Ill as I was, the sight of such a dish restored my appetite, and I smiled my appreciation. Chungnya was the only Chinaman
we ever saw who appeared to be able to think and act independently.
The others, like so many sheep, ate, drank and slept strictly according
to orders.

'That boy should be the next Chinese Ambassador to the U.K.,'
said Harrop, as Chungnya departed.

I was inclined to agree. Chungnya was a perfect example of everything that is good in China. No amount of political indoctrination or
'thought reform' could subdue his strong individual personality. He
refused to be forced into the common intellectual mould which shapes
the minds of the young people of new China.

Darkness was failing when Fatty came in bearing a small oil-lamp
which he set on one of our tables. He signified that the light must be
left on all night to allow the guard to see inside the cell. This was a

new departure. Either it was intended to keep an eye on my condition in case of complications or was simply to facilitate observation through the window during the long night. We didn't object, for at least we could sit up and see something. At the moment life was almost one barely interrupted, endless night.

I ate no dinner that night, but my companions assured me that I had missed nothing. The meal consisted of yak entrails and rice with about a pound of chillies added. Both Damodar and Harrop had to give up after a mouthful or two, the chillies burning their mouths, the tears streaming down their faces.

At 6 p.m. Chungnya entered followed by the Dzongpen, plus a Tibetan interpreter and a medical orderly with a stethoscope slung round his neck and a gauze mask protecting his nose and mouth. Finally, to crowd the cell, came Schickelgruber and several of the guards. The Dzongpen bowed to us and extended his good wishes through the Tibetan, who spoke Nepali. His plausible *bonhomie* might be genuine, but he had made promises which he had not kept and, for all we know, he might have led us into a trap.

The medical orderly, who seemed to be in his early twenties, asked me to undo my shirt. Harrop became annoyed with this futile attempt at diagnosis as the orderly examined my chest with his stethoscope.

'Tell the clot that Syd's suffering from dysentery, not a ruddy cough.'

The message was passed on, but the orderly took not the least notice. When he had finished his examination, the Dzongpen asked how long I had been having these bouts of illness, and we informed him that I had carried the dysentery for three and a half months.

It was explained most carefully that the pills the soldiers had confiscated were intended to relieve or possibly cure my illness, and the Dzongpen promised that they would be returned the following day. There was, too, a qualified doctor in Taklakot and a visit from him would be arranged. Also the doctor had his own drugs which would prove superior to mine.

We took the opportunity to voice our protests concerning our treatment, mentioning the awful food, and the brutality of the guards that same morning. I was informed that we had started the fracas by attacking the guards. Schickelgruber had testified to that and, as we were to learn, the Peoples' Liberation Army is never wrong. As for the food, if we sent a note in Hindi or Nepali stating just how we liked our food cooked, arrangements would be made to ensure that it was made to our liking. The question of exercise would also be taken up with the commanding officer, and, as no one could speak English, an English-speaking officer had been sent for and was expected within a few days.

The visitors departed, but not before the Dzongpen had promised that he would pay us a daily visit to attend to our wants. It seemed to us that there was little point in the Dzongpen making all these promises unless he intended to keep them. In fact, however, my pills were never returned, the doctor failed to appear, the food deteriorated still further, and the Dzongpen did not make his daily call. I believe now that he meant every word he said and that he wished to carry out his duties in a humane and civilized manner, but was prevented from doing so by the military in charge of administration at Taklakot.

The next day was November 5th. I decided that the incident of the day before should be forgotten unless the Chinese themselves became rough, in which case we would retaliate. So, for the time being, the routine was back to normal. The bowl of washing water between 8.30 a.m. and 9 a.m., and breakfast of boiled turnips, minus meat.

Harrop suggested that I would feel better if I sat in the sun, and he and Damodar carried out my sleeping-bag and air mattress, and I settled down to idle away yet another day. Chungnya came out of the kitchen, waving an enamel mug decorated with a red star and a clenched hand, shouting, 'Chai?'

'Yappa do,' I said, rising to take the proffered cup.

As I did so I looked across the river towards the grey barracks, and something caught my attention. Two tall wooden masts had been erected at either end of the roof and between them I caught the reflected gleam of an aerial wire. A radio, which had not been there a couple of days before, had been erected. This might well mean that the interrogating committee from Gartok was now drawing near and that everything was being prepared for the transmission of messages direct from Lhasa or Peking.

I drank the tea abstractedly. Koila should by now have reached our base camp and passed my message to the other members of our expedition. It was almost certain that the outside world would learn of our predicament within a few days and, I hoped, before we had been packed off by mule to Lhasa.

In any case, things were reaching a critical stage, and we should soon know our fate. Anything was better than this endless waiting in a filthy, rat-infested, freezing cold cell. I decided that we must keep close watch on all movements at the other side of the river and warned Harrop and Damodar as to what had happened.

After that we kept up a constant watch throughout daylight hours, with frequent trips to the lavatory, over the wall of which we could command a view of the river and the bridge. The usual activity was going on at the top of the hill. Although the new fort was out of sight of the prison, we could still see the endless line of men, animals and load-carrying Tibetan women winding their way up and down the track.

In the early afternoon a fatigue party of soldiers emerged from the grey barracks and started ferrying furniture across to the red building about three hundred yards away. I was surprised to see seven modern tubular steel chairs followed by a small table. The Chinese were obviously preparing for someone to occupy that building, and we must figure in it somewhere.

The guards emptied all our kit, including tents, out of the small room next door to the guardroom and carried it all away to the grey building at the other side of the river. The reason for that move was obvious. Without the tents, stoves and fuel, our chances of getting over the mountains, if we escaped, were virtually nil.

I went and leaned against the lavatory wall and watched our precious high-altitude equipment being carried over the wooden cantilever bridge. With it vanished our last hope of an early release. A group of Tibetans I had not noticed before glanced up at me from the other side of the wall. They were sitting in the open dishing butter tea out of an urn. Behind them smoke billowed from the top of a large conglomerate boulder which had evidently been detached from the cliff face many years before.

To my surprise, one of the Tibetans walked over to the boulder, which must have been about twenty feet square and almost as high, and drew back a ragged curtain that concealed a hole leading to the interior of the great clay and pebble block. Most of the people living at that side of our prison appeared to reside inside these boulders, which are so soft that they can be hewn with primitive tools. In some instances one family lived inside the boulder and another family lived in the shadow of an overhanging side which had been partly bricked up. A hole had been made in the top to serve as a chimney and smoke spiralled up from these great stones throughout the day.

One of the Tibetans came over to the wall, looked up at me and held an empty bowl in outstretched hands, begging for food. I sadly shook my head and turned away. The guard, coming out of the kitchen, waved me away from the wall.

I went and sat on my bed. Damodar was leaning against the wall of the guardroom with his head a few inches from the glass window, and he appeared to be listening to something.

'Come away from there,' I said, 'or you'll get into trouble.'

He came over. 'I think,' he said, 'that the Chinese have a small cat.'

'Don't talk daft,' I replied. 'We haven't seen any cats in Taklakot. They wouldn't live long with all the big Tibetan mastiff dogs prowling around at night.'

Every family in Taklakot appeared to have one of these large dogs, which protect the herds of sheep from the savage wolf packs that roam the plateau in winter. The dogs are always let loose at night, and heaven help the unwary traveller who should chance to be abroad during the hours of darkness. Strangely enough these same dogs are gentle and docile in the daytime. We saw Tibetan children and even Chinese soldiers playing with them.

Damodar, to prove that he was right about the kitten, walked over to the door of the guardroom and called, 'Puss, puss, puss.'

The guard on the roof shouted to Damodar to get away from the door, cocking his gun and lifting it to his shoulder to show the seriousness of his intentions.

Chungnya came out and said, '*Yappa mindo?*'

The answer was no, but we would not accept it and started an argument. Finally Chubby came out carrying a pretty little black kitten, a piece of string tied round its neck and the other end attached to a heavy stone. The kitten was set down in the middle of the yard, its freedom being limited to the three feet of its string. Damodar and I undid the string. The guards tied it on again, and we undid it once more. We persisted until they gave up and the cat was allowed to roam about the yard.

Watching the little creature frolic about I thought that it might be that these people had a common level of understanding with us. In this I was utterly wrong, for the kitten never enjoyed a moment's respite from persistent cruelty from the day Damodar brought about its freedom.

Before the cat had played half an hour, Marlo picked it up and blew cigarette smoke down its nose. Then he stubbed the lighted cigarette against the helpless creature's nose. That was the beginning. Later in the day one of the guards took a running kick at the kitten and sent it flying across the yard. Our intervention was of no avail. The cat was taken indoors, where its plaintive cries announced that it was being subjected to further cruelties.

Monkey Face had his own technique of cruelty, grabbing the cat by its tail and swinging it round and round before throwing it with all his might against the wall. The wretched thing soon showed signs of injury, and, within a few days, died. That they might not lack amusement, the guards brought in a Tibetan mastiff on a lead. The dog was large and savage-looking, but it was, in fact, the gentlest of creatures. It was kept tied to a post and subjected to the same inhuman treatment as the cat. Lighted cigarettes were used to burn its nose and mouth, and it was kicked in the body and face. Schickelgruber was the most adept at the kicking. He did not wear tennis shoes, but clumped about the yard in heavy boots, the soles of which were of leather. He took pleasure in kicking the dog until he had provoked Harrop or me to protest. Then, while the guard on the roof threatened us with his sub-machine-gun, he kicked the dog all the more.

During a lull in the activity we slipped the noose from the dog's neck and let it fly through the yard door left open by the kitchen wallah who had gone to the river for water. The animal, perhaps having been rendered witless by its painful treatment, ran only a few yards and then sat down, thus allowing Fatty to chase out to it and bring it back again.

We tackled Chungnya about it and he placed his finger to his lips in an admonitory manner. When it was his turn for guard duty and the others had all disappeared indoors, he untied the dog and chased it out of sight.

Harrop claimed that to the Chinese Communists cruelty is a form of humour, and I was inclined to agree. But I could not ignore the thought that, as they treated animals savagely, and as they had admitted liquidating no less than 2,000,000 'Reactionaries', our own chances of escaping death were slender in the extreme.

On the same day that I noticed the radio masts, I heard sounds of activity coming from behind our prison, in the region of the cliff face. Soldiers in fatigue dress of light khaki drill tunic, trousers and tennis shoes kept disappearing and reappearing. Something was afoot. I looked to the top of the cliff that stood a few yards behind the prison. A crowd of Tibetan children who had gathered to see what was going on were not allowed to stay long. Schickelgruber ran up to the cliff top and drove them away with his Tommy gun.

My apprehension did not decrease when Chungnya came over and tried hard to convey something to me. He pointed over the lavatory wall to the Lhasa track and, pointing his gun, said, 'Tatatatatatatat.'

Then, turning in the other direction, he looked through the yard door towards the Indian frontier, pursuing the same performance and saying, '*Hindustan yappa mindo.*'

I could not fathom what he was trying to tell me. Then he pointed to my climbing boots and motioned up the cliff face behind, pressing the palms of his hands together and closing his eyes. He was talking about the cliff and about the night-time. Finally he stamped his foot on the ground and said, 'Booooom!'

'Oh no, not land mines!' I exclaimed.

But that was exactly what he meant. With a pencil stub he traced the shape of a mine in the dust. Scraping away some of the dust, he placed a pebble in the hole and then covered it over. I was still incredulous. Admittedly the cliff face was one way of circumventing the track at night, and thereby reducing the risk of running into guards, but the laying of mines seemed to be a big step to take merely to prevent the escape of two Englishmen and an eighteen-year-old Nepalese youth.

The idea that the Chinese regarded us as Very Important Prisoners did nothing to assuage my anxiety. We began to gain the impression that what lay in store for us made escape imperative—even a matter of life and death—and the Chinese were taking every precaution to see that escape was impossible.

Thereafter, during daylight, there was always someone with a loaded gun sitting on top of the cliff, ready to drive away any Tibetans who chanced to come near the cliff edge.

On November 6th a group of officers came down the track that ran north to Gartok. Using the usual excuse of visiting the lavatory, I looked over the wall. There were six men on mules riding along the track towards the grey barracks. Three were dressed in the usual khaki and three in navy blue serge uniforms, the collars buttoned right to the neck. This was the outfit of the full-time employees of the Communist Party. These were, indeed, the men from Gartok. Our waiting was at an end.

I scrutinized the faces of the guards standing near me. They were watching the arrival of the officers as intently as I was, and all conversation had ceased. For the first time since the day of our arrest I felt afraid. Schickelgruber detached himself from the group and went indoors, to emerge moments later carrying a machine-gun. He joined the guard already on duty and they had a conversation punctuated by glances in my direction.

Finally he came over, held the barrel of the gun against my chest, and motioned me towards our cell. We had long since ceased arguing when robbed of a few precious hours of daylight, for protest had no effect. Harrop and Damodar, sunbathing on the far side of the yard, were awakened by kicks on the soles of the feet and forced to join me indoors. Their sleeping-bags were thrown in after them, disturbing the usual clouds of dust.

My companions were annoyed and bewildered by what had taken place, and Damodar was still a little dazed from his morning snooze.

'They are here,' I said, cutting short their complaints.

'Who's here?' Harrop demanded.

'The big shots from Gartok.'

'How do you know?'

'They've just arrived, six of 'em. I've read that in the New China the political people always wear blue drill tunics and trousers. The jackets button right up to the neck like the Russian army uniform.'

It was Damodar who broke the protracted silence. 'Didn't some-one say they had an English-speaking officer at Gartok?'

'That's right, and the time factor is right as well. They've had just about enough time to send a rider with our kit, maps and diary to Gartok for these blokes to scrutinize them and for the officers to ride down here. It all fits. This will be the interrogation committee, or——'

'Or what?' Harrop prompted.

'Or a Peoples' Court.'

Damodar, who had read little about world politics, asked what a Peoples' Court was supposed to be.

According to Chinese internal propaganda, I explained, the Peoples' Courts were an essential part of the machinery to stamp out what were called deviationist and counter-revolutionary tendencies in the people. China herself had admitted that these Courts had con-demned to death no less than two million people. By the time we had suffered our final interrogation all of us knew that the outcome of such a trial is a foregone conclusion. The law allows of no defence. It is the prosecution alone which produces evidence. All that is re-quired is a signed confession.

The proceedings always followed the same stereotyped pattern. The victim acknowledges and laments his faults and shortcomings to the Court, and the judges nod their heads in agreement with the re-formed views of the penitent. The accused, if regarded as suitable, is subjected to several months' 'thought reform', or what the American newspapers call 'brain washing'. After passing further interrogations he is assigned to labour or 'volunteer work brigades'. At all times he is under the close surveillance of the political agents who watch and report on his every movement. It is obvious that such a system lends itself to the furtherance of personal grudges, ambition and petty spite. To be denounced is enough to ensure a conviction. This is reminiscent of Caligula's Rome, where a denounced person was arrested and his property handed over, lock, stock and barrel, to the informer. It provides an almost irresistible temptation to those envious of a neighbour's possessions or who were anxious to accelerate their own promotion by eliminating rivals.

Ominously for us, no European tried by a 'Peoples' Court' had escaped with less than three years' imprisonment under the most frightful conditions.

The outlook that day was decidedly unpleasant, and we detected anxiety in each other's faces as we discussed our position. We were talking when one of the soldiers locked our cell door. From that moment it was kept locked whenever we were indoors.

At 3 p.m. dinner of yak entrails and rice was brought in. As it was indigestible we ate some of our pemmican and meat blocks. The stocks of our own food were being carefully eked out, but it was obvious that a month in prison would see the end of our precious reserves, which were intended at the outset to last only twelve days. As it was we enjoyed what we called a cup of 'Nestea'—Chinese tea with Nescafé added. Only half a teaspoonful for each mug.

The little oil-lamp was lit early and the face of a guard was present at the window all the time. Precautions were being carried to the most stringent lengths, and our chance of escape while subjected to such vigilance was too trifling for consideration.

There was a different atmosphere that night. Into it had crept an urgency which affected us all, even the guards. Their faces were expressionless as they stared glassily at us through the window. Our efforts to crack jokes failed pathetically. Even Damodar, the born tumbler and court jester, failed to raise a laugh when he gave an imitation of Fatty. With remarkable aptness he reproduced the belch, throat clearing, spitting, flea-hunting and, finally, reading, an occupation which Fatty always carried out with a sagging jaw.

My own thoughts were unhappily engaged with the dread possibility that perhaps Koila had not been able to cross the 19,500-feet Urai Lagna pass under the hostile conditions. If so, our friends would have no knowledge of our fate. We would be presumed dead, and the Chinese would be able to hold us as long as they wished—maybe for ever. The blow would fall most severely on my wife and nine-year-old son. At least we would know what was happening to us. But for them there would only be a sudden ending to the regular air mail letters and then silence and the torment of anxiety.

I slept badly and kept dreaming of the Chinese 'Peoples' Court'. In my nightmare the characters had the ugliest and most evil faces I had ever seen. One, who looked remarkably like a horse, kept putting a gun to my head and I sweated, waiting for it to go off. At last the explosion came, and I awoke with a violent start. Outside it was daylight.

Chapter 12

OVER THE RIVER

BREAKFAST was eaten in a silence disturbed only by the sounds of the rat making his daily attempt to nibble sustenance from the ancient chupatty in the corner of the cell.

I knocked on the cell door and it was unlocked by Lofty, who followed me to the lavatory and back to the kitchen where I signified that I wanted a shave. If I was to be interrogated then I intended to put up a reasonable front and appear in good order.

To my surprise my request was granted and Chungnya produced a cheap bakelite safety razor of Indian manufacture. There was only one blade and that as blunt as a barrel-hoop. I had but little soap, and making a lather minus brush and with lukewarm water was virtually impossible. Nevertheless, I managed to remove a month's growth of beard, but not without considerable suffering, and my face resembled a raw beefsteak.

That done, I reversed my filthy sweater so that the hole formerly in the middle of the chest was now in the middle of the back and conspicuous only in retreat. For footgear I wore the bulky high-altitude boots that kept my feet warm and comfortable. My efforts to involve the guards in the usual sign language this time proved unavailing. Obviously they had been given strict instructions not to fraternize with their captives.

Monkey Face was on the roof, his gun following my every step. After a few minutes Fatty came out of the guardhouse equipped with gun, spare magazine and grenades, and with a tubular cloth bag slung over the shoulder and under the opposite arm. Through the thin material gleamed the copper-nosed bullets that it contained. Allowing for the loaded gun, the four spare magazines in a hold-all at the waist and the cloth bag, he was carrying no less than 250 to 300 rounds of 9 mm. ammunition, a sizable arsenal for one small Chinaman.

Later in the morning Marlo also shouldered his gun, and for the first time we had three armed guards on duty. New guards arrived in the yard, appearing at frequent intervals to stare through the cell window at Harrop and Damodar, or to survey me with avid curiosity as I sat with assumed indifference on the yard step.

Every few minutes one of the soldiers went to the outer wall, climbed on to the firing step and looked towards the grey and red buildings. I made repeated trips to the lavatory to record any interesting developments.

At 11 a.m. a group of khaki- and blue-clad individuals left the grey barracks and walked across the intervening three hundred yards of rubbly ground towards the red building. From my vantage point I recognized the Dzongpen and noticed, much to my surprise, that one very short fellow was carrying a rifle, the first I had seen in Communist Tibet. All other Chinese carried the mass-produced sub-machine-guns which, though modelled on identical lines to the Russian prototype, were, in fact, manufactured in China, the date—which was always 1953—being stamped in Arabic numerals on the top of the breech.

These uniformed figures sauntered along the track, some, like small boys, kicking a stone before them. Half-way to the building one of the blue-clad figures stopped and relieved himself over the edge of the cliff that overhung the Karnali river. He was immediately joined by the rest, all of whom joined in a contest to see who could urinate the furthest. One, on second thoughts, dropped his padded trousers and squatted in the middle of the track. These were the representatives of the new China!

Schickelgruber screamed at me for looking at the officers, and I was forced to return to the centre of the yard. By standing at the top of the steps I could see as much as from the lavatory, and I kept my eyes glued to the red building over the river.

Harrop and Damodar came out and we watched the last of the blue-coated figures disappear indoors. As the last one, a chubby individual carrying a brief-case, stepped through the doorway, he turned and looked back towards our prison. I pulled a bright red handkerchief from my pocket and gave him a wave, but a glance at the face of the guards told me the joke was not appreciated. At the end of a few minutes the soldier with the rifle who had accompanied the officers stepped outside the doorway of the red building and waved a hand.

That was the signal.

Schickelgruber tapped me on the shoulder and called Fatty and Marlo over. They pointed to the yard door, and I stepped outside our prison for the first time since our arrival at Taklakot eleven days before.

The two guards did not walk on either side of me, but kept a careful ten paces behind, their guns levelled all the time. We passed a crowd of Tibetans who, realizing that something unusual was afoot, had formed up outside the boulder residences we had to pass on our way down to the cantilever bridge.

The bridge was larger than it had appeared from our prison, being wide enough to take two yaks or mules side by side. A group of young Chinese soldiers in fatigue kit, some minus jackets and sporting bright green cotton sweaters, passed in the opposite direction and stopped one by one to have a closer look as I went by.

The lower part of the hillside below the red building was dotted with mud-brick, roofless enclosures, some of them newly built. They were intended to house troops in transit, when a tarpaulin supported by poles would suffice for a temporary roof. Lack of exercise and the effects of dysentery had left me somewhat run down and I arrived at the door of the interrogation building panting for breath.

The man with the rifle barred my way, so I came to a halt and had a close look at his gun. It was a U.S. Army 30-calibre semi-auto-matic carbine, probably a souvenir from the Korean War. I turned to look back, to see Harrop and Damodar standing on the top step in the centre of our prison yard. They gave me a cheery wave, and I felt in need of moral support at that moment. 'Thank God I am not alone,' I thought.

A call from inside the yard prompted the guard to step to one side and motion me through the doorway.

Inside the courtyard stood a group of impassive-looking Tibetan officials who indicated a curtain-covered doorway to my left. I walked over to it and paused, wondering what would happen when I entered. Someone pushed the curtain aside and stepped out. It was the self-styled Indian trader who had tried to trap us on the day of our arrival at Taklakot. He gave me a weak smile and with that my fears vanished. This slimy eel was no monster, no unknown quantity. The emotion he aroused was one of indignation and disgust. All I wanted to do was punch him in the face and knock his gold teeth out.

Ignoring his sickly grin and bending to avoid the usual bump on the head when negotiating Tibetan doorways, I stepped inside.

That one step took me out of a world of reason and sanity into Orwell's 1984. Inside the illumination was poor and I hesitated on the threshold while I tried to adjust my vision to the twilight per-vading the room. The only light admitted came through a small window, covered with thin white paper.

My eyes becoming accustomed to the dim light, I was able to take in my surroundings. The room was only some ten feet square, and part of it was hidden by a folding screen that stood just to my right. To the left was a small stove made out of an old five-gallon oil drum which, in the absence of a chimney, sent smoke coiling to the ceiling where it hung in blue wreaths.

Straight ahead was a single bed equipped with blankets. Obviously the occupant of this room did not sleep on the floor as we did. Beneath the bed was a tin trunk and, unexpectedly, an old gramophone. Above the bed a revolver in a leather holster hung from a hook, the belt studded with cartridges. Was the gun put there to tempt me into making a grab for it? If so those who set the trap were not very bright, or perhaps they credited me with the same I.Q. as they themselves possessed? Anyway, the date was November 7th, and seven was supposed to be my lucky number. I had no intention of committing suicide on my lucky day.

The two guards pushed me past the screen and my interest sharpened as I noticed a number of people sitting around a small table behind the screen and to my right. There were six of them. This was Big Brother's interrogation committee.

Chapter 13

THE INTERROGATION COMMITTEE

NONE of the six addressed me, and most of them ignored my presence. Occasionally one would glance up from his notes and say a few words in subdued tones, as if they feared I understood Chinese and might overhear what was being said.

They were a decidedly unpleasant-looking sextet. On the whole I preferred our guards, even Schickelgruber. The ones in the blue suits wore peaked caps and the khaki-clad individuals wore hats with ear-flaps trimmed with beautiful Tibetan fox fur. The familiar red star badge, with the Chinese equivalent of the numbers One Eight in the centre, was pinned to the front of the hat. The table before them was spread with dishes of nuts and Indian sweetmeats. A pot of tea was passed round frequently, and with their tea they took milk and sugar, a luxury not to be enjoyed by the ordinary soldiers of Taklakot. Their professed equality had no reflection in reality.

Above and behind the seated figures were two army recruiting posters, striking because of their bright colours and bold style. One depicted Mao-Tse-Tung standing on a balcony waving to a crowd of young people. He was garlanded with flowers and beamed down on his youthful flock like a Dutch uncle. On the second poster he was joined by General Chu-Teh, supreme commander of the Peoples' Liberation Army. Both were waving, this time to battalions of young, goose-stepping soldiers who gazed up at their self-appointed leaders with faces glowing with youthful adulation.

As I write, the newspapers are filled with the story of the downfall of the 'Cult of Personality' in Russia and her satellites. Stalin is no longer remembered as the 'Little Father' of all the Russians. It now appears that he built for himself a spurious reputation as a genius and military strategist.

How does all this affect Mao-Tse-Tung, who, in thirty years, has built for himself a reputation as great as that of Stalin? For many regard Mao as Asia's man of destiny. I had read just about everything that had been written about China. The end of the Manchu dynasty at the beginning of the present century. Sun Yat Sen's three principles of democracy. Chiang Kai Shek's breakaway from the Kuomintang-Communist Party coalition in 1926. Mao's long march across Southern

China to Yunnan, where he and his supporters set up the first of their three autonomous border republics.

In those days Mao was supported by the liberal element in China who, for many years, had suffered under the corruption and intolerance of Chiang Kai Shek's autocratic regime. After gaining power the Chinese Communists subjected their intellectual non-Communist supporters to restrictions on speech, activity and personal freedom which surpassed anything they had suffered at the hands of the tyrant they had so recently overthrown. Intolerance has run riot in a nation where freedom and liberty were the passwords that allowed the few to gain power and bring about a new kind of slavery for the masses.

No doubt Mao's turn will come, and when it does his posters at Taklakot will be cut up by the Tibetans and used for prayer-flags.

My ruminations were interrupted by a voice saying, 'Hello!'

I looked down to see that the chubby-faced fellow in blue seated on the right-hand side of the table had spoken to me.

'Hello to you,' I said.

'Do you speak Chinese or Tibetan?'

'Neither,' I told him.

Having passed this information on to the others, he said, 'Please, sit.'

He, like his companions, was seated on a modern tubular steel chair. Looking behind me I was surprised to see a tubular steel chair folded up and leaning against the wall. I reached for it and opened it out. The chubby character watched my every move, and I was about to take my seat when he said:

'No. You must sit on the floor.'

I went hot with anger as I realized that, in accordance with Chinese tradition, I had been deliberately made to lose face. The foreign devil had to be shown that he was inferior to the 'Peoples' representatives'.

'No, thanks,' I said. 'I'll stand, if it's all the same to you.'

He glared and snapped a command at my two guards, who took up positions on either side of me. One snatched the chair away and the other brought the butt of his gun to within six inches of my head.

Not feeling inclined to have my skull split, I sat down on the dried-mud floor. My captors were running true to type, and as I looked at their inscrutable, mask-like faces a shiver swept down my spine.

'Who are you?'

With that I was on the defensive. 'First I demand to know who holds us prisoner and by what authority? Unless I receive such information I shall not answer any questions.'

The English-speaking Chinaman, whom we identified by calling him 'Smoothy', was visibly shaken by what he regarded as unprecedented impertinence on the part of a prisoner.

'You must not ask questions, only answer them.'

I shrugged.

'If I and my friends are to be held prisoner we demand to know with whom we are dealing. I repeat that unless we are told we shall refuse to talk.'

After pondering this for some time, he pointed to the left-hand side of the table.

'You will not know the names and ranks, but to show you we are reasonable I will explain who we are.'

Before our interrogations were over we had christened each member of the committee with an appropriate sobriquet.

The man on the left, a wizened little figure in army kit, was the C.O. from Gartok. Because of his facial expressions and his walk we called him 'The Ape Man of Taklakot' or 'Monkey Face'. From that moment we stopped calling one of our seven guards 'Monkey Face' and rechristened him 'Shorty'.

Next to the Ape Man sprawled an ugly brute who had the unenviable distinction of being probably the most unpleasant-looking character I had ever seen. He had large protruding ears that were slightly pointed at the top. His long face was practically innocent of forehead, and his nose was both flattened and long, unlike all the other Chinese I had encountered. His jaw seemed equal to a horse's in size and it sagged loosely. Chin on chest, he looked at me from under very bushy eyebrows, and all the time he sat there he drooled, the saliva running down the front of his stained and grubby khaki tunic.

His head closely resembled the plaster models of the heads of Neanderthal man that are to be seen in museums. This character was the C.O. of Taklakot, who had shot a soldier before the rest of the garrison only some weeks before. I did not like the look of him and had the feeling that he was all the time mentally measuring me for a coffin—if such a luxury is afforded the victims of Chinese Communist law in Tibet. We nicknamed him 'Ug-Lug' because that was the sound that issued from his lips whenever he spoke. It was unlike the Chinese dialect spoken by the others, and we never figured out his origin or place of birth.

Next to Ug-Lug sat a bue-coated figure, none other than the

Governor of West Tibet. He looked most unimportant to me, being smallish and about fifty, his gaze constantly wandering about the room as though he expected interesting events to take place on the walls or ceiling. On the odd occasions when his gaze met mine it was instantly averted. On the whole he was mild-mannered, and only once lost his temper, and that at the third interrogation when I called him a Fascist. He always spoke very quietly, and when he ventured an utterance all the other members of the star chamber courteously fell silent.

Next to him sat a blue-clad youth, a nondescript little character who took no part in the questioning. He served as a secretary, copying all questions and answers in a minute book on the table. At least, I thought that everything went down in it until I noticed at later proceedings that he only entered my statements when they conformed to the answers his superiors required. If my answer failed to conform to their ideas of Communist truth, it did not rank in the records. We called this pencil-pusher 'The Bookworm', and he looked to be no more than eighteen years old.

The fifth member of the committee was another army officer who carried a Russian version of the Leica camera slung round his neck. We refrained from giving him a nickname because he never made a second appearance. His was strictly a one-night stand and his job was simply to take identification photographs, for the record.

The sixth member, of course, was the chubby little fellow with the bland unsmiling countenance, 'Smoothy', the only Chinese in West Tibet who could speak English. After he had made his brief and very sketchy introductions, silence reigned for a few moments and a cosy little tea-party developed. Small handleless china cups were passed round, Smoothy pouring the tea to which milk had already been added. Sugar was available in a small silver bowl. Occasionally the silence was broken as a member of the committee cleared his throat and spat on the floor.

I was surprised and disgusted to find that the highest officers in West Tibet indulged in the same awful habit of expectoration as their common soldiers. Had there been any awards going for frequency of expectoration and noise, then Ug-Lug and Smoothy qualified for first prize. The Indian sweets looked particularly tempting and they ate these to the usual accompaniment of chewing and sucking sounds reminiscent of our prison guards.

I opened my mouth to speak, only to be silenced by a quick 'Hello, shut up!' from Smoothy.

I had the feeling that all this waiting and tea-drinking enabled them to size me up and to keep me in a suspense which, they hoped, would make me feel nervous. But the longer I sat the less scared I felt. Their performance roused my indignation, helping to win the psychological battle for me. It was impossible to lose face in the presence of such an ill-mannered group. The wizened little Ape Man wiped his nose on his sleeve. But the Bookworm went one better by blowing his nose on the floor. Everyone went on eating and nobody seemed to mind.

I reached into my pocket for a handkerchief, only to be prodded painfully in the ear with the barrel of a Tommy gun. I persisted and produced the handkerchief, which brought smiles to the faces of the guards. It seemed that the idiots had feared that I was about to produce a bomb or a gun.

After a while the Governor spoke a few words to Smoothy and Smoothy, examining his notes, said:

'Hello. We are going to ask you some questions and these questions you must answer honestly. You must not speak other than to answer a question.'

The proceedings had begun.

Smoothy cleared his throat and spat a couple of inches from my feet.

'First, what is your name? Also we must know your age, your nationality and your address.'

I delivered this information and then was asked my mother's name, and had to explain that my father was no longer alive. Then my wife's name, my son's name and age, my occupation and so on. It was very like applying for a job, only in this case the term of employment could be anything from five years to life.

To the question of nationality I replied, 'British and bloody proud of it.'

Smoothy interrupted to say: 'You must not swear. You must conduct yourself well at all times when you are in our house.'

The question of nationality was repeated and I answered, 'Same as before.'

Smoothy exchanged a few words with the Governor and doodled with his pen. Then, without looking up, he said, 'You are not an American then?'

Knowing just how unpopular Americans were with the Chinese Communists, I was thankful that I was not indeed a citizen of the United States. Had Harrop and I been American I have little doubt that our treatment would have been rougher and that they would never have let us go.

'Take a look at my passport,' I said. 'My nationality is entered inside it.'

Smoothy turned to the Bookworm who produced my passport from inside a brief-case. Smoothy then thumbed through the pages and did not repeat the question. Holding up the passport, he pointed to the photograph inside. 'Is this you?'

I could appreciate his difficulty in not recognizing me from the picture, for it was a poor photograph in the first place and I had lost weight since it was taken. I replied that it was, but had the feeling that he was working up to something.

'We believe that this document is fictitious and that it is not your true passport. It is forged.'

I asked how he reached such a conclusion.

'Because you say you are an engineer and it says on this passport you are a manager. Either the document is false or you are lying.'

Patiently I tried to explain that, before joining the expedition, I had been a branch manager of an engineering company in North Wales and that I had been trained as an engineer in my youth. Smoothy rejected this and kept repeating the same question over and over again. I was told that I was not co-operating and that I should answer more honestly.

Finally losing my temper, I told Smoothy that he was a damned fool, to which he gave the stock reply, 'You must conduct yourself well while you are in our house.'

He warned that the question would be raised again at some future date and now would I tell him what my wife's occupation was. I replied that she was a housewife. Smoothy looked incredulous.

'But how does your wife live if she does not work?'

I pointed out that the majority of English wives are supported by their husbands, an answer which immediately caused me to be classed as a bloated plutocrat. I could only presume that in the Peoples' China every able-bodied woman must go out to work, and that home life is regarded as terribly bourgeois and deviationist.

Smoothy even wanted to know how it was that while I lived in North Wales, my mother lived in Cheshire, fifty miles away. He evidently believed in the Confucian ideal of filial piety and of maintaining the unity of the family. They seemed to be wasting a great deal of time, but as the questioning proceeded I perceived that there was method and reason for every word and act where the Chinese are concerned.

It all seemed tedious and childish, but they were displaying a typical oriental cunning. They were looking for a flaw in my story. If I was a spy, then my passport, personal history and family background would be fictitious. The questions asked at this first interrogation were repeated with variations at all subsequent enquiries. It was their hope that I would make a mistake, giving an answer that did not conform to the ones I had given on previous occasions.

Throughout they received from me the same replies, but I gained the impression that they believed not a word that I was saying, regarding me as a very able liar.

The preliminary questions over, Smoothy asked his most critical question.

'Who sent you here?'

I replied that nobody had sent me, and that I was in the Himalayas simply because I wanted to be there. His reaction was one of complete unbelief.

'What you say is a lie,' he retorted. 'Answer more honestly.'

I was beginning to think that of all the people who could fall into the hands of the Chinese Communists, none could be more unfortunate than Harrop and myself. We were the first mountaineers to be arrested by the Chinese and now we faced the inevitable and unanswerable questions, 'Why do you go to the Himalayas?' or, 'Why do you climb mountains?'

It is impossible to explain this even to an Englishman who does not share the passion for climbing mountains. Obviously it was fantastic to think that any acceptable reason could be conveyed to the Chinese. Particularly when I am not sure that I know the answer myself.

'I've always wanted to visit the Himalayas,' I said. 'Ever since I read my first book about it fourteen years ago.'

'That is not a reason. Why do you climb mountains? What is the purpose?'

'I do it for pleasure. It's my hobby.'

Smoothy interpreted that one for the rest and disbelief and scorn appeared on their faces.

'*What is the real reason* for going up mountains?' Smoothy demanded forcefully.

I repeated that there was no reason save that of pleasure.

'It will be very difficult for you if you do not answer honestly,' he cut in. 'Now, who sponsored the expedition?'

'The Mountaineering Club of North Wales and the *Liverpool Daily Post*.'

This caused the Governor to demand more information about these two imperialist organizations.

'How did you know about this club?'

'Easy. I am one of the founder members and a member of the committee.'

'What is the club's purpose?'

'To bring together those in North Wales who are interested in mountaineering.'

'Ah, yes. But what is the club's other purpose?'

At this I laughed, but was brought to order when Ug-Lug and Monkey Face objected. Smoothy reproved me for not treating the investigating committee with the respect their positions merited.

'You cannot hide the club's purpose from us,' he said. 'We will find it out from the other two. Now, what are the club's politics?'

'It's a mountaineering club and strictly non-political.'

'That cannot be true. Every organization has politics.'

'Not this one. It's a private club; not an instrument of the State.'

'You are being deliberately obstructionist,' Smoothy accused. 'You will only make things difficult for yourself and your friends. Please give the answers that are truthful.'

I exploded at that.

'Do you think I'm to pervert the truth and tell stupid lies that will fit in with the answers you want? The only truth you recognize is what you want to hear. If you don't like what you hear, then you say the answer is a lie. There are no grounds for common understanding between us. We come from different worlds.'

Smoothy choked as he swallowed his indignation. Nor were my words interpreted for the benefit of the others.

They started to sort out the next set of questions and Smoothy kept making alterations to his questionnaire. The Ape Man kept pointing to me and smashing his fist into the palm of the other hand. Ug-Lug smote the table with a gross ugly hand, causing the pots to leap in the air and chatter together. The Bookworm, in his attempts to steady the crockery, was distracted from his note-taking.

The Governor remained very placid. He sat, his hands resting on his crossed knees, his gaze pursuing its eternal wanderings. Ug-Lug's voice reminded me of water going down a drain with its unvarying 'Ug-lug-glug'. The character with the camera kept sighting at me through the viewfinder and twiddling the rangefinder.

A Tibetan brought in a bowl of nuts and a further pot of tea. I was feeling thirsty and the sight of tea, sugar and milk tempted me to ask for a cup. Pride, however, prevented me from making the humiliating request, and I suffered in silence, and my captors, of course, did not offer me a drink.

The interlude ended, the questions started again.

'Who is the big leader of your club?'

'The President of the Mountaineering Club of North Wales is Mr. Eugene Brunning, C.B.E.'

'What does C.B.E. mean? Is it part of his name?'

'Of course not. C.B.E. is a decoration awarded by the King or Queen for services to the Commonwealth.'

Smoothy glowed with satisfaction.

'You admit, then, that this Eugene Brunning is a British agent?'

I was fast beginning to realize how hopeless it all was. To them a C.B.E. was an organizer of spies. I had to grin to myself. Had Eugene heard all this he would have rolled on the floor with laughter.

'What was that you said?'

Smoothy's shout made me realize that I had been talking half aloud.

'Nothing at all. I was just thinking how stupid and damned ridiculous the whole business is.'

'Be careful,' he warned. 'You are not conducting yourself well.' Then, 'Why did this Eugene Brunning send you here?'

'He didn't send us here.'

'Yes, he did. We know all about your imperialist spy organization. This Brunning sent you to spy on the Peoples' Liberation Army. He sent you into Tibet——'

'We had never been in Tibet until kidnapped by your troops,' I interrupted. 'They arrested us while we were making a reconnaissance in the mountains of Nepal. As we were in the mountains, how can you claim we were in Tibet? There is no true frontier. It is as yet undemarcated and has never been agreed between the Governments of Nepal and Tibet.'

Smoothy was simmering with rage.

'You were arrested by the Peoples' Liberation Army. That is proof that you were in Tibet.'

Their disregard of reason and logic was worse than I had imagined. No matter on whose soil you happened to be standing, the fact that you had been arrested by the P.L.A. was proof to them that you were

H

in China. It was impossible to reason with such people; but worse was to come.

'This leader of your organization in England. He is the organizer of an illegal invasion of China.'

'How can two men and an eighteen-year-old boy comprise an invasion?'

'It is an invasion,' he insisted. 'Its intention is to spy on the Peoples' Army.'

'What is there to spy on in Tibet?' I countered. 'There is nothing here but semi-desert and a rocky plateau.'

Smoothy translated that one, and they all smirked self-righteously, conveying the impression that there was plenty for an imperialist to spy on.

I was convinced that their actions and attitude were those of people who definitely had something to hide. The restriction on the making of maps; the tightening up of security measures; the objections to pilgrims, and the banning of cameras added up to something important which they were determined to conceal.

Our guilt was already established in their minds. Of that I was certain. I was utterly weary of the ridiculous, maddening situation. Of the senseless questioning, the tedium of repetition, the naked hostility and disbelief. There is a proverb that 'Patience was made in China', and there is the adage that constant dripping will wear away a stone. The Chinese were pursuing a wearing-down process, trying to break down my resistance by a means which they had so often tried and so rarely found wanting.

'What was the name of the mountain you intended to visit?'

'Nalkankar. It's 24,062 feet high and we hoped to prove that it has an unnamed summit not shown on the map that might be almost 25,000 feet. Had things gone in our favour we would have made an attempt on it. But the weather conditions made that impossible.'

'Where is this mountain?'

'Just south of Kojarnath. It's half in Tibet and half in Nepal.'

'Why did you wish to climb it?'

'I don't know.'

'Admit the truth. You intended to occupy the mountain for some purpose. What was it? Why did you wish to occupy it?'

I had never heard the like of this before. According to the new Chinese mentality, mountains are not climbed, they are occupied.

I had read newspaper reports of the political trials in Eastern Europe and the set-up here was very much the same. There is no escape. You can talk only to your interrogators. You have no companions, no reading matter. After several months of this type of questioning the victim feels that he must escape to preserve his sanity. He signs the ready-made confession required by the Peoples' Court, and thus signs the warrant which sends him to his death or a slave labour camp.

God help China, I thought. God help Asia and God help the world. Six hundred millions of them; their numbers increasing every day. The radio and Press in the hands of a party with no intellectual freedom whatsoever. To think that such people had supreme power over the immense area of Tibet. The members of this interrogation committee were in themselves a condemnation of the authorities who had appointed them.

Smoothy was writing something, not in Chinese calligraphic symbols, but in longhand. I waited for the result.

Chapter 14

THE CONFESSION

SMOOTHY pushed the document over to me.

'Please read this and sign it. Your guilt is already established.'

I took it and read, 'I confess to participating in an illegal invasion of China. . . .'

After a cursory examination I handed it back.

'I cannot sign it because it is not true. I have never invaded China. We were arrested in Nepal. I have no intention of putting you in the clear in the event of a diplomatic protest from the British Government. When word of our arrest gets out, the British Foreign Office will protest in the strongest possible terms. All your propaganda about friendship and world peace is just so much eyewash.'

'By what authority do you state that you were in Nepal?'

I listed the reasons one by one.

We had made careful enquiries in West Nepal and all the people we had questioned claimed that Jung Jung Khola was part of Nepal. The Governor of Baitadi, Mr. Prasad, had also assured us that the frontier lay much farther to the north. The three recognized camp sites in the Khola all possess Nepalese and not Tibetan names.

Smoothy then revealed that neither he nor his friends had the least idea where the border lay, nor had they even a clue as to the configuration of the countryside.

'We have further proof of your guilt,' he said. 'You have constantly admitted that you were in the Jung Jung Khola, and all the people living in the Jung Jung Khola pay taxes to the New China.'

I was no longer inclined to laugh, not even at this extremely comical claim.

'That's impossible. No one lives in the Jung Jung Khola. It's uninhabited and always has been. It is a high mountain valley unsuitable for habitation, agriculture or grazing.'

I was accused of lying and told that many Tibetan houses were situated in the Khola and that I must have seen them and spoken to the inhabitants. I could only suggest that they should go up to the hills and take a look for themselves. Ignoring this, they made another effort to persuade me to sign the confession.

'You and Mr. Harrop have sent many letters asking for better food and conditions. Sign this confession and your requests will be granted. Also your punishment will be light.'

Having told Smoothy to consign his improved conditions to the appropriate place, I remarked that I had no wish to see their stinking country and that, if they didn't want visitors, why didn't they adopt the simple expedient of deporting us?

He answered that we had attempted to commit a crime against the Peoples' Republic of China and that we must be punished as a warning to other imperialist agents. When I asked what form the punishment might take, I was simply told that confession would result in light punishment and failure to confess would mean severe punishment.

Nothing but injustice can result from such an attitude. The guilty man confesses and is punished lightly. The innocent man, having nothing to confess, is sent up the river for a long stretch. I decided that the British judicial system would always do for me.

They now reverted to the earlier questions about my family, trying to discover a discrepancy in my replies. But my answers were always the same, for I had only the truth to tell.

At one stage Smoothy produced the expedition flags we had hoped to fly from the summit of Nalkankar. He held out the flags of the United Kingdom, Wales, Nepal and U.N.O. Pointing to the Union Jack, he asked if it was the British flag, and then he held up the pale blue symbol of the United Nations.

'This is the United Nations flag. Why did they send you here? And what is the connection between this U.N.O. organization and your illegal expedition?'

I explained that the U.N.O. flag had been flown from mountain tops by practically every expedition since the war. That involved me in another round of questions.

'Why didn't you say there were other expeditions? Who are they? Where do they come from?'

I sighed heavily, exasperated by their incredible ignorance.

'There are scores of expeditions. I can't remember where they all come from, but I can tell you that none of them has any connection whatever with ours.'

Having talked that one over with the Governor, Smoothy said:

'You have admitted that there are many organizations such as yours operating in the Himalayas. We know for a fact that they are all part of the same illegal espionage organization and that you all receive instructions from the same headquarters. Tell us everything and it will be much easier for you. The Peoples' Republic of China is very lenient with repentant criminals.'

That was the signal for them all to start shouting across the table. Evidently they thought they were on the verge of uncovering an international spy organization.

'Is the international headquarters in England or America?'

I decided that it would do no harm to pervert the truth slightly and lead them up the garden.

'The central H.Q. for British expeditions is the Everest Foundation.'

'Who is the big leader?'

'A man called John Hunt.'

'Is he connected with the British Government?'

'No. He's a Brigadier in the British Army.'

This last answer really set the kettle boiling. Smoothy felt that he was on to something at last, and the Bookworm was scribbling furiously.

The faces opposite were keyed up with anticipation. The heart of the British Secret Service was about to be laid bare.

'Is this John Hunt retired?'

'No, he's still a serving officer, and he received a decoration from Her Majesty the Queen a couple of years ago.'

'Have you met him?'

'I've only corresponded with him.'

'Ah! You admit, then, that you have received your instructions from him?'

'Nonsense!'

'Tell us about this organization. Have you visited its H.Q., and what is its address?'

'I can't tell you any more about the organization because I've never been there and don't know any of the permanent staff. Its H.Q. is in South Audley Street, London, only a few doors from your own Chinese Chargé d'Affaires' residence. I wouldn't be surprised if John Hunt hasn't got his telephone line tapped and his mail opened.'

That startling disclosure gave me a few moments' peace while they argued back and forth among themselves.

When the questions started again I looked at my watch. I had been sitting on that hard, filthy floor for two and a half hours. I'd had more than enough for one day.

'I would like to go back to my cell,' I said. 'I'm not answering any more questions.'

'You have not been kept in a cell,' Smoothy retorted. 'You are being quartered in a house and you are being well treated.' Then, 'What is the penalty for espionage in Britain?'

When I did not reply, he worded the question differently.

'What would happen to a foreigner wearing your uniform and emblem if he were caught spying?'

'In wartime it would mean death.'

That seemed to satisfy him, but I had the feeling that he was leading up to something.

'What are you getting at?' I demanded.

He reached over for the Bookworm's brief-case and produced from it a flag. It was the red flag of the Chinese Republic, decorated with five gold stars. I understood his objective now. I could almost have asked the question for him.

'You brought with you the flag of the Peoples' Republic. What was the purpose?'

'The purpose was a very simple, but obviously misguided, one. The summit of Nalkankar is half in Tibet and half in Nepal. Had we been fortunate enough to make the first ascent of that mountain we would have flown all the flags from the summit, including the Chinese flag. We would have flown the Chinese flag as a gesture of goodwill.'

He took no pains to conceal the fact that he believed not a word of what I said.

Stabbing his fat finger at me he cried:

'You carried our flag as a subterfuge to help you make an illegal occupation of the mountain.'

His Chinese impassivity had deserted him. The sight of the Communist flag in the hands of a 'Western imperialist' was enough to establish our guilt in his eyes. I wondered what made us decide to take that hideous piece of red bunting in the first place. As a gesture of friendship with people like these? But it was impossible to make friends with such thought-conditioned sub-humans.

I looked at Monkey Face, whose eyes protruded as if on stalks as he raved in true Schickelgruber fashion. They appeared to lose their tempers in an abnormal and uncivilized manner. At least, the Taklakot types did. I could well understand how these people enjoyed torturing a helpless animal.

The Governor displayed the least agitation, though he did nothing to restrain his comrades in their hideous display of savage temperament. Perhaps he was hoping that this unpleasant outburst would frighten me into a confession.

The truth failing to convince them, the lies required in the form of a confession could only hasten our doom. At the worst certain death. At the best a long term of imprisonment.

Ug-Lug came from behind the table to thrust his foul face close to mine. I could see the tiny veins in his bulging bloodshot eyes. Quivering with rage, he screamed in my face. Then, turning to the table, he snatched up the 'confession' and thrust it within inches of my face. I shook my head. The Governor spoke a few barely audible words and Ug-Lug summoned the guards to crowd me more closely. They did so, their Tommy guns cocked, the barrels touching the sides of my temples.

Smoothy pointed to the 'confession'.

'You would be very wise to sign. The punishment would be very light.'

I hesitated. Was it worth while getting my brains blown out? Why not sign? Perhaps we would escape with a short prison sentence. But how long could I stand confinement in one of their filthy, dark, rat-infested cells, to be restored to daylight ten years later a physical and mental wreck? I would take a chance on the immediate future— without a confession.

Perspiration filmed my forehead as I said, 'You can go to hell!'

There was silence for a moment. Those who could not speak English must have divined what I had said.

The Governor rose and spoke to the photographer, who sighted his camera at me. They evidently wanted my picture for the record, perhaps to pin it to the death certificate.

But no. They would not shoot any of us. Not yet. This was our first interrogation and we knew that they were in touch with either Lhasa or Peking or both. The men at the top would never sanction our execution until they had all the facts in their possession. The Tommy-gun threat was merely a trick.

Smoothy asked me to look at the camera. The light was very poor and I wondered how on earth the photographer could hope to get a decent picture. No suggestion was made that I should step out into the sunlight. Furthermore, the ever ready case kept swinging in front of the camera lens as the operator held the instrument vertically.

It was the sort of thing that happens to every photographer, and being something of an amateur photographer myself I tried to point out that he would get a useless negative. I was rewarded by Smoothy commanding me to 'Shut up'. So I said no more, and the photographer pressed the shutter release and wasted his exposure.

Smoothy rounded off the day's proceedings by saying:

'You have not answered honestly today. Next time you come to our house we will ask further questions and we expect you to answer them honestly.'

The two guards prodded me with their guns, and I stood up, cramped and stiff after more than two and a half hours of squatting on the floor. The curtain was pulled aside and, bidding my hosts a very good day, I walked out into the yard. My first interrogation was over.

Chapter 15

SOLITARY CONFINEMENT

OUTSIDE, blinded by the sunlight, I paused for a few seconds to shield my eyes. The Dzongpen and the Indian *agent provocateur* stood by the yard door. Both greeted me, but I gave no sign of recognition. I was in no mood to exchange pleasantries with them.

Out in the open and away from the confines of the red building I began to feel brighter. It was too nice a day to feel miserable. My guards stopped to light a cigarette and I sat on a rock to take advantage of the view.

Down below, the bright green Karnali river rushed along on its journey south to Nepal. Its surface was dotted with ice fragments that must have had their origin at the foot of the mighty glaciers of Gurla Mandhata, whose virgin 25,350-feet summit towered above our prison. A crowd of Tibetans, who must have been waiting some time, had gathered to see me come out. They did not appear to resent a stranger in their midst and returned my smiles quite openly. As we exchanged friendly expressions I felt sad that such a proud and free-dom-loving people should have to suffer domination by the mis-guided individuals sitting in the interrogation room.

Overhead a pair of lammergiers circled round in the cloudless sky, surveying the landscape for carrion, their broad wings casting great shadows wherever they flew. At this point I could see the Taklakot ridge from the end, and its narrowness surprised me. The great Lamasery at the summit took on the appearance of a huge ship seen from the bows.

All too visible across the river was our prison, and the thought of returning to its filthy, confining dreariness was depressing. I had only a few moments to take everything in, and sights and sounds I would not have noticed at any other time assumed an unusual and poignant significance. Everything that was new I tried to register indelibly on my memory. 'This is Tibet,' I said. 'In spite of the Chinese, it is wonderful to be here.'

A group of Tibetans rode by on horses, their appearance and their posture in the saddle betraying the fact that they had been indulging the Chang bottle much too freely. Dressed in their best, gold and silver was much in evidence, particularly on the wood and leather saddles which were finely decorated with most beautiful engraving and filigree work. One carried an instrument that looked like an ordinary trumpet, but sounded like an oboe. He was so drunk he was unable to play it and the queer noises he produced from it sent his friends into near-hysterics. My guards enjoyed the joke as much as the Tibetans. For once their faces showed their youthfulness and their Tommy guns and uniforms lost their harsh significance, leaving only the vision of two Chinese boys who were enjoying a piece of slapstick comedy that needed neither caption nor sub-titles. It was international in character. An Eskimo or Hottentot could laugh at a Tibetan. They are the world's number one clowns. What makes the Tibetan so lovable is the fact that his humour is not the unconscious type of the village idiot. Far from it. The average Tibetan is keen and intelligent and because of that his wit is sharper than most. The Tibetan peasant certainly seemed to enjoy life much more thoroughly than his Indian or Nepalese counterpart.

One of the riders was bearing a flag furled round a ten-feet pole with a heavy silver top piece. This flag-bearer fell off his horse to the accompaniment of loud guffaws from his companions. Leaving the flag on the ground, he remounted with great difficulty. The flag lay at the horse's feet and the rider eyed it ruefully. Holding on to the saddle with one hand, he swung down to retrieve the flag. He was hanging almost upside down when the saddle slipped right under the horse's belly, precipitating the rider into the dust. As with the ponies we had ridden from Kathan to Jitkot, none of the saddle-girths of these animals were fitted with anything so modern as a buckle. The girth was tightened with home-made rope finished off with one or two knots.

The flag-bearer lay motionless while he gathered his wits, his friends riding round him shouting good-natured taunts. When he had sorted himself out, he rose and leaned against his patient animal, which viewed the proceedings quite unconcerned. The episode ended with the flag-bearer staggering along leading his horse by the reins, the saddle hanging underneath the horse's belly. One of the Chinese picked up the flag and handed it to the oboe player.

Resuming our journey, we passed some fifty Chinese soldiers in their shirt-sleeves filling four-gallon drums with water, all the cans bearing the trademark of an Indian firm of mustard oil dealers. The majority of the soldiers wore the usual tennis shoes, though a few sported cheap brown leather shoes of very inferior quality. Green or maroon army issue cotton sweaters were worn by some, each having numerals of white cotton cloth sewn on the back. The most common numbers were 29 and 33, but what they signified I did not know.

A couple of dozen mules stood around by the river bank, saddled with the crude wooden carrier frames for transporting the water-cans, four per mule. At the side of the bridge another group of soldiers was cleaning the stomachs and intestines of sheep and yaks in the fast-flowing river-water. A large pot boiled merrily on top of a stone fire-place, the type in which, according to tradition, missionaries used to be boiled. It was large enough to hold three average-size people. A few Tibetan children hung around the soldiers hoping for a few scraps, and occasionally a couple of feet of intestine was thrown their way. The children eagerly seized their booty and made off.

As we passed over the bridge the offal-washers looked up from their task and shouted questions to my guards, who shook their heads in reply. We prisoners were evidently top secret. I paused in the middle of the bridge and looked down into the cold, translucent water sweeping along with such immense force, hurrying south to the Indian Ocean.

With a raft we might have sailed down the Karnali to freedom, for there are no rapids or waterfalls on the Tibetan stretch, and within hours we could be in Nepal. But we had no raft, and the soldiers were too watchful for us to make use of one even had we possessed one.

We moved on up the hill to our prison. I stepped through the doorway, having to climb over a newly delivered bundle of brush-wood that must have been about six feet high. A Tibetan had delivered it by yak a few moments before, and was now haggling about the weight and price. Chungnya wrote down the supposed value and amount in an exercise book while the Tibetan screamed blue murder. I had covered less than half the distance across the yard when Schickel-gruber threw the firewood man bodily through the door. The poor fellow ran down the hillside wailing and lamenting his fate, followed by his yak at a more leisurely pace.

Damodar was sitting with his back to the wall of our cell and Harrop was standing at the top of the steps that led to the higher part of the yard. The yard was full of Chinese troops, most of them new to me and all of them armed with machine-guns.

Harrop started down the steps to greet me, but was stopped by two guards who thrust the muzzles of their guns into his stomach. Two others waved me across the yard, keeping me covered all the time. With my hands raised, I stood with my back against the lavatory wall. Schickelgruber walked over, pointed a finger at his mouth and then at mine, warning, '*Mindo.*'

I was now to keep my mouth shut.

'How did it go?' Harrop shouted.

'These Chinese are bloody impossible,' I replied. 'They're convinced we are spies.'

Schickelgruber screamed in rage at my defiance, one hand on the cocking-lever of his gun.

'Then it's Lhasa or Peking next stop,' Harrop shouted back.

'I'm afraid so.'

Schickelgruber reversed his gun, holding it by the barrel, waving it in the air and muttering under his breath. I had reached a critical moment. Another word and my skull would be shattered.

Everyone gradually quietened down, but the last word came from an unexpected quarter. It was spoken in English with a slight Nepalese accent. 'All Chinese are bastards.'

'Brother,' I thought, 'you can say that again.'

The guard Chubby stood on the firing step looking over the wall towards the red building. He answered a signal with a wave of his hand, and it was Harrop's turn to appear before the interrogation committee.

When he had gone I was forced to sit on the yard floor opposite Damodar, while armed guards menaced each of us, their gun-barrels pointing at our chests all the time. I fumed at our impotence. How I hated the Chinese at that moment!

Chungnya came out of the kitchen and stood behind the guards, looking curiously at me over their shoulders, doubt and confusion clearly written on his face. Our inability to speak each other's language and the different mental outlook of East and West had not prevented a friendship from developing between us. Chungnya could think for himself, and it was clear that he was endowed with a generous measure of human feeling. He might not have heard of Christianity, but he practised it.

Chungnya had good cause to look troubled. He was fighting a battle for which he was not mentally equipped. His education was limited to the stereotyped Communist interpretation of history and world events. His knowledge of other peoples was such that he could think of them only as bourgeoisie and proletarian.

There is no dividing line in Marxist philosophy. I do not believe that any man who is naturally intelligent can accept Communist social philosophy indefinitely. Sooner or later the errors are seen and reason prevails. Thought-conditioning has its limitations. The subject must, if he is to accept Marxian ideology without question, be of a simple mentality and, even more important, he must remain ignorant of how the rest of the world lives. Otherwise the façade of lies and propaganda is penetrated and collapses.

Chungnya had now met two of the so-called imperialists, and he had sufficient objectivity of outlook to see that they were nothing like he had been led to believe. All the other guards, Chubby excepted, regarded us as enemies. Obviously the local political officers had been to work on them, and they viewed us as enemies because they had been deliberately conditioned to do so. Chungnya, I felt sure, would win the battle of his own mind. But whether he would be the happier, when he was unable to escape from his associates and the atmosphere they imposed, is a question I cannot answer. Independence of thought under Communism must make one very much the odd man out.

Chungnya's assertion of his individuality came weeks later, on December 14th, when I was knocked down from behind by a Tommy-gun butt. Chungnya intervened and forced my attacker to put up his gun.

I grinned at Chungnya and he grinned back. 'Damodar isn't quite right,' I thought. 'Not all Chinese are bastards.'

Schickelgruber gave Chungnya an order, and he went into our cell to emerge carrying my sleeping-bag and air mattress. He took these to the small cell at the right of the yard, the door, situated in a small dark passage, being immediately opposite the guardroom door and only three feet from it.

At a signal I followed Chungnya inside. Although this was an obvious move, it had not occurred to me. We would be kept separate from now on, and would probably not be allowed to so much as speak to each other, to prevent us, of course, from exchanging notes concerning our respective interrogations.

I was allowed to return to the larger cell for a few moments to sort out a few of my possessions. I shared out the last of our Nestlé's chocolate and Kendal mint cake and our last tin of boiled sweets. I also shared the condensed milk, which was in small tubes. Finally, we had about half a pound of sugar cubes each. Soon these remnants would all be gone and there would be nothing to supplement the atrocious diet or to improve the taste of the brick tea.

Along with a torch and one of the tiny Tibetan tables Chungnya had given us, I went back to the cell that was to be my new home. The smallest room of all, it had once been used as a vegetable store.

There was a raised ramp at the back which had held bags of *chigada* (small turnips) and a few dried-up specimens of these still littered the floor. My cell boasted two windows. One looked out on to the court-yard and the other provided a grandstand view of the interior of the lavatory enclosure.

The ceiling was too low for me to stand upright, and a heavy beam ran across the centre, making it essential for me to stoop when passing. After pitching my bed I had less than six square feet of floor space and, if anything, the cell was filthier than the one I had vacated. The lower parts of the walls were so extensively riddled with rat-holes that it resembled a miniature edition of Greater Taklakot.

A piece of white paper glued to the wall by the window proved to be the remains of a Chinese calendar. As a little space remained, I scribbled in the date—November 7th—adding, *My lucky day*.

There was so much noise in the yard that afternoon that I did not hear Harrop return or Damodar leave for his interrogation. The door was kept locked, being opened only for excursions to the sanitary arrangements. Dinner consisted of half-cooked cabbage, the mess being overloaded with chillies. I ate what I could, but had to give up when the tears began to stream down my face. The chillies were hot enough to burn a hole in the plate. After dark, on being allowed out for tea, I took my pint mug into the kitchen. Harrop was there, as well as Chungnya and Chubby. The latter placed cautionary fingers to his lips, indicating that there must be no talking. I decided that we would observe the rule for the time being.

I looked at Harrop, and it was obvious that he was bursting to tell me what had happened in the interrogation room. I grinned at him and he laughed, blurting, 'Silly lot of beggars, aren't they?'

I nodded agreement.

Chungnya shook his head admonitorily at Harrop. '*Mindo.*'

Schickelgruber, Fatty and Marlo, the most disagreeable of our seven guards, were in the guardroom, otherwise Harrop and I would have been expelled from the kitchen 'chop chop'.

I reached under the table, which consisted of an old door set on brick supports, and pulled out a bag of chillies. Shaking them on to the greasy wooden surface where all the food was prepared, I said, 'Syd, John, Damodar, *yappo mindo . . . mumbo mumbo*,' the latter being Tibetan for a large number.

Chungnya, who was eating a bowl of cabbage—left-overs from dinner—understood, and nodded his head to assure me that he did so. There would be no chillies in our food when Chungnya was cook.

Three days out of twenty-one, which, at least, would be a slight improvement. He picked up about half a dozen chillies, crushed them in his hand and dropped them into his cabbage. I was horrified. Not so Chungnya. He was quite unperturbed. The diet that seared and threatened to skin my mouth had no ill-effect, apparently, upon his constitution. I could only conclude that he had been brought up on the stuff.

At a signal from Chungnya, Chubby thrust his hand inside his tunic and produced two packets of Chinese cigarettes, one decorated with the emblem of a flying horse, the other with a clenched fist. I was given one packet, Harrop the other. When I signified that I did not smoke, Chungnya went out and pushed my packet into Damodar's cell. There could have been no guard on duty, otherwise the action would have caused pandemonium.

Chungnya called me out and pointed to the cell next to the one which had served as our communal prison. Damodar had been moved to this room, Harrop now occupying the original cell on his own. 'Damodar,' Chungnya said as he pointed.

The thoughts that must be plaguing Damodar disturbed me deeply. A few months before he had been studying at Benares in India. This was his second expedition, his first occurring earlier in the year when he had accompanied the Kenya expedition to Himalchuli in Central Nepal. He had voiced his anxiety the previous day when he said that he had already missed half a term at college. I did not dishearten him further by telling him that there was a serious possibility that he might miss many more terms at college and possibly live— if he lived at all—to draw his old age pension in Communist China.

For a boy of eighteen, he had a dauntless spirit and a sense of humour equal to almost any situation. Nothing seemed to depress him. Nevertheless, he could not be indifferent to his future and the prospective ruin of his career.

It was dark now and long past our normal bedtime. I went outside and looked south towards the great peaks of the Himalayas—Nepal, and freedom, such a few short miles away and yet so utterly inaccessible to us. The last of the sun's rays bathed the topmost pinnacles in pale yellow light, and the first stars were pricking themselves out across the sky. What a wonderful place for an observatory, I thought. But how could such a thing ever be? How could one hope to explain its 'purpose' to the Chinese?

Chungnya came out of the kitchen bearing a Tommy gun, which

Full complement of the Welsh Expedition at the base camp, Saipal

Standing : left to right : Damodar, John Harrop, George (Scotty) Dwyer, Geoffrey Roberts. *Seated :* Humfrey Berkeley, Syd Wignall, John Henson. Dhotial porters *kneeling :* Pongya, Ratti, Koila, Giddy, Ungya

The author after his 200-mile march from Taklakot

River crossing in the foothills of the West Nepal Himalaya. Roberts seated on the far bank —Harrop suitably dressed in mid-stream

A 4,000 feet descent to the Kali-Gad river. The Nepalese liaison officer is 18-year-old Damodar-Narayan-Suwal who is seen in the rear

This Hindu shrine is set in the cliff face in the lower Seti gorge

Sorting out our expedition stores at Dhuli . . . the last habitation before setting out on the last lap of the 85-mile march from Pithoragarh to Saipal trader camp site near the Nepal-Tibet border

Below: Exploration of the watershed of the Seti river and the Jung Jung river. The author on high snow col to the West of the Urai Lekh, looking into the 'Hidden Valley' which according to the Indian survey map, does not exist

Above: Harrop is seen here erecting survey cairn near the 19,500 feet Ura Lekh pass on September 17th, 195

Tibetan traders camped at Saipal camping ground in the upper reaches of the Seti valley. The comedian in the foreground is doing a dance for the amusement of the expedition members.

This old Tibetan is seen wearing a letter from the author's wife as a hat

The village idiot whom the expedition members called 'Mad Willy'

Koila who was beaten on the head and shoulders by Chinese troops

The hidden valley
or 'False Tinkar'

Above : Panorama of peaks to the west of base camp, forming the divide between the Seti and the upper reaches of the Salimor Khola

Right : Looking north from the snow col. The Jung Jung Khola lies beyond the foreground snow edge. The lower slopes of 25,355 feet Gurla Mandata in Tibet are seen in the distance. The faint snow-capped line of peaks beyond is the trans Himalaya. . . . Kailas—sacred to both Hindus and Tibetans alike—is the snow peak nearest to the lower slopes of Gurla Mandata

One of the regular daily avalanches which
fell to the north and south of the base camp

Peak opposite the base camp, covered with deep fresh snow

Facing page : En rou
for the final reconna·
sance. Crossing av
lanche debris on t
way up to the 19,5
feet Urai Lekh pa
October 19th, 1955.
a normal post monso·
season the foregrou
is clear of snow

Looking back from the head of the Seti. Rokapi in the centre distance

In the Jung Jung Khola, October 22nd, approaching a trading camp site known as Tharedhunga. The Kathan Pass lies several miles to the north on the left-hand side of the valley

Looking back towards the head of the Jung Jung Khola, October 21st, 1955, from about 18,000 feet

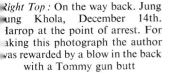

Above : A point half-way back to Urai Lekh, December 16th, 1955

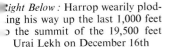

Right Top : On the way back. Jung Jung Khola, December 14th. Harrop at the point of arrest. For taking this photograph the author was rewarded by a blow in the back with a Tommy gun butt

Right Below : Harrop wearily plodding his way up the last 1,000 feet to the summit of the 19,500 feet Urai Lekh on December 16th

Facing page : The four porters and Damodar approaching the first of the Tharedhunga lakes in the Jung Jung Khola region

Above : Harrop and the author on the summit of the Urai Lekh, December 16th, 1955. Harrop is making unprintable remarks about the Chinese Communists and the author is unfortunately suffering from a frozen nose

Right : Damodar-Narayan-Suwal, 18-year-old student from Khatmandu. He was the official expedition liaison officer and accompanied Wignall and Harrop into captivity in Tibet

Above : Our four Tibetan porters for the return trip. The big fellow in the foreground claimed that he had been an erstwhile brigand

Our Tibetan porters brew Yak butter tea near the old expedition base camp site at Saipal

Descent of the south side of the Lekh. One of our Tibetan porters has slipped on the ice

Left : Starting to negotiate the rock pitch which crosses the top of a several hundred foot deep gully. The passage of 30 feet took three-quarters of an hour. December 18th

Below : The old expedition base camp lies beyond the ridge in the foreground. The summit of Kapkot lies in cloud . . . snow is falling on the way down from the Urai

Below : One of the difficult parts in the Seti gorge. Damodar is negotiating a place where the track has collapsed into the river 1,500 feet below. He was forced to edge along under the boulder projecting from the cliff face. Harrop is standing in the shadow under the overhang. Beyond the man-made steps the track has again collapsed into the gorge

indicated he was to be the guard. He was the only one who laid aside his gun when Harrop and I were in evidence.

It was now bitterly cold and I returned to my tiny cell, Chubby following with a very small oil-lamp. It was not for my benefit, for I had no reading matter.

I donned my down-filled jacket and climbed into the comfort of my double-skinned Everest sleeping-bag. I had many things on my mind, and had no intention of going to sleep immediately. Some record of the day's interrogation would have to be made. I had to remember the important points and set them down in correct sequence. The minor questions and answers would be remembered later. With the oil-lamp in evidence, writing sitting up in bed would be detected very quickly.

I was interrupted by the catch on the cell door being undone. Chungnya came in carrying the plywood lid of our food-box. From his trousers pocket he extracted a very dilapidated pack of playing cards, their backs adorned with a daring pin-up of one of the current Indian film glamour girls.

The board was slapped down on my knee and I was handed the pack.

I held out my hand, Chungnya shook it and then, standing the Tommy gun against the wall within easy reach of my hand, he sat down on the edge of my air mattress. We sat looking at each other for some moments. I felt that this lad had a great deal on his mind, and that he wished to convey a message to me. There was little we could do other than show him that we did, indeed, appreciate his kindness.

I offered him my last bar of chocolate, but he shook his head. He called it 'coffee' and, like the others, he would accept nothing that we offered to him. In all probability the guards had been strictly forbidden to receive anything from us.

He tried to show me a Chinese game of cards, but it seemed to consist simply of slapping the individual cards down hard on the table. He who slammed the cards down the hardest and fastest was, it seemed, the winner. Being unable to make head or tail of the game, I had to give up after a couple of hands.

My attempt to play patience was defeated by my inability to concentrate. My mind remained with the events of the day. At eight o'clock I heard voices raised in the guardroom, followed by the clank of metal as someone shouldered a Tommy gun. Chungnya looked quickly at my watch, stubbed out his cigarette, snatched up his gun and adopted a businesslike pose. The door was pushed open

I

by Lofty, who looked in, nodded a greeting to Chungnya and went out into the yard. Chungnya grinned, gave me a playful cuff over the ear and departed.

Fishing down at the bottom of my sleeping-bag I found a few pieces of chocolate wrapper and toilet paper. Armed with a pencil I sought sanctuary inside my bag and, with the aid of Damodar's torch, I made a record of the events which had taken place during the day.

The diary completed, I relaxed with my hands linked behind my head. Sounds of scuttering on the floor told me that the rats had started to explore again. Very soon they would be crawling all over my sleeping-bag. I would have to do something about these disagreeable cell-mates.

A voice beyond my cell took up a chorus. It was Damodar. There was no mistaking his vocal efforts, always off key. He was singing a song Harrop and I had taught him; one which had been very popular in England just before we left. We had arranged our own parody of the words, and it was these that Damodar was singing with such gusto.

Lofty went from one cell window to the other to see if this was a conspiracy, for both Harrop and I took up the tune with Damodar. Outside, the Tibetan mastiffs supplied a far from musical accompaniment, and across the bleak, desolate Tibetan plateau drifted the strains of 'They locked up my lover in Taklakot gaol. . . .'

Chapter 16

THE GRAPEVINE

EARLY on the morning of November 8th I was awakened by Chubby entering my cell with the usual bowl of hot water with which I was supposed to wash. While setting it down he managed to spill a good half of it. The last of our soap was now no more than a wafer-thin piece the size of a postage stamp, and was in Harrop's cell. So I decided to remain dirty. The fact that I was reasonably clean-shaven made me feel a little better.

I sat up, wrapped against the cold in everything I possessed, and waited for the inevitable bowl of boiled turnips that would soon be along. At least it would be hot, and that was something.

When Chubby brought it in I went through the motions of having a dry wash, and signified that I would appreciate a piece of soap. He shook his head and leaned across my bed to point through the window towards the grey barracks where the officers were quartered. With that he stood to attention, saluted, shook his head once more and said, '*Mindo.*'

By means of such simple sign language the guards could by now convey a great deal to us. A salute and a nod or shake of the head meant that the officers had taken a positive or negative attitude to our requests. '*Mindo*' was the order of the day, every day. We could have nothing. The guards used 'Sunlight soap' made in India, but our requests for a supply were repeatedly refused.

I usually took half a cup of the very inferior tea to bed every night in order to relieve the dry throat that invariably brought on the bouts of coughing which interrupted my sleep. I reached for the cup, thinking cold tea would provide all the drink I needed, but found that it was frozen hard in the cup. Intending to go and help myself in the kitchen, I donned my boots, but had no sooner started for the door when I went flat on my back. The water spilled by Chubby had turned to ice.

I was in the act of pocketing two cubes of sugar and a tube of condensed milk when an idea occurred to me. What had Harrop said to the interrogators the day before? It was essential for us to know each other's statements, for the slightest difference in our explanations

131

would be bound to complicate matters. As we were forbidden to talk, I must find some other means of getting a message to him.

I had heard of the American prison system called the 'Grapevine', which was a simple 'Morse' code tapped out on the water-pipes that ran through the cells. Such a system was impossible here, not only because of the absence of hot or cold water-pipes, but also because I did not understand Morse. I decided to write Harrop a brief note underlining the salient points and to make an effort to pass it to him in the yard.

Returning to my bed, I scribbled a message of some four hundred words on a sheet of toilet paper. This I had to do sitting up with my hands just concealed beneath the top of the bag. Occasionally, Schickelgruber would peer in through the cell window. When I saw the shadow of his figure fall on the floor I suspended my writing and stared straight ahead.

The message completed, I went out for my mug of tea. Harrop and Damodar were seated on either side of the yard, Schickelgruber standing between them, his gun held at the ready. There was little hope of passing the note under such circumstances, and I collected the tea and returned to my cell.

Another method had to be found, and one which could be carried out quite openly in front of the guards without them being any the wiser. One lump of sugar went into the cup, followed by a tiny squeeze of condensed milk from the tube. It was in that moment that the solution to the problem occurred to me.

The tube of milk provided the answer. If I unrolled the bottom of the tube I could slip a note into the cylinder. But how I was to prevent it becoming plastered with condensed milk presented a further problem. The answer was provided by the half-dozen polythene bags that had once kept our pemmican ration waterproof, and which now resided in the pocket of my Anorak. Cutting out a small square of polythene, I wrapped the note in it and, having scooped some of the condensed milk into my cup, pushed the note into the tube.

Dragging my sleeping-bag outside to serve as a seat, I took up a position against the wall of my cell and waited for a few moments, hoping that Schickelgruber's vigilance would relax. But not for a moment did he cease to look from one to the other of us. Mentally I consigned him to the nether regions, at the same time wondering whether to wait until the following day when everyone had settled down after the excitement of the first interrogation.

Such a course, however, did not commend itself as it was probable that there would be another interrogation that same day, when there would be further risks of answers which were apparently at variance with those already given. Although I did not know it at the time, a certain amount of accidental harm had been done already. For, whilst I had said that the expedition had been sponsored by the Mountaineering Club of North Wales and the *Liverpool Daily Post*, Harrop had stated that the sponsors were the Royal Geographical Society. This organization had, in fact, trained three members of the expedition in survey and had also supplied a photo-microptic theodolite for our use.

That apparent discrepancy was all the Chinese needed to convince them that one or probably both of us had resorted to lies. With Harrop and me it was merely a question of degree. We could quote as sponsors any one of half a dozen different organizations, the above three ranking, perhaps, as the most important. With the Chinese there could be no question of degree. If we gave answers that were not completely identical in detail then we could only have a sinister purpose in doing so. We must be trying to conceal something of an incriminating nature.

Deciding that the message had to be passed without delay, I squeezed a little of the milk into my cup, ostentatiously in order to draw attention to what I was doing. Then, screwing the cap back on, I threw the tube over to Harrop. As he had his own supply of condensed milk, he must have thought my action very peculiar.

The tube landed about three feet short of him, and before he could move Schickelgruber dived and snatched it from the floor.

I felt as though the bottom had fallen out of my stomach. Schickelgruber, apparently suspecting something, was turning the tube over in his hand and inspecting it with no little curiosity.

Walking away from Harrop, he seated himself on the top of the steps that led to the lower part of the yard. Turning round, he surveyed all three of us individually, and while I tried to appear unconcerned I felt sure that my mounting anxiety must reveal itself, thereby betraying me. Harrop caught my eye and his expression assured me that he realized something was afoot.

After a few moments, which for me stretched to as many years, Schickelgruber unscrewed the cap from the tube and pressed some of the milk on to his forefinger. He grinned and said, '*Newfan.*' To make sure, he tasted it and then spat it out. The top was replaced and Schickelgruber walked back to Harrop. I was becoming so keyed up that I could hardly restrain my impulse to shout, 'Give it to him, you fool!'

To my disgust he accentuated my apprehension still further by opening the tube again and squeezing some of the contents into Harrop's cup. He turned and was on the point of throwing the tube back to me when I pulled another one like it from my pocket, at the same time shaking my head. With that he shrugged and handed Harrop the tube. The grapevine had begun to work.

I looked hard at Harrop, and the moment Schickelgruber turned his back I was reassured by a knowing wink.

Harrop had more sense than to go indoors right away. He pocketed the tube, making no move until the guards had been changed and Schickelgruber had departed across the river. After that the sergeant of our guards made a daily trip to see the officers, no doubt to report on our behaviour.

I decided that diary-keeping called for the use of pen and ink. Repairing to the kitchen, I washed out my sludge-filled pen and, taking advantage of Schickelgruber's absence, asked Chungnya for ink. The sight of my pen was enough and he supplied me with ink immediately.

Unable to exchange speech, we had to do something to while the time away, and Harrop set to with a few bouts of gymnastics. Although some of the guards tried to emulate him, none succeeded in doing so until Chungnya took a hand. Then he revealed an unsuspected virtuosity in this realm. He began with some remarkable handstands. He ended them by creating the false belief that he was about to fall flat on his back. But half-way to the ground his body arched like a spring and, propelled by one intense movement, he restored himself to the upright, standing smartly on his feet.

He followed this with several other feats. Lying relaxed on Harrop's mattress, he doubled up his knees under his chin and sprang straight up into a standing position. We were so intrigued by this performance that we persuaded him to do it half a dozen times.

Lofty watched the proceedings with a slightly amused smile while knitting himself a vivid blue pullover. All the guards knitted, including even Schickelgruber. The monkey-faced little character whom we now rechristened Shorty, to distinguish him from Monkey Face of the interrogation committee, knitted no less than three pairs of gloves while we were in prison.

Chungnya displayed greater intelligence. He gave up after the first glove and went about collecting wool from the sheep the Chinese had bought for slaughter. When he had enough, he passed it through the yard door to the only pretty Tibetan girl we ever saw. She came

once a week and Chungnya handed over enough wool to almost fill
the wicker basket she carried on her back.

He did quite well out of the deal, gaining for himself a pair of
nicely made mittens knitted with a pattern that closely resembled 'Fair
Isle'. Later she handed over three pairs of socks, thick and heavy, but
innocent of heel. They were the same shape from top to toe.

The girl called that afternoon and Chungnya and Chubby stood
at the gate and carried out a bit of courting. The girl acted coy, giggling
and hiding her face, while the two soldiers grinned like a couple of
Cheshire cats. But later, when Schickelgruber returned, the guards
abandoned their joyous attitude.

The meticulous way in which the guards carried out their instructions, interpreting every command in the most literal manner,
amused rather than annoyed us. Once, I went over to the wall and
climbed on to the firing step to have a look across the river. I was
immediately challenged by the guard on duty, who made it known
in no uncertain terms that he would shoot if I did not step down.
Whereupon I walked back across the yard, up the steps and over to
the wall of the communal cell, from which vantage point I had a much
better view than from the firing step. This the guards allowed without
the slightest protest. In the Chinese Army, as in all others, orders are
orders and must be carried out however absurd they might be.

Schickelgruber returned with a sheaf of papers, and he handed
one to each of us, at the same time pointing over the river. For some
inexplicable reason we were to write to the officers, but no indication
was given as to the nature of the communications. Did they expect a
confession? If so, unless they stretched us on the rack, they were
doomed to disappointment. I decided to take the opportunity to
furnish them with an impressive list of complaints, which occupied
almost a full sheet of foolscap. Later I discovered that both Harrop
and Damodar had done the same thing. Nothing came of it, but it
helped to kill a little time, the only commodity of which we had an
excess supply.

On the second day in my solitary cell I decided to darn a pair of
socks and stitch a patch on both the knees and bottom of my very
decrepit drill trousers. My first efforts to secure the needed materials
were unavailing, but, later in the day, I persuaded Chubby to furnish
the necessary items. After that, Schickelgruber added to our restrictions by forbidding any further repairs.

Feeling sick during the afternoon, I lay down indoors. Harrop,
although I did not know it at the time, seized the opportunity to send

a reply to my note. It was much easier for him to pass a message than for me. I had no legitimate reason to go anywhere near his cell, but he had to pass mine on his way to the toilet. He waited until I was indoors and then flipped a screwed-up note through the open window as he passed. The window was on the same level as his shoulder and for a fractional moment he was out of sight of the guard.

As my eyes were closed I did not see the note come through the window, but I remember Harrop muttered 'Damnation to the Chinese' as he passed, and that I replied, 'Hear, hear!'

The note lay on the floor until the following day when I discovered it quite by accident. That I found it at all was due to my unwelcome cell-mates, the rats.

The previous night these creatures had awakened me several times. On the last occasion I had found one about to enter my sleeping-bag. When he scurried away I found that another large hole had been chewed in the neck of my sweater. The rats, I felt sure, were not feeding on the wool, but were more probably purloining it to build their nests.

Determined to put an end to their depredations, I set about sealing up all the holes in the walls. The door had a raised step over which one had to climb, and it let out doorways which allowed the rats ready ingress. My task was that of finding stones of the right sizes with which to block the holes. I scoured the yard and also managed to break pebbles away from the lower part of the wall which consisted of conglomerate blocks.

One by one the holes were blocked until only one remained. I was in the act of picking up a stone to jam into this last aperture when I noticed a tiny screwed-up ball of paper on the floor. I opened it to discover that it was a reply from Harrop. I might well have over-looked it indefinitely.

Damodar could not, of course, be brought into the secret corres-pondence without making the system too unwieldy and complicated. So Harrop suggested that, as his cell door was only three feet from Damodar's and exactly facing it, he should whisper a few words across or, in an emergency, toss a note through the door during the daytime.

To help while away the time, I decided to make a sketch map of the mountain ranges that stretched away across the skyline to the south. From my cell window I could see the whole of the West Nepal Himalaya from the Urai to the Tinkar Lipu and almost to the Lipu Lekh pass on the border of India. I was, in fact, occupying a wonderful survey station, for no surveyor had ever been granted permission to enter the Tibetan plateau and survey the mountains of Nepal from this excellent viewpoint.

I made my sketch on a piece of toilet paper in the form of a panorama. As the paper was not long enough for my purpose, I had to draw the sketch in sections of some five inches each in length, using four sections. To ensure accuracy of detail I pursued my task in a leisurely manner, thereby occupying three days and introducing a welcome diversion from the usual tedious routine. The need to avoid detection caused me to maintain a constant vigil throughout.

Each day, when sketching was over, I hid the partly finished record inside the double lining of my spare windproof trousers, pushing it through a convenient tear in the outer cloth. At the end of the three days I managed to insert the finished sketch inside the plastic backing of a small mirror I had purchased from Woolworth's in Cologne for 4d. This hiding-place assumed greater importance when Harrop accidentally came into possession of a tiny identification photograph of Smoothy, our English-speaking interrogator.

That day we were furnished with a further illustration of oriental logic. My companions were sitting in the yard and I made a trip to the kitchen to discover in what state of lukewarm mediocrity the tea might be. Looking across the river I noticed the khaki- and blue-clad figures of the officers ascending the hill via the track that led up to the new barracks. They sat down for a breather half-way up the track and passed round a pair of binoculars with which they surveyed our prison. As soon as the guards saw that the officers were looking at us they ushered us back into our cells and locked the doors.

The next morning I was sitting in the yard alone and the same thing happened again. I lost my temper and swore at Fatty and Schickelgruber, but to no avail. Into my cell I went. The reason for this curious action was one that remained unexplained.

On the morning of Friday, November 11th, Schickelgruber entered my cell and signified that I should hurry my meal. I was destined for my second interrogation.

As I was by no means looking forward to the prospect I lingered over the meal as long as I could. It was a nice day and I would have much preferred to sit on in the yard. In any case, why the rush, and why so early in the morning?

Damodar and Harrop came out of their cells hoping to discover what sequence of interrogation had been planned for them. As I looked at Harrop he gave me the 'thumbs up' sign.

Outside the doorway the Governor's personal bodyguard, armed with his American carbine, was waiting to escort me. I moved off downhill in the direction of the bridge, but was brought to a halt by the barrel of his rifle barring my way. He pointed along the track in the other direction, indicating the way by which we had entered Taklakot. It was to be a different interrogation room this time.

Chapter 17

'ARGUMENT ABOUT IT AND ABOUT'

THE new interrogation chamber turned out to be a Tibetan house built partly into the cliff face and situated about fifty yards from our prison. Half a dozen army mules were tied to a rail outside the door, and two guards stood in the doorway talking to the gold-toothed Indian who served the Chinese.

I was ushered down a passage so dark that I tripped over a saddle and bumped another armed soldier accidentally in the stomach. Within a very short distance I had picked up no less than six armed soldiers as escort. Could it be that, after assessing the answers I had given at the previous interrogation, they had decided that I was a very dangerous person indeed?

The new interrogation room proved to be smaller than the previous one and there was barely sufficient room for everyone to crowd inside. Most of the armed guards had to remain jammed in the doorway. The room boasted but one small window, and this only some nine inches square. Through this tiny aperture enough light percolated for me to see and recognize the faces of my inquisitors.

All were familiar, except that the photographer had been replaced by a much smaller man wearing the largest fur hat I had ever seen.

The same small table was in evidence and the committee occupied the usual tubular steel chairs. Glancing behind me I was not surprised to see a chair folded and standing against the wall as before. The drill, too, proved to be the same. I was reaching for the chair when Smoothy said, 'Hello, you must sit on the floor.'

I sat cross-legged on the ground waiting for the usual two or three minutes' silence to end. They all smoked English cigarettes, a tin of which stood on the table. Tea was poured out as before and, as before, there was no cup for me. The tea-drinking ended, Smoothy cleared his throat, spat on the floor and said, 'Hello.'

I did not reply and looked him straight in the face, an action which he found disconcerting, for he deliberately looked away from me.

'We have brought you here to answer some questions. This time you must answer honestly.' He paused. 'What is your name?'

'Sydney Wignall.'

Smoothy doodled with his pen. 'We want to know your real name.'

I replied as before.

'Have you any other names?'

I assured him I had not.

'What you say is a lie. You have used other names. You will tell them to us.'

Not knowing what he was getting at, I remained silent.

'We now have proof that your passport is false. We have evidence which shows that you use other aliases.'

With that he fished about inside his brief-case and threw a handful of visiting cards on the table.

'We discovered these amongst your belongings. Now confess that you are a British agent.'

He handed the cards to me and I burst out laughing as I saw what they were. I had collected these cards on the 6,500-mile road journey to the Himalayas. They included the names of a newspaper reporter from Aachen, Council officials from Wiesbaden, the British Vice-Consul at Innsbruck, a Reuter's correspondent, a Customs officer on the Greek border, an American civil engineer in Istanbul, a student in Istanbul, a gentleman in Teheran who was a close confidant of the Shah of Persia, an Afghan accountant from Kandahar and, finally, a card bearing the names of a British couple who were travelling from the United Kingdom to Australia by car.

How on earth was I to talk my way out of this one?

With difficulty I explained how the cards came into my possession, going through the names one by one, trying to convince them that my identity as S.W. was the only one to which I had ever laid claim. When I reached the Turkish student Ozcan Kocabiyikoglu, I decided that this was the one that would get me hanged.

'What does the name mean?' Smoothy demanded.

My feelings were very mixed as I replied, anticipating what the reception would be:

'Ozcan is his first name. The other name means "Son of the Big Moustache".'

Discarding his usual aplomb, Smoothy told me that I was insulting his intelligence.

I thought that the last card might prove my point.

'I may be this chap Field,' I said. 'But how the hell can I parade as his wife Mary as well?'

Unconvinced, Smoothy took back the cards.

'There is the evidence that proves you are a foreign spy,' he said. 'A great deal of trouble will be saved if you sign this confession.'

The by now familiar document was produced, and again I refused to have anything to do with it.

The Governor interposed to say a few words in a very soft voice. Smoothy listened and then smiled. Everyone around the table began to grin and I wondered if the Governor had just remembered a shaggy yak story and had told it while he happened to be thinking about it. But Smoothy soon dispelled that illusion.

'Who is the big leader of your expedition?'

This served to underline their obtuseness. Not once during the previous interrogation had they raised this point. Perhaps because it had not figured on the question form that had been radioed from H.Q.

'I am,' I replied.

That wiped the grins from their faces. They had not expected me to tell the truth. They all looked puzzled, and Smoothy gave voice to their curiosity.

'If you are the big leader, why did you come here? Why did you not send someone else?'

This reminded me of the story of a group of Chinese watching Europeans playing tennis. After the game was over one of the Chinese mentioned to the players that he noticed that they employed boys to retrieve the balls from the side of the court. He could not understand why they paid boys to do this task and at the same time did the most energetic work themselves. 'Why don't you employ someone to play this very strenuous game for you?' he asked.

That epitomizes the Chinese attitude to all things. Those in authority must not lose face by doing work that could be undertaken by hirelings.

I repeated that I was in the Himalayas for climbing and exploration and for nothing more. I added that I objected strongly to being kidnapped by the Chinese and held against my will in Tibet.

'This,' I went on, 'is China's second aggression against Nepal.' Before he could interrupt I gave him the rest of the story. 'Two years ago, Chinese troops illegally entered Nepal north-east of Khatmandu and were arrested by Ghurka soldiers. One of these Chinese soldiers was still a prisoner last year and our liaison officer saw the man being exercised in the streets of Khatmandu. He was escorted by unarmed soldiers and given far more freedom than you allow us.'

Smoothy translated that choice piece of news to the others and they reacted by screaming, their eyes bulging. I marvelled that officers could conduct themselves in such an undisciplined manner. Only the Governor remained calm. He was a shrewd old character and I felt that he had more intelligence than the rest of them together. The others were merely a pack of savages.

He raised a hand and they quietened, giving him undisputed possession of the floor. In subdued tones he made a brief statement to Smoothy, who passed it on to me.

'The Peoples' Republic of China has never committed an act of aggression against any nation. China's peaceful record is proof of that.'

I acknowledged that I was somewhat ill informed about China's 'peaceful record' and asked for more details. That provoked the stock reply:

'You must not ask questions, only answer them.'

He lifted his hand and the Governor's bodyguard pushed the barrel of his carbine against my chest and put his finger to his lips. Meanwhile, Smoothy was busy writing on a sheet of foolscap. When he had finished, he handed the document to me along with a pen.

'Sign this.'

I read: 'I confess to having ORGANIZED an illegal invasion of China.'

'Sign and your conditions of imprisonment will be improved.'

'What kind of improvement have you in mind?' I asked. 'Will the guards carry only two grenades instead of four? Or is it your intention to reduce the number of mines at the back of the prison by half?'

Smoothy tried to summon a magnanimous smile.

'You will receive cigarettes and soap and any other small item you might desire.'

So I was to trade my future for fifty cigarettes and a tablet of soap! Once again I declined to take advantage of his offer.

He tried another avenue, resorting to one of the oldest tricks in the world.

'Your two companions have confessed. You are the only one left. Your punishment will be much heavier than theirs.'

I asked to see the signed confessions, but, of course, they were not forthcoming.

My captors were uneducated and illiterate, but they were not without cunning, as their next move revealed.

'The cards we have shown you prove that you have more than one name and that you are a spy. We also have evidence that you travelled secretly in Tibet carrying out espionage before you were arrested by the Peoples' Liberation Army.'

As we had never been any farther north than our camp site in the Jung Jung Khola I was at a loss to understand his claim. Thinking that he was venturing a shot in the dark, I displayed no outward signs of emotion. Smoothy produced a piece of heavy paper, folded in such a way that I could not see what was written on it.

'This is sufficient evidence to prove that you have lied and that you have been attempting to subvert the Tibetan people.'

The paper was handed to me and I opened it out. It was a fine example of Tibetan script, but it meant nothing to me.

'This document was printed in Tibet, and was found amongst your belongings with several others like it. It is proof that you were in Tibet at some time before you were arrested.'

I realized then that the script was one of those that Harrop had purloined from the Chorten outside Jitkot Lamasery. I didn't think that I would have any difficulty explaining that one away. But I reckoned without the cunning of the quiet-spoken little man, the Governor.

'Our possession of this sample of Tibetan writing,' I said, 'can be explained easily. It is one of many that Harrop collected while we were being held at the Tibetan monastery at Jitkot between the 25th and the 28th of October.'

My reply was translated to the Governor, who then took complete charge. Addressing me through Smoothy, he spoke deliberately, emphasizing every word.

'One of our officers found these items in your equipment on the 28th of October, *the day of your arrest*. You were not arrested on the 25th of October and you have never visited Jitkot Monastery. From your place of arrest in the Jung Jung Khola you were brought straight to Taklakot.'

Astounded at this claim, I saw that we were being framed. The facts were being distorted to provide the evidence the committee needed to show that we had been operating in Tibet before our arrest.

I could think of no way to meet this obviously serious charge save that of demanding that they should bring the Dzongpen and Gin-Din-Rhou, the High Lama of Jitkot, to give evidence. Smoothy retorted that I was merely attempting to hold up the proceedings. It seemed that we were certain to be railroaded.

Or was this an attempt to make me doubt the evidence of my own senses? The first step in a process designed to undermine my sanity? We could never talk our way out of Taklakot. If there was any hope of deliverance, it lay elsewhere. We could only hope that the Foreign

Office would exercise its influence to such purpose that we were granted our freedom. It was either that or an attempt at escape. But the latter course might be the one our captors wished us to take, thereby giving them an excuse to shoot us in the back.

I understood now, however, the extent to which these people would go in order to obtain a confession. Interrogation is not designed to discover truth. It is to persuade the accused to accept a decision arrived at by his accusers before the first question has been asked.

The Governor was smiling now. No doubt he believed that he had sprung the trap and that there was no escape from it.

'Take a look at the diary you confiscated,' I said. 'Opposite the relevant dates you will find full details of our stay at the monastery. A full explanation as to how we came into possession of the script is there also.'

'We have examined your diary. There is no such entry. It states that you were arrested on the 28th of October.'

'That's a lie!' I shouted. 'You are all crooked. So this is how you fake your trials.'

Smoothy ignored my outburst.

'It also states in your diary that you intended to try to escape.'

Knowing that no such entry had been made, I asked him to show me the particular passage. He then read the following extract: ' "Events that were entirely unexpected have brought a sudden end to our plans. We are now in the hands of the Chinese Communists. We may not now be able to climb a mountain, but our further *escapades* should make an interesting story. . . ." '

'What does that prove?' I asked.

'I have looked up the word ES-CAR-PARDS,' said Smoothy triumphantly, producing a green cotton-backed dictionary. 'It means escape.'

I told him that it meant nothing of the kind, and that I had used the word to indicate 'adventures'. In addition, his pronunciation was all wrong.

It was obvious that I was wasting my time. It was futile to answer questions, futile to argue. The result had been predetermined before the opening of the 'enquiry'. I could tell them to go to hell now, but how much of this sort of thing can the mind stand? The only possible course, it seemed to me, was to argue stubbornly and mislead them as much as possible.

The proceedings were interrupted by the entry of an aged Tibetan servant bearing a large pot of tea. After serving the officers he turned and asked me in Hindi if I would like some. I replied, '*Acha*,' but before he could reach for a cup he was bundled out of the doorway. He evidently did not know the score in Communist-ruled Tibet. The guards who saw him through the door were far from gentle. The type of treatment that the Chinese Communists meted out to their Tibetan 'Comrades' reminded me of the popular quotation from George Orwell's *Animal Farm*: 'All animals are equal, but some are more equal than others.'

Marx's lesson about the social equality of man was one of the chapters that the Chinese have not read, or maybe they have dismissed it as old-fashioned.

There was a pause in the proceedings while the interrogators drank their tea. Smoothy handed me an exercise book and said, 'While we have a small rest you must write here the complete history of your life from the age of eight years.'

Having nothing better to do I complied. I entered the names of the schools I had attended, where I had lived, when I started work and similar items. Having filled in four pages I gave it back to him. He perused it and selected the phrase, 'Worked in Marine Engineering'.

'Is this Marine Engineering the name of a firm?'

'It is an industry.' As he still did not understand, I added, 'It means shipbuilding.'

When he asked why I had not said that in the first place I told him that I had not realized that his intelligence was so limited, but that I would make due allowance for it in the future.

'I have told you before,' he shouted furiously, 'conduct yourself well when in our house. When you return to your cell today, you must examine your thoughts and think great criticisms of yourself.'

I told him that, while he might control my activities, he would never be able to control my mind.

Losing his temper completely, he shrieked at me: 'You will think differently when we have finished with you. We will force you to admit the bankruptcy of your bourgeois way of life. We will help you to reshape your pattern of thinking so that you will see and recognize the truth.'

I remarked that I was weary of sitting on the hard mud floor and that the only thing that might be reshaped would be my backside. Everest string vests can produce a very painful diamond-shaped design.

K

Chapter 18

'WHY DID THE BRITISH OCCUPY EVEREST?'

'WE are only questioning yourself today,' Smoothy said. 'We are in no hurry and are prepared to wait until you take a more reasonable attitude and sign the confession.'

At that I lost my temper.

'Give me one good reason why your army invaded Tibet. Why don't you carry out your promise to take Formosa?'

Smoothy's cup halted abruptly halfway to his mouth.

'I have told you before. We have liberated Tibet from the threat of foreign domination. Formosa is not our task here. This is a different army. Our task is the complete emancipation of the Tibetan people.'

'But all the Tibetans are already in your hands, aren't they?' I was puzzled by his statement, but not for long, for he evidently took for granted certain aspects of the 'Liberation' of which I was ignorant.

'You must be aware that there are parts of Tibet that have not yet been liberated.'

I was not aware of any such thing, but I was quite willing to have a Chinese geography lesson as a change from the usual questionings.

'We will not allow our subjects to live under foreign domination,' he said.

His claim opened up considerable possibilities. Could it be that they included as their subjects all the people of Tibetan origin who lived in various parts of Nepal? Surely not, for to claim suzerainty over the Bhotias and Sherpas was nothing less than an open threat to annex parts of another country. I had seen and heard enough to know that anything is possible with these warped doctrinaires. If Comrade Mao claimed the Sherpas as Chinese subjects, that would be good enough for the Peoples' Liberation Army.

'Are you,' I asked, 'referring to the Sherpa and Bhotia people of Tibetan origin who now live in Nepal?'

Smoothy deliberated a few seconds, and then:

'They do not live in Nepal. You are lying again. Where Tibetans live, there is Tibet, not Nepal.'

'Don't be ridiculous. The people you refer to have long since renounced Tibetan nationality and live in the border areas of Nepal.'

'Again not a true statement. A Chinese subject can never renounce his true nationality. Where these people live is still Tibet. They have seen the peaceful liberation of Tibet and are looking forward to the day when they too will be liberated.'

That distortion of fact obviously suited them nicely.

'Name these areas,' Smoothy demanded.

I asked for a map and my own eighth-of-an-inch scale map of Nepal was produced.

'Haven't you any maps of your own?' I asked.

His reply amazed me.

'This is the first map of Tibet we have ever seen. We have always been given to understand that Tibet is unmapped.'

'Then you're wrong. This is a map of Nepal.'

'Some parts of this map represent Nepal,' he retorted quickly. 'But others represent the Republic of China.'

When I asked him to indicate the areas of Nepal over which the Chinese claimed rights of ownership, he pointed to the Tinkar valley, the area around the Nalkankar basin in West Nepal, the Manangbhot area north of the Annapurna range and the Sola Khombu region near Mount Everest. There was no denying that the Chinese knew where the Sherpas and Bhotias lived.

For some strange reason I was asked to draw a map of the areas in dispute, and, the map having been taken away, I was handed a pen and cheap exercise book. I drew a sketch map, shading in the areas populated by Sherpas. The six inquisitors passed the book round, nodding as they did so.

Smoothy looked troubled.

'Surely the rest of the world recognizes this ground as part of China?'

'No,' I replied. 'On the contrary, it is recognized internationally as part of Nepal. If you try to "liberate" it you will fall foul of the United Nations.'

Smoothy was silent for a long time. He must have realized that he had dropped a large-size brick in discussing the matter with me. Had the political education department assured him and his comrades that some of Nepal was really Tibet and that the rest of the world, acknowledging this fact, would not interfere when China made her just territorial claims? It sounded like the Sudetenland all over again.

Here was something to tell the Foreign Office when we got home —provided we got out of Tibet alive. I could not help reflecting that my inquisitors were not overbright and that I appeared to be obtaining from them information of much greater value than they were gaining from me.

These exchanges, however, wore a serious aspect. Someone amongst them was bound to realize that we could do them immense harm in the event of our release. It seemed that our prospects of leaving Taklakot by any means other than 'over the wall', as Harrop put it, or on a shutter, were remote indeed.

Smoothy's arguments had served to jog my memory a little. I had heard these claims of Chinese dual citizenship before, but on those occasions in relation to the people of Chinese ancestry who lived in Malaya and Indonesia. I was persuaded that my interrogators were in no way being consciously hypocritical when expressing their opinions concerning the Sherpas and Bhotias. From their viewpoint, they were honest and sincere. The peoples of Tibet *were* Chinese, and had long awaited liberation and reunification with the homeland. Leave it to the P.L.A. and all would be well.

The terrifying thing about the new China is not her military might, but the total ignorance of those who exercise power: the power to send a huge army over a frontier at a word of command, the Korean War being a classic example.

My thoughts were restored to the immediate present by Smoothy, who might have been following my train of ideas.

'There is a resurgence of nationalist feeling in Asia today,' he said. 'All Asiatics see in the new China the embodiment of their desire for political emancipation.'

It might have been taken bodily from a Marxist pamphlet, and I could not prevent myself grinning at Smoothy as he said it. He started to smile self-consciously and I burst into laughter.

The usual prod in the ear from a Tommy gun silenced me, and I took opportunity to protest at the brutal treatment. Smoothy spoke to the guard and throughout the rest of the hearing I was silenced by an impolite but painless 'Shut up!'

The Bookworm handed a leather case to Smoothy, who plunged a hand into it and ferreted about until he had what he was searching for. But he did not extract it. Instead, he sat there with the air of a magician about to perform his most astonishing trick. After the visiting-card 'aliases' and the alteration of the date of arrest, I was, I felt, prepared for anything. I was to discover, and quickly, that I was wrong.

'What was the real reason for wanting to occupy this mountain Nalkankar?'

'We simply wished to be the first to climb it.'

'That is a lie. What did you hope to find on the mountain?'

'Only snow.'

Smoothy smirked. Upending the leather bag he scattered the contents all over the table, disclosing the fossils Harrop and I had collected near the summit of the Kathan pass the day before our arrest.

'What are these?' he asked.

'Fossils of shellfish that lived on the ocean bed millions of years ago.'

Smoothy then perpetrated a first-class howler:

'You did not collect these in the sea. You found them in Tibet.'

I could not suppress an audible sigh of despair.

'Millions of years ago,' I explained with weary patience, 'Tibet was under the sea. We found these fossils near the Nepal-Tibet frontier at a height of about 16,500 feet.'

Smoothy's expression betrayed that he believed not a word I had said. The idea of a foreign spy trying to persuade him that Tibet once lay beneath the sea was too absurd for serious consideration. Everyone knew, even the most ignorant, that the sea was thousands of miles away.

'Tell us the real reason for wanting to illegally occupy the mountain.'

Words failing me, I remained silent.

'You were sent by the British Government to look for radio-active materials such as these. You hoped to find them on the mountain.'

Apparently our interest in fossils and Harrop's geological knowledge gained at Leeds University were to result in our execution.

I tried to explain that we had intended to present our fossils to the British Museum. To my surprise, the answer sufficed, and I could only conclude that they believed the British Museum to be part of the British Government.

The Governor diverted Smoothy to another tack.

'How many expeditions are there in Nepal today?'

Having not the least idea, I hazarded a guess that there would be 'half a dozen' merely to keep the party alive.

'How do you keep in touch with them?'

'We don't. I've never so much as met any of the members of these other expeditions.'

'Surely you have met them at the place where you were given your instructions?'

'We do not receive instructions. We are a free people and we go where we please without asking permission from anybody.'

'Where is the nearest expedition?'

'Maybe a couple of hundred miles away.'

'Who is the big leader?'

'I don't know. Perhaps Raymond Lambert.'

'Who is he?'

'A Swiss guide. Surely you've heard of him. He went very high on Everest in 1952.'

Smoothy then provided a further revelation of his ignorance.

'This Swiss will be from Switzerland?'

'Yes.'

'Is Switzerland in Asia?'

'No, Europe.'

'Is it a Peoples' Democracy?'

'Not the type you would understand.'

I felt sorry for Smoothy. His knowledge of geography was of the sketchiest, and I realized how easy it would be to mislead him. But I was not prepared for his next question.

'What is this Everest?'

My hands went ceilingwards in despairing supplication. There was no limit to his ignorance.

In the simplest terms I explained that Mount Everest, or Chomolungma, was the highest mountain in the world and that the first ascent had been made by a British expedition, the first men to reach the summit being Edmund Hillary and the Sherpa Tensing.

Smoothy, apparently eager to know more about the matter, was also unwilling to reveal the true extent of his ignorance of world affairs.

'Where is this mountain?'

'In the Sola Khombu area of Nepal. The summit is half in Nepal and half in Tibet.'

That upset him.

'We have already told you that the place you call Sola Khombu is part of Tibet. This expedition had no right to be there and was therefore illegal.'

Being weary of this type of merry-go-round I did not answer.

'Why did they climb this mountain?'

I was about to say they did so because they wanted to as it happened to be the highest mountain in the world, when an idea occurred to me. They would not believe the truth, and would be happier with the sort of answer they wanted. I was convinced that they would merely dismiss my story as a feeble attempt at a joke, but I was due for another surprise. They eagerly accepted every word of it.

'I don't know so very much about it,' I said. 'It was all kept so very secret.'

'Go on.'

'John Hunt organized the expedition.'

'You refer to the man you have mentioned before, the man who is the big leader of the organization in London?'

'Yes. He handed some oxygen bottles over to Hillary and Tensing which they carried with them when they made the first ascent.'

Smoothy discussed the matter seriously with the Governor. They were all interested now, and I was anxious to keep the story alive without them detecting its falsity. It seemed that the more improbable the story the more they were inclined to believe it. Honest answers were far too simple.

Quiet and intent, the inquisitors hung on every word.

'What did they do with these oxygen bottles?'

'They deposited them on the summit in accordance with instructions received from John Hunt.'

I thought this would be the end of the matter, but had not reckoned on the curious workings of the oriental mind.

'What was inside these oxygen bottles?'

I barely succeeded in restraining my laughter.

I was about to reply, 'Oxygen, you idiot!' but the game was beginning to get interesting, so I offered a more tempting bait.

'I don't know,' I said.

That precipitated an argument amongst the inquisitors. They were close to the truth about the Everest expedition, they were certain, and they were not to be denied now.

'That is a lie. You must tell us what was inside those oxygen bottles.'

I thought for a moment. The first thing that came to mind was the fossils and Smoothy's suspicious interest. The figures seated before me all revealed excitement with the exception of the Governor, who, imperturbable as ever, puffed away at his cigarette and regarded me shrewdly.

'Uranium,' I said.

Smoothy's face was a picture. He passed on my answer to the others and, judging by the serious, heated discussion that took place, there could be no doubt that they had accepted my story completely.

Smoothy had a final question on the subject.

'Why did they place these bottles on top of the mountain?'

My fantasy was becoming too involved and I wriggled out by

saying that I was not in John Hunt's confidence at the time. The question was repeated some twenty times, and in each instance I gave the same answer. After a while they must have decided that this was a reasonable reply and the question was dropped.

Smoothy wrote in the same exercise book in which I had sketched my map. Having finished he said: 'Is this a correct interpretation of your statement: "On an unknown date in May 1953 a Mr. Hillary and a Mr. Tensing illegally occupied a mountain in Tibet and left on the summit two oxygen bottles filled with uranium—for an unknown purpose"?'

I agreed that the statement was textually correct. Smoothy proffered a pen and the statement, saying, 'Please, sign.'

'With the greatest pleasure.'

Having signed, the document was passed round the table and everyone appeared to be happy with the day's work. Deeming this to be an opportune moment to obtain a concession from my captors, I asked to have returned to me an envelope full of coloured photographs of my wife and son. Smoothy passed the request on to the Governor, and he, in a mood of generosity, consented. The photographs were produced from Smoothy's brief-case, and I was asked to count them and then sign a receipt.

Once again I was asked to sign the much-thumbed confession, but declined.

'You have been more co-operative,' said Smoothy, rounding off the day's proceedings. 'Next time you must also be co-operative and answer honestly. We now give you three minutes to reconsider signing your confession.'

I sat there in the dull silence, waiting for the three minutes to end. I was numb from the waist down from sitting close on four hours in that same cross-legged position. When the time was up, the guards had to help me to my feet and I leaned on them as I stumbled towards the door.

Chapter 19

FIVE DAYS ALONE

THAT proved to be the longest of all the interrogations. I emerged from the Tibetan house weary in mind and body. A Tibetan official, or Bonpo, was standing outside the door and he took my arm as I stumbled into the open. Shading my eyes, I looked at him. He was not unlike old Gin-Din-Rhou, being kindly of countenance and dressed in good-quality clothes and leather riding-boots. He had a dignity and bearing far transcending that of the local villagers. In his left ear he wore a gold earring which must have been fully six inches in length.

Although I did not know it then, he had come from Gartok to arrange for the reception of the Viceroy, or Garpon, the highest official in the area of Ngari Korsum, of which Taklakot was the main trading post. The Garpon holds a very exalted position in the Tibetan hierarchy, his civil position being that of the fourth rank. Between him and the first rank are the members of the government and high religious officials. Highest of all are the members of the Dalai Lama's family and, finally, the young King-god, who occupies the throne in the Potala Palace, just as much a prisoner of the Chinese as we were ourselves.

The old man's face was wreathed with benevolence and kindness as he escorted me to the yard door. I noticed that the guards stepped back deferentially and only prodded me with their gun barrels when I was beyond his protecting influence. At the yard door I turned and salaamed the old gentleman. Delighted to witness this sign of respect from a European, he salaamed me three times in return, saying, '*Kali Phe-Kali Phe.*' Tibetan, a poetic language, is difficult to translate into English. A free rendering of the above, however, might read, 'Go gracefully and go well.'

At the entrance to our own building four of the armed escort deserted me, leaving me to enter with my two original guards. Dinner was being served early that day, and Harrop and Damodar, each seated by his own cell wall, were eating their meal of rice and cabbage. Today there was a welcome addition which the Chinese call 'Pin-sa'. This was a flat cake of dough about twelve inches across and an inch thick, baked on a tin lid placed over the fire. Innocent of rising agents, it was, by European standards, very stodgy, but we liked it. It was as near to bread as we could get and appeared on the menu only once every eight or ten days.

With my back to my cell wall, I sat with legs outstretched to relieve the cramp that tormented me from the thighs down. I took a bite of the Pin-sa, and it hit the bottom of my stomach like a piece of lead.

As Harrop walked past for his tea ration he muttered, 'Sign any dud cheques?' To which I replied with a shake of my head. Schickel-gruber came over to stand some three feet from me throughout my meal. He produced a piece of paper and a pencil and pointed to the path by which I had returned. Was he still on about that bloody confession?

I decided to ignore him, but Schickelgruber was not to be ignored. He unclipped the magazine from the underside of his machine-gun and held it out to me so that I could see the brass-jacketed copper-nosed bullets it contained.

Replacing the magazine he pulled the cocking lever back to the full cock position. I paused, my mouth full of Pin-sa, wondering what the ugly little savage was cooking up. He aimed the gun at my head and, after a pause of a few seconds, pulled the trigger.

I jumped visibly as I saw the action of his trigger finger. He grinned at my reaction. The gun had not fired because the safety catch was in the 'On' position. This was one of Schickelgruber's little jokes. Thereafter, he pulled that one on me about every other day, sometimes using an empty magazine so that the breech block slammed forward with a nerve-tearing 'clack'.

My anxiety was of short duration. The 'safety-catch trick', as we came to call it, was intended simply to coerce me into signing a confession. But I took refuge in the thought that there was little chance of getting a bullet through my head as long as my name was not on that all-important scrap of paper. Nevertheless, I was rather appre-hensive about the mechanical reliability of a mass-produced gun manufactured in China, which had perhaps a 32nd of an inch of metal on the end of its safety catch as the only thing between me and kingdom come. I decided that the sooner Schickelgruber tired of his little game the better it would be for all concerned, and especially for me.

I was not allowed to eat the main meal of cabbage out of doors and was ushered inside at the early hour of 3 p.m. Apart from trips to the lavatory, I had seen my last bit of sunshine for five days.

When I protested at being thrust inside at such an unseemly hour, the door was slammed and locked. This was a new routine. I was to stay in that cell, where the temperature was never above freezing point night or day, until I signed that confession.

I looked out of my tiny window into the courtyard and voiced my thoughts aloud.

'You can all go to hell, you miserable, cowardly little yellow bastards.'

Hearing me, Harrop and Damodar encouraged me with a cheer, with the result that a guard came and stood with his back to my window to prevent me seeing outside. I still had one window left— the one that overlooked the lavatory hole. I spent the rest of the daylight hours wrapped in everything I possessed making a social survey of the sanitary and hygienic habits of the P.L.A. Chungnya and Chubby were the only ones who used toilet paper. After a while the guards noticed me watching them and I enjoyed their obvious embarrassment. They glared at me and I grinned or favoured them with insulting expressions.

By five o'clock it was beginning to grow colder in my cell. The sun was fast disappearing beyond the mountains. I had on two sweaters, a windproof jacket and a down-filled coat, plus a muffler and a balaclava helmet. In spite of this protection it was too cold to sit outside my sleeping-bag. At 5.30 p.m. Marlo came in and lit my oil-lamp. Donning my high-altitude boots, I walked around the cell, space allowing me only three steps before reaching the opposite wall. Then I had to turn and repeat the performance. Twice during each circuit of the room I had to duck to avoid banging my head on the low beam that ran from north to south.

At the end of half an hour's exercise I gave up and tried to play a game of patience with the cards Chungnya had given me a few days before. Again my luck was out, but I stumbled on a means of getting a message to Harrop informing him as to what had taken place at my second interrogation.

The plywood box lid was the answer. The layers of wood had started to part company and it was a simple matter to push a note well down between the layers. Harrop would have to find a means of fishing it out. With the note well concealed, I called for Chungnya. When he came in I gave him to understand that Harrop would like a game with the cards, and without question he took the lid and cards to Harrop's cell. I could only hope that John would understand my motive in sending him the cards.

Later that night I heard Harrop bang on his cell door to be let out to the lavatory. As he passed my cell window he whispered, 'O.K., I've got it,' and with that he flipped a note into my room.

On the morning of November 12th I was wakened by the noise of the breakfast dishes being rattled in the kitchen. I rattled on the door and Fatty opened it, but when I tried to step outside he rudely pushed me back with the barrel of his gun. Schickelgruber came over waving a piece of paper and a pen. I told him to go to hell and the door was slammed in my face.

I dressed with everything I had and walked around the cell to keep warm. A simple calculation told me that if I walked round the room 176 times I would cover about a mile. Soon, because of the small diameter of the circles, I became dizzy, and I countered this by doing twenty-five trips clockwise and twenty-five anti-clockwise. This involved ducking my head 352 times for each mile. Between meal-times I managed to complete about three miles a day. After the first day I no longer needed to count, for I could judge the distance by recording the walking time on my watch.

The guards never ceased to marvel at this performance and vied with each other to push their fur-hatted heads into the window space to witness my peregrinations. Boredom was my most dangerous enemy, and I was determined that, come what may, I would emerge from that cell as sane as when I went in.

Rats invaded my solitude again, and I discovered that they ignored the holes I had blocked up with stones and now burrowed through the soft crumbly dried-mud walls. I now regarded the rats as company, liking them better than the Chinese. They could go out whenever they wished.

I let one rat in and then bunged up the hole. He scurried round the floor taking not the slightest notice of me. I tossed him a slice of boiled turnip, a left-over from breakfast, and he turned up his nose at it. When he started to chew a corner of my sleeping-bag, I opened up the hole by which he had entered and piloted him out. Thereafter I let him in once a day. I had only to remove the stone and he tore straight in across the room. When there was meat he had some; when it was yak meat he had the lot.

On the third day of my isolation dysentery attacked me again. I started to pass blood and was running a temperature. In spite of the coldness of the cell I perspired profusely, alternating between feverish spells and fits of shivering. When I stood up to go to the lavatory my legs felt like jelly. I sent another note to the officers explaining my condition and asking for medical attention. The note, needless to say, was ignored.

All this time the guards never once went for a walk or indulged in any form of exercise. I now understood why they thought that there must be a 'purpose' in climbing mountains. If there was no purpose, why undertake it? Our Chinese lifted not so much as a finger unless inspired by the hope or certainty of material gain. Looking out of my cell window I reflected on all the wonderful snow-clad peaks that lie inside Tibet and that will almost certainly never be climbed as long as the Chinese Communists rule the country.

By the late afternoon, realizing that something was wrong, Chungnya came to visit me. He pointed through the window at Schickelgruber's back, then pointed over the river towards the officers' quarters. For some reason he wanted Schickelgruber out of the way. Pulling paper and pencil out of his pocket he thrust them into my hands. Surely Chungnya had not joined the chorus of those trying to persuade me to sign a confession?

I satisfied my curiosity by writing the officers a letter in which I described them as Fascist and stated that their treatment of prisoners was no better than that meted out to those who fell into the hands of the Gestapo and the Japanese 'Kempitei' or 'thought-control' police. I stated further that their treatment of Harrop, Damodar and myself would receive the widest publicity when we were released, and addressed the letter to the 'O.C. troops, Taklakot'.

Chungnya handed the note to Schickelgruber and he, mistakenly believing that he had my confession, tore off eagerly over the bridge to the grey barracks. Chungnya went back to the kitchen, to return some fifteen minutes later with a bowl of noodles and shrimps with a poached egg crowning it. Good-hearted, thoughtful Chungnya! He sat watching me eat it and Shorty and Chubby joined him to watch also.

Chungnya kept saying, '*Yappa do, Chid,*' and ruffled my hair. Chubby and Shorty leaned against the wall, each knitting himself a glove. Later they were joined by Marlo, who, to my surprise, was spinning wool, drawn through the fingers of his left hand and wrapped around a wooden shuttle that spun below his right hand, dangling on the end of the thread. It must have been handicraft week in the P.L.A.

Shorty temporarily suspended his knitting and pulled two paper-backed books from inside his padded tunic. The others grinned and joshed him good-naturedly. I asked for the books and they passed them over. One was a simple text book with which Shorty was learning to read. The pages were full of tiny sketches, each one adjacent to the appropriate Chinese symbol. I was struck by the fact that the majority of the pictures were of a military nature, although it was not a military manual as it contained pictures of houses, clocks, children and animals. Three pictures out of every four represented weapons of war. Rifles, machine-guns, helmets, mines, tanks and many other items. It was, indeed, a miserable vehicle for education, I thought.

The second book was a form of Chinese comic paper, being a magazine about 5 inches by 3 and consisting of about a hundred pages. It told one long story in picture form, the story of the Chinese equivalent of the American comic strip character 'Superman', only their protagonist was a super ape, a super ape which lived in a palace on a mountain top surrounded by thousands of his chimpanzee subjects.

The villains of the piece were the Mandarins and plutocrats who tried to lure him away from his friends and environment in order to wrest from him the secret of his strength and apparent immortality. By the use of wine, women and more wine he is eventually won over to respectability and a post in the government. Sickening of it all, he flees back to the hills, whereupon the emperor sends out huge armies which are all defeated by the ape kingdom. By a ruse, the ape god is eventually trapped. They try to behead him, but the swords break on his neck. They boil him in oil in a giant cauldrom, but he breaks free, smiting left and right with his favourite weapon, a long bamboo pole which, conveniently, seems to appear from nowhere when needed. We leave the ape god back on his mountain, seated outside his palace lifting up his wine cup in a toast, with all the minor apes seated around gazing up in admiration. The moral seems to be that it is better to be a good ape than a corrupt member of the bourgeoisie. But such a book will probably now be banned in China because it pays tribute to the now discredited personality cult.

At 7 p.m. Lofty came in and handed his guard duty over to Shorty. The boys retired for the night and I was alone once more. For a long time I sat looking at the photographs of my wife and son. I did not hear Schickelgruber return; no doubt because he was being reprimanded by the officers for not producing the confession.

The next morning I was awakened by sounds of the most frantic screaming. It was Schickelgruber in the guards' quarters, and he was altogether berserk. I dressed and waited to see what the result of my note would be. My patience was not taxed. Schickelgruber stormed into my cell, his eyes bulging with rage. His screams eventually simmered down and his mouth frothed as he mumbled away like a pot about to boil over.

Once, he clenched his hand and, after placing the forefinger of his left hand on the tip of his nose, he pointed it at me, inferring that I was due for some rough treatment. Weak though I was, I decided that the man was a bully and a coward and that I would call his bluff. Standing upright I caught hold of the front of his jacket with my left hand. He jerked away from me and fell backwards over the raised doorstep. I followed him out and he backed to the guardroom. I had one leg inside the doorway when I noticed a Tommy gun standing some three feet away from me. Schickelgruber was about the same distance from the gun.

He screamed for the guards and I was seized from behind by Lofty and Fatty. I swung round on Fatty and he let go and retreated. Lofty was made of much sterner stuff and was much stronger than me. I felt too ill for further fight, and retired to my cell.

Schickelgruber, who had certainly lost face in front of his men, would now be even more unpleasant.

They took Harrop and Damodar over the river again that day. That night Harrop flipped a note through my window, which informed me that they had asked him how we kept in touch with our headquarters. He had informed them that we had blundered badly by leaving our carrier pigeons in Bombay. They had accepted his story without question.

At about 6 p.m. Chungnya came in, to my amazement bringing half the book of poetry that Harrop had brought over from base camp and which the Chinese had confiscated on the day we had been moved to Taklakot. Harrop had repeatedly sent notes requesting its return, and the officers, no doubt feeling that he had co-operated by giving information about the carrier pigeons, had duly rewarded him. They would be greatly displeased were they to learn that I now had half of the book.

The volume had been divided dead in the middle, so that I could read only the first half of the 'Ancient Mariner'. What a joy it was, and how it boosted my morale! Here, on this desolate Tibetan plateau, I was able to appreciate what I had previously missed. I read and re-read every line, learning Byron's 'Don Juan' by heart and scribbling passages from other poems on the cell walls. One of Alexander Pope's was significant indeed, and he might have had my cell in mind when he wrote:

> In the world's worst inn, with mat half hung.
> The floors of plaster and the walls of dung.

Chapter 20

A TASTE OF COMMUNIST DEMOCRACY

NOVEMBER 15th marked the fifth day of solitary confinement. Each day I had looked through the window to see Harrop and Damodar sitting in the yard enjoying the sunshine. But I had to stay in this filthy hole until my resistance broke down.

Dizzy spells were more frequent now and I felt light-headed all the time. When I stood up nausea assailed me and the room started to spin round. I could no longer so much as look at the boiled turnips at breakfast-time. Climbing back into my sleeping-bag I tried to sleep, longing only for rest. A little fresh air and sunlight would have helped, too.

At midday I was prodded by a gun-barrel, and I looked up to see Schickelgruber and the Governor's bodyguard complete with his American carbine. This could only mean another appearance before the interrogation committee, and I shook my head and turned the other way. It was no good. They grabbed hold of the sleeping-bag and rolled it over, depositing me face down on the mud floor. I felt too weak even to curse them as they dragged me to my feet. Shorty and Lofty joined the escort and I leaned on them for the pull up the river bank after we had crossed the bridge.

At the top I was puffing like an old man and evinced no interest in the characters standing around the doorway of the red building. This questioning was to take place in the same place as the first on November 7th. I stumbled across the yard and through the curtained doorway.

I waited for the usual, 'Hello, sit down on the floor,' but as no one asked me to sit I simply continued to stand, feeling all the time a tremendous longing to lie down and sleep.

There were no formalities this time and the usual waiting period was ignored. There were six people sitting round the table and they all seemed to be shouting at me. All, of course, except the Governor who sat cross-legged, puffing away at a cigarette. I looked vaguely at them, not doubting that their rage was inspired by my note of two days previous.

I leaned against the wall behind me.

'Stand up straight!' Smoothy screamed.

'You go to hell!'

His chubby little face was working with passion. He waved my note in the air.

'You sent this insulting letter to us. You likened us to the German and Japanese war criminals. We are not Fascists. We are democratic. You are being treated very well. We do not usually treat criminals as well as this.'

I was harangued in this manner for about ten minutes before they simmered down. There was a momentary silence and then Smoothy said:

'Hello. Please sit.'

He asked the same questions as before. Name, address, family details, occupation and so on. I struggled through about twenty minutes of it and then said:

'I'm ill. I want to go back to my cell.'

The request being ignored, I repeated it.

'I've got dysentery. I must go out every hour or so. I will have to go now.'

Smoothy glared at me.

'You will stay where you are until told to move.'

'I keep passing blood. I'll have to go.'

He called the guard.

'You will be allowed three minutes only. You are only doing this to avoid being reprimanded for your insulting letter.'

I went outside and had to squat in a corner of the yard surrounded by a curious crowd of Chinese soldiers and Tibetans. I was much too ill to experience any feeling of embarrassment. The Tibetans shook their heads and tut-tutted. I was helped to my feet and guided back to the interrogation room.

The guards gave a long description to Smoothy, for they had seen the pool of blood I had left on the floor. He could no longer claim that I was malingering.

I seized the opportunity to ask for medical attention, and Smoothy retorted that it was already under consideration and that the question would be raised later in the proceedings. He came back to the question of my enforced solitary confinement.

'You are being kept in that cell because you have illegally invaded China. You are a criminal and as such will be punished according to Chinese law.'

'According to the basic principles of democracy recognized the world over,' I retorted, unable to stomach his self-righteousness, 'a man is not punished for a crime until he has been tried and found

L

guilty by a properly constituted court. You cannot punish us without a conviction.'

Smoothy's reply was typical of the modern ideas on justice dominant in China.

'You will be tried by a Peoples' Court. You will be convicted and you will then be punished heavily.'

The trial was a mere formality.

'Who will represent us as defence counsel at the trial?'

'You do not need a defence. We know that you are criminals.'

That did it. Ill as I was my loathing and hatred could no longer be restrained. Pointing to the Governor, I cried:

'Tell that parchment-faced old bastard that he's a Fascist.'

Smoothy passed on the compliment and the old man exploded. That was the only time he ever lost his temper. Jumping to his feet he looked me straight in the eye, all his oriental passivity gone. His face contorted with rage and his eyes bulged, revealing his essential inhumanity. I now saw that he was the most dangerous member of the committee. The guards came over to stand on either side of me, their guns held close to my head.

'You must apologize,' Smoothy said.

'You can tell him to go to hell.'

Smoothy made the same request about ten times, and I refused to reply.

'Do you know what your sentence will be if you do not repent?' he demanded. 'You and your companions will all be sentenced to life imprisonment. Please sign this confession and we will lighten the punishment.'

I ignored him.

'You have very little time to change your mind. Your trial will be held shortly. We have taken every precaution to prevent your escape. The rest of your illegal party cannot help you. They are now hiding in Hindustan.'

I paid no attention to his transparent bluff.

I began to day-dream and the voices kept fading away, and the guards constantly prodded me into wakefulness. I said that I would like to lie down, and Smoothy responded by giving an order to the guards, who promptly hauled me to my feet. Thinking that it was all over I made for the door, only to be stopped by the Governor's bodyguard.

'You refuse to co-operate. You will stand until you sign this confession.'

I leaned against the wall again, to be roughly pushed away from it by one of the guards. When I fell down, one of the soldiers caught me and held me upright. I was feeling feverish and the voices seemed to be reaching me down a long tunnel. Faintly I heard a voice saying, 'Please, sign this.' I felt a pen thrust into my hand.

'Sign and all will be well.'

At that moment I felt I would willingly sign anything to escape from that nightmare chamber. I had one last defence.

'I'm sick. I need medical attention. I want a doctor.'

'That will be arranged. Sign this confession and we will see that you get the best medical attention available.'

'And if I don't sign?'

'Then there will be no medical attention.'

I looked at their cold impassive faces one by one. They were the most inhuman, cold-blooded set it had ever been my misfortune to see.

'I'll see you all in hell first!'

I have never been one to hate easily. I have never had it in me to bear grudges for very long. Now, for the first time in my life, I hated passionately and so fiercely that, had I possessed a gun, I would cheerfully have killed every one of them. Given the opportunity, I would have snuffed out the life of any one of them with no more compuncton than I would a candle.

Smoothy, after a chat with the Governor, handed me a sheet of blue notepaper.

'Take this back to your cell and write a criticism of your insulting behaviour. Tomorrow is self-criticism day for the soldiers in our command. You, too, must criticize yourself.'

I stuffed the paper into my pocket and was shown through the door. I remember nothing about the march back to my cell. I tumbled into my sleeping-bag and lost consciousness immediately.

The following morning I was turned out of my bed at 9 a.m. To my astonishment my sleeping-bag and air mattress were taken out of doors and placed in the sunniest part of the yard. My enforced stay indoors was ended. It had failed to produce the oft-demanded confession and my accusation of Fascist treatment had struck a sensitive spot.

That day was like a holiday. I basked in the sunshine and read Byron. At midday Harrop and I exchanged our respective halves of the book. He was learning Gray's 'Elegy'. Damodar, reading Shorty's book about the apes, roared with laughter to such a degree that Shorty, frowning, snatched the book back and took it indoors.

The toilet-paper situation had now become desperate. We had none left and my condition was such that my need was urgent. I went into the kitchen and appropriated an old quilted cotton army tunic the guards sometimes used when cooking. When Marlo argued and tried to take the stained and greasy garment from me, I raised loud protests, claiming that I needed it as a pillow. The guards relented and I retained the jacket.

Taking it indoors I tore open the lining. It was padded with soft cotton wool. Harrop meanwhile was in the process of using up one of his two tattered shirts. Damodar reverted to nature, and a problem which assumes such immense importance for the European had for him no significance at all.

That night the guards brought in a sheep for the kitchen table. Looking through my cell window I saw Marlo and Shorty tie up its legs and then start kicking the terrified, helpless creature. Tiring of kicking it in the ribs, they went to work on its face. Marlo wore tennis shoes, which could not inflict much pain, but Shorty wore leather boots and, judging by his expression, was receiving immense sadistic pleasure. When the animal was too numb and stunned to struggle further they dragged it outside and slit its throat.

On November 17th I made a special entry in my diary. While dressing, I took my morning look out through the window. The usual line of men, women, mules and yaks threaded its way up the hill opposite, bearing loads of equipment and raw materials for the new barracks at the summit. My gaze wandered to the base of the hill. From the far side of the grey barracks a solitary yak emerged, on its back a long aluminium or steel radio mast. One end of the mast hung close to the ground some thirty feet to the rear of the animal, and was held clear of the ground by two Chinese soldiers in fatigue dress. They were obviously making very sure that it would not be damaged by the large stones that littered the track.

The first mast was about halfway up the track when another yak appeared bearing a similar mast. The new barracks was to be an up-to-date radio station, not a temporary affair like the one set up in the grey building following upon our arrest. The two wooden masts still stood and, no doubt, carried messages back and forth concerning us prisoners.

The guards had not carried out their 'self-criticism' duty the day before, as Smoothy had promised, but today they set about the task with gusto. For most of the morning our seven guards sat writing little essays concerning themselves and, presumably, of a derogatory nature. Shorty and Fatty, who were still learning to write, were having the greatest difficulty and had to be helped by Chungnya and Chubby.

The writing completed, each in turn stood at the top of the yard steps and declaimed their faults. The others sat below, cross-legged, nodding their heads in agreement. Every now and then the penitent would place his forefinger on his nose to emphasize some point about himself.

Needless to say, I did not write out any self-criticism. Everything I had said and written about the Chinese officers I had meant with the utmost sincerity. The sheet of blue notepaper became part of my secret diary, which I was still keeping.

The days passed with irksome tedium, and on the fifth day after my interrogation I expected to be taken across the river again. This, however, did not happen. The attitude of the guards, in fact, lost some of its hostility, although there was no relaxation in the measures to ensure our security. It occurred to me that we might have been tried in our absence and were already serving our sentence. I decided that, at the first opportunity to converse with Harrop and Damodar, we would plan to go over the wall. It would be a most hazardous undertaking, but anything was better than years—perhaps a lifetime—in Chinese hands.

I began to feel better and the bouts of dizziness ceased. But other symptoms remained and I was destined to suffer from dysentery until I received medical treatment in India after our release.

On the sixth day three interesting events occurred. An old Tibetan accompanied by a young boy delivered a load of firewood, argued about the price and was thrown out of the yard. Later, a concentration of armed troops came marching down the Lhasa track. I judged by their weapons and equipment that they had come no great distance and that a much bigger concentration of troops lay farther to the north-east of Taklakot, out of sight of the Indian traders.

When Marlo, who was standing on guard on the roof, saw me watching the column of marching men over the wall, he shouted down to the guardroom and we were all driven indoors.

The final and most surprising event of the day took place after dinner. We had just eaten the most awful dish of yak entrails and rice smothered with chillies when Schickelgruber picked up my air mattress and carried it into the communal cell Harrop had been occupying on his own. Without more ado, all my kit followed it and then Damodar's. Our period of silence and isolation was ended.

The news caused us to rejoice, and our delight seemed to infect the guards. As we sorted out our kit we sang all sorts of songs. I sang cowboy songs and attempted to yodel, causing the Chinese to shout for more. In deference to Harrop and Damodar, however, who had pained looks on their faces, I declined.

We went out into the yard and celebrated with a mug of most atrocious tea. I put on a song and dance act in the raised part of the yard, and favoured them with my prison music-hall speciality, 'Burlington Bertie from Bow'.

I had an old pair of yellow woollen gloves that my wife's mother had knitted for me years before, and I waved them about ostentatiously when I came to the line, 'I walk down the Strand with my gloves on my hands and I walk down again with them off.'

This amused Shorty and, astonishingly, Schickelgruber as well. They asked me to sing it again complete with actions, and when I reached the appropriate line, although they could not understand a word, they each whipped out a pair of knitted gloves, and stalked up and down the yard, imitating my gestures. Thereafter, 'Burlington Bertie' was requested almost daily by the guards.

That first night together in our communal cell we had much to discuss. We went over the interrogations in an effort to fathom the Chinese mentality. That serious questioning was ended was beyond doubt, otherwise we should still have been kept apart. But whether this was a desirable development we could not say. It might mean that we were to be released fairly soon or that we were to be sentenced. We had no means of knowing what the change portended.

We decided to give the Chinese a couple of weeks in which to reveal their intentions. If nothing promising emerged during that time then we would attempt to escape. In the meantime we had ample opportunity to determine the course most favourable to our purpose. Escape during daylight hours being out of the question, we discussed the problems of a departure by night.

Our first task would be to silence the guard, which would have to be done when making a midnight trip to the lavatory. It could not be earlier than midnight as there was a distinct possibility that the guards would be playing cards until that hour. To delay beyond midnight would allow us insufficient time to reach the Lipu Lekh pass on the Indian frontier before daylight.

That, however, highlighted another problem. The guards were changed every two hours, which meant that we must silence the guard at the end of his period of duty before he wakened his relief. That would also allow the previous guard two hours in which to go to bed and fall asleep. The plain truth was that we had not the least chance of reaching the Lipu Lekh before one of the guards awoke to find that no one had called him for his spell of duty. The success of the plan, therefore, hinged on one thing—silencing the entire garrison of seven guards. This could not be an easy task when every one of them slept with a Tommy gun standing against the wall alongside his bed.

The most difficult decision of all was to determine which guard we should attack first. The answer was only too obvious. The only two guards who did not regard us as enemies and who were not particularly strict about security at night were Chungnya and Chubby. It would have to be one of them—ironically, the very men who had been most friendly and considerate.

The weapon had already been decided upon. Harrop had borrowed a nice smooth, river-washed stone from the kitchen which the guards had used to grind salt. I dropped it into a stocking, thus creating a lethal weapon if used with any force. By tacit agreement we did not broach the question as to who would strike the blow, for there could hardly be any doubt about the matter. It would have to be me. Damodar could not be considered as there might be loss of life and we did not know how he would stand with his government.

I ruled out Harrop because of the incident in the yard when he provided Marlo with a headache. His wild nature made even Chungnya and Chubby regard him rather uneasily, for they never seemed sure whether he would pat them on the back or hit them on the nose. Because of my illness and because I accepted the minor irritations of prison life with a certain degree of composure, they regarded me as incapable of violence. I was more patient than the others and often had to restrain Harrop from taking the law into his own hands when provoked by Schickelgruber.

Of all the people I had met since being apprehended by the Chinese, the last one I wished to harm was Chungnya. Happily, that unpleasant possibility could be left in abeyance for a time.

Meanwhile, we were together again and that was a much happier state of affairs. I am not given to making speeches, but I ventured to deliver a short one that night. I was most grateful to my two companions for the way they had behaved while in Chinese hands and for their friendship. 'If I ever go to prison again,' I ended, 'I shall choose you two as my companions.'

Harrop thanked me for the dubious honour, then said:

'What do you mean, going to prison again? You're not out of this one yet.'

We sang well into the night, venturing some sort of rendering of every song we could remember. The Chinese objected only when Damodar wailed some awful Indian film music. After a while we tired of singing and I lay back in my sleeping-bag, thinking of home. For some strange reason the music of Sibelius entered my mind and I found myself humming part of the first movement of his Second Symphony. Gradually my memory pieced the whole fabric of the thing together and I was surprised how much of the score I could remember. Sibelius may not have had the Tibetan plateau in mind when he composed his music, but it could not have been more appropriate had he done so. My reflections were disturbed by Harrop's snoring and Damodar's wailing interpretation of 'Giddy Aye Eh for the One-eyed Reilly'. I pulled the top of my sleeping-bag over my head and turned in.

Chapter 21

THE EDGE OF WINTER

THE fine, sunny days became less frequent. The sky was now often overcast and the great range of mountains that stood between us and Nepal was screened with snow-bearing clouds.

We were looking at it one morning when Harrop said:

'Thank God, we won't be going back over the Urai Lekh. When they decide to release us we will go over the Lipu into India.'

The 19,500-feet Urai Lekh, which was many days' march from the nearest Nepalese village, was not to be traversed without serious risk at that time of the year. Happily, we thought, it was not for us. We were to discover that the Governor had his own ideas on this matter.

Schickelgruber and Fatty never adopted the more liberal attitude of some of the guards. Fatty always made a point of closing the yard door whenever he saw us looking through it. We were never allowed to go within twenty feet of that door when it was unlocked. We discovered that, if we paid no attention to what was happening outside, Fatty did not mind, and so, in order to annoy him, we would all stare intently through the doorway as if something of great importance claimed our interest. Fatty's curiosity thus excited, he would leave his perch on the roof and look out through the doorway. After favouring us with a dirty look he would lock the door and return to his point of vantage.

It took him a long time to discover our little game. We pulled the trick on him only when one of the guards had gone down to the river to bring water for the kitchen. The water was carried in two mustard-oil tins of about four gallons capacity each, the cans being suspended on either end of a pole carried across the shoulders. The total load was in the region of 90lb. and must have been quite a haul up from the river bank. When the water-carrier arrived back he found the door locked on the inside, and he would curse and shout at Fatty who was too lazy to come down. One guard had perforce to climb the wall when his comrades in the guardroom declined to render assistance. Day in, day out we repeated this joke, which gave us something to do.

The weekly slaughtering of sheep and yaks took place on a Saturday or Sunday. Schickelgruber could always be relied upon to tell us the exact number slaughtered. The carcases were piled up on the river bank by the bridge and groups of soldiers from various companies came to claim their rations. The record kill during our stay was just short of four hundred sheep. A great mass of stomach and intestine was piled up by the water's edge and more than fifty soldiers were busy cleaning it in the ice-cold, fast-flowing Karnali river. Hearts, liver and kidneys were boiled on the spot in large cauldrons and the usual crowd of Tibetans stood around waiting for largess.

On that particular day the proceedings were abruptly and unexpectedly terminated by the most violent dust storm we had ever seen.

These dust storms were always heralded by a biting wind leaping out of the north at gale force. Our prison, being sheltered under the cliff face of the great Taklakot ridge, never received the full force of the storm. Nevertheless, there were times when we had to endure the discomfort of being choked with stinging sand particles. The dust penetrated to every corner, finding ready ingress through the open windows of the cells and quickly spreading a fine layer of grey dust on all our possessions.

On this occasion we first sighted the storm sweeping over the plateau towards the mountains of Nepal. By-passing the ridge, it took a course parallel to but west of our prison. Very quickly the hamlets surrounding Taklakot and Jitkot were overwhelmed by the huge grey pall. In a matter of minutes the sun vanished and the landscape took on the appearance of a dead planet. The carcases by the river were abandoned and the Chinese and Tibetans dashed for cover. Harrop and I stayed out to the last moment to witness this awe-inspiring sight. The area of the storm was spreading. Its widest part was approaching Taklakot and would soon smother our prison.

Through occasional breaks in the grey wall we caught sight of one or two untethered mules tearing around in frenzy on the far bank of the river. The tiny clusters of poplars growing outside some of the Tibetan houses bent almost double under the fierce pressure of the wind. The storm, we estimated, was about ten miles in length and some three thousand feet in height. Low moaning sounds came from the cave dwellings in the nearby cliff face as the wind swept through the galleries.

I tried to speak to Harrop, but my words were snatched away by the wind.

Then the storm enveloped us. Choking with dust-filled lungs, we stumbled to our cell. Damodar was already there, brushing a layer of dust from the top of his sleeping-bag.

Incidents such as this caused us to ponder on the relative merits of the Chinese soldiers. Regardless of their training and large supplies of armaments, they remained at heart very simple people with the hill peasant's inherent fear of the more savage and unpredictable moods of the elements.

We spent the next morning cleaning up our cell. That finished, Chungnya came in bearing a home-made broom of brushwood. The floor was hidden beneath a thick carpet of dust that was years old and was better left undisturbed. We had to restrain Chungnya's enthusiasm when his actions provoked a cloud of dust almost as deadly as that brought by the storm.

When the dust had settled, Chungnya came and sat on my bed, and I made another attempt to discover his real name. After a while he told me, and even went so far as to write it in Chinese symbols on the fabric side of my air mattress. For obvious reasons it is impossible to reveal his real name, and we must employ 'Chungnya', which cannot compromise him with his superiors.

Later in the afternoon, when I was sunbathing in the yard, Chungnya came out of the guardroom. He glanced down at my air mattress with a troubled look. His name was fully visible on the side of the bed. He squatted beside me, his gaze fixed on his bright blue tennis shoes. When the guard on the roof had walked to the far end of the building and was out of sight, Chungnya held out his hand and said, '*Be*.' Regretfully I handed him my pen and he scored through the Chinese symbols rendering them indecipherable. That done, he was his usual cheerful self once again.

Any form of fraternization with the prisoners identified by the officers would, no doubt, have had dire consequences for any of the soldiers in our prison.

The nights no longer seemed endless. We had a pack of cards and an oil-lamp, and we sat up playing rummy and pontoon until 8 or even 9 p.m. Once we played until midnight, retiring with frozen fingers. Damodar knew rummy, but had never heard of the old British Army game of pontoon. I still had about fifty rupees in one-rupee notes and we shared this out between us. When the game ended I pocketed our combined funds, so that the result was always the same. We could not be accused of gambling.

We could always detect the value of the cards Damodar held from his expression, for he betrayed his reactions to his 'hand' on all occasions.

The advantage went his way when teaching us a Nepalese card

game. This was similar to the one played by the Chinese, in so far as it consisted entirely of slapping all the cards down one by one as hard as possible. I could understand neither the tricks nor the scoring, nor, for that matter, could Harrop. When all the cards were played Damodar snatched the pile of rupee notes from the centre of the table and announced that he was the winner.

Being unable to figure it out, we resumed pontoon. In the middle of the game we were interrupted by Chungnya who was on guard duty. He had been watching through the window and had noticed the small pile of money on the table. He came in with Marlo, Shorty, Chubby and Lofty, who smilingly gave us to understand that people who play for money quickly fall out. Gambling in the P.L.A., apparently, was illegal.

Lofty and Chungnya gave a first-class demonstration of their thesis by each trying to scoop up the winnings and ending with a mock wrestling match on the floor. We put away the money and resumed playing rummy. This incident was to have its sequel the following afternoon, when we were locked in at the unusually early hour of 4 p.m., Schickelgruber being in one of his more hostile moods.

The other Chinese, with the exception of Fatty who stood guard, started playing cards, using an old ground sheet as a table. We watched them whack the cards down one by one swiftly and furiously, Lofty keeping the score in a cheap Indian exercise book. The second hand was played in a far from cordial atmosphere, Chubby continually grumbling at Marlo. The third hand saw the end of the game and the most wonderful mêlée in the middle of the yard. Schickelgruber came tearing out of the guardroom to try to restore order, but he retired from the fray nursing an ankle kicked by someone who had been wearing something much stouter than tennis shoes. When it all ended, the only casualty was Marlo, who went indoors lamenting a damaged ear.

November 27th was celebrated by the Chinese as a holiday, although what the day was dedicated to we never discovered. Its importance was brought home to us, however, when some of the guards even went so far as to put on a clean shirt. For the first time since our imprisonment began, and only heaven knows how long before that, Marlo changed his long underwear. It soon became obvious that great effort was being put into the preparing of dinner that afternoon. One by one we were conducted to the kitchen, and, for our edification, Schickelgruber counted the number of the courses on his fingers.

There were noodles, eggs, pork scraps, mutton, shrimps imported from China, 'Pin-sa' bread cakes, 'Mien-Bo', a form of steamed dough, *chigada* (turnips), peanuts and one or two dishes which we could neither identify nor describe. Schickelgruber beamed all over his face. He was really putting on the dog, showing the infidels that China can outshine the Ritz when it so desires. Chinese soldiers from other encampments kept dropping in to see what good things graced our menu. Regardless of its ingredients, this dinner might well have been as unpalatable as any other had it not been that Chungnya had been cook for that day. After sampling the dishes we came to the conclusion that he was the best cook in Taklakot.

The Tibetans were brought into the celebrations, and small groups passed our prison bearing flags and trumpets. We were utterly indifferent to whose death, birthday or victory inspired the festivities. We rejoiced simply because we were sampling food that was properly cooked, provided much-needed variety and wasn't over-larded with the palate-blistering chillies.

In the middle of the feast two strange guards came in bearing a gramophone and a box of records. Lofty assumed the position of Master of Ceremonies and set the wicked contraption in motion. It was far worse than Damodar's Indian songs. Half the records were devoted to military marches, with an exaggerated oriental resort to timpani, and the other half consisted of moanings and wailings with noises off or background effects that sounded like cocks crowing. The young soldiers were thrilled with this canned music and allowed their food to go cold as, open-mouthed, they watched the records, calibrated at 78 r.p.m., spin round at about 100 r.p.m., on a machine that possibly was innocent of a governor. Damodar suggested that the Chinese officers had probably sent the machine over with the hope that we should willingly sign a confession to escape its scarifying din.

After the entire repertoire was exhausted, the most awful tune of all was replayed about a dozen times. In the evening the whole box of tricks was carted back to the place where I had first seen it—under the small cot in the interrogation room.

The following morning we breakfasted on scraps left over from the previous day's dinner. Even they were better than the usual *chigada* stew.

Just before midday Shorty came in carrying a gigantic yak head, complete with skin and horns, which was intended for our dinner that night. This was a disagreeable surprise which quickly restored the true perspective after the dinner of the night before. While we watched, Shorty and Schickelgruber began to dismember the head. A chopper removed the horns, and was then used to attack the skull. After several minutes, their efforts having failed to achieve their purpose, they gave up and tossed the whole thing into the largest boiling pot they could find. Skin and hair were left on the head and no attempt was made to clean it. We went on hunger strike that night.

Fortunately each of us had hidden a couple of pieces of 'Mien-Bo' in the cell, left-overs from the night before. We dined off this steamed dough, leaving the head to the guards, who peeled off the boiled flesh while leaving the skull intact.

The following day Shorty managed to split the skull with the axe, and he and Marlo disputed with each other for possession of the brains. Both Harrop and I were surprised at the smallness of the yak's brain in comparison with its huge head. The tit-bit that Marlo finally secured was no bigger than a large sausage. Damodar later informed me that Shorty had eaten the animal's eyes the night before and that he and Marlo had had an argument about these morsels.

A dust storm sprang up in the afternoon and the dismembered head was left outside, exposed to the onslaught. The storm over, Chungnya went out to cook dinner. He took one look at the dust-covered monstrosity and decided that his stomach was too sensitive. We went back to fried cabbage and chillies, offset by a piece of 'Ma-Hwa'—dough fried in mustard oil.

Shorty and Marlo, having blown a little of the dust off the yak's head, ferreted about with a knife seeking tasty scraps. What was left over was later given to a very old and feeble Tibetan woman who came begging at the yard doorway. Fatty, on guard, threw a stone at the old woman, hitting her on the arm. He was in the act of aiming a second stone when our shouts distracted him. Before he could throw it, Chungnya came down and handed the woman the remains of the yak's head. It was obvious that she was grateful and regarded the head as a feast. She had the greatest difficulty in climbing out over the yard doorstep unaided. From the wall I watched her vanish into one of the nearby boulder dwellings accompanied by three ragged, hungry-looking little urchins.

By now we were into December and hopes of an early release were dwindling. We started to go over our escape plan and decided that, if there was no indication of release within a week, we would accept the risks and make a break for it at night. We were discussing this plan one morning when we accidentally came into possession of a photograph of Smoothy.

Harrop, Damodar and I were sitting against the wall enjoying a brief sunny interlude, a now increasingly infrequent occurrence, when Schickelgruber arrived from a trip to the officers' quarters. He carried a stiff-backed book, with green cotton cover, which I recognized as Smoothy's Chinese dictionary.

Schickelgruber seated himself against the wall of what had been my solitary cell and became engrossed in his own highly complicated language. At the end of half an hour he gave up and was turning to go indoors when Harrop asked if he might look at the book.

Being in a more amiable mood than usual Schickelgruber handed the dictionary over. As Harrop was flipping through the pages an identification photograph, no larger than a postage stamp, fell from between the pages. It was, indeed, a picture of Smoothy. None of the guards having seen what had happened, I slipped the picture into my pocket. Later that day, when indoors, I had a close and careful look at it. The picture revealed a much younger Smoothy wearing the padded army uniform with the P.L.A. flash on his chest. His promotion to the blue tunic political corps had obviously come at a later date.

Harrop was determined that we should have a copy of the army flash which decorated the jackets of the soldiers, but his efforts to copy this were quickly detected and the drawing was immediately confiscated. After that he worked very surreptitiously, copying the symbols, one stroke at a time, in pencil on his thumb nail. In this manner he escaped detection by the guards, and once or twice when he thought the Chinese were paying him too much attention he erased the pencil marks from his nail with one rub of the underside of his forefinger.

In this manner it took him three days to copy all the symbols, but, as he said, it was, at least, something to do. We were curious to see if these symbols represented a regiment, but in this we were destined to be disappointed. When we reached Delhi we had the flash deciphered, but it simply said, 'Peoples' Liberation Army of the Republic of China'.

Both the copy of the army flash and Smoothy's picture were carefully concealed inside the backing of my small mirror. I now had enough incriminating material on my person to ensure a very uncomfortable time should I undergo a close search before our release. The seven weeks' diary, much of it unfavourable to the Chinese Communists, in itself would create trouble.

Later that day Fatty, seeing that Harrop was whiling away his time with a pencil, demanded to see what he had been drawing. Prepared for just such an occasion Harrop was not caught unawares. He produced a neat sketch of a rather fat and ugly sow. It required little in the way of sign language to inform Fatty that the sketch was supposed to represent his unpleasant and offensive self. He growled at us both and marched off with the drawing. Chungnya and Chubby, who probably shared our sentiments regarding Fatty, regarded the matter as a joke. But Fatty, Shorty and Schickelgruber took the matter up and spent half an hour showering us with curses and insults. To our surprise, Harrop's little joke was raised at our next interrogations.

On the morning of December 6th we watched the officers march across from the grey barracks to the red interrogation building. A group of soldiers carried the familiar tubular steel chairs across and Harrop had barely swallowed his last mouthful of boiled turnip before he was hustled off for his third inquisition. Within half an hour he was back. To my surprise neither Damodar nor I was sent over the river during the next half-hour. The procedure was new, but not without purpose. Harrop had been instructed to try to persuade me to sign the confession, although, of course, he had no intention of doing any such thing.

'You stick it out,' he advised. 'Keep telling them to go to hell.'

I asked Damodar if he thought that a wise course and if he believed that there was the remotest chance that the Chinese might release us once they obtained my signature on that critical document. He replied that his intuition assured him that we would soon be on our way home. It was curious to hear a young man who had the advantages of a college education speak of signs, omens and portents concerning travel. He confessed that he had originally intended joining our expedition a day earlier than he had done so, but had been persuaded by his father to postpone the trip for twenty-four hours. His father had consulted a soothsayer who had given him this advice.

I felt reassured by the outlook and conduct of my companions. If they were willing to stick it out, then so was I. In addition there was, as Damodar said, hopeful portent in the morning's happenings. The interrogation had taken place in the open air in the yard of the red building and Harrop had been offered a tubular steel chair. He nearly dropped dead when Smoothy offered him an English cigarette and then added, 'Keep the tin.'

To prove it, Harrop pulled a nearly full fifty tin of cigarettes from his pocket. He also told us that, in the middle of the interrogation, Smoothy had produced Harrop's drawing of a pig, saying, after Harrop had identified it, 'It is forbidden to draw pictures of the guards.'

Harrop had also presented a letter to the officers addressed to his family in England, requesting that it be handed to one of the Indian traders in the vicinity for despatch to India. It contained nothing that might offend the Chinese and was simply intended to inform his father and mother that he was a prisoner in Tibet and in good health. Smoothy declined to accept the letter, saying, 'There is no official postal service from Tibet.'

Harrop, not to be put off, insisted that the letter be handed to the Indians.

'It is impossible to send letters through Hindustan,' Smoothy said. 'All the passes are blocked with snow.'

We doubted the truth of the statement, and were soon to discover for ourselves that Smoothy had, in fact, lied.

When the guards considered that we had had sufficient time for Harrop to persuade me to sign the ever-to-be-disputed document, I was ushered out of the prison yard. I was climbing the far bank of the river when I noticed that the line of human and animal transport wending its way up to the new barracks at the top of the ridge was now carrying desks, chairs, tables and even carpets. The building work apparently was completed.

My interrogation, like Harrop's, took place out of doors in the courtyard of the red house.

The committee sat round the table puffing at cigarettes and occasionally spitting on the floor. The atmosphere was somehow different from that of my three previous interrogations. I had the feeling that we had won the two-months-long battle of wits and would soon be on our way home. Everyone smiled when Smoothy said, 'Please, sit down,' adding as an afterthought, 'on this chair.'

A guard came out of the interrogation room and deposited a tubular steel chair in the middle of the yard. The chair had clearly been taken indoors after Harrop had left, so that a great display could be made of their very gracious and hospitable act.

I accepted the seat and thanked Smoothy for his courtesy. He communicated my appreciation to the others and everyone smiled broadly, even Ug-Lug, who nodded his head to me in a very friendly fashion. They were under the impression that Harrop had talked me into confessing and that their ostensible kindliness was having its effect.

M

I opened the proceedings by producing a letter addressed to my wife and making a request similar to Harrop's. Smoothy was profusely apologetic about the heavy snow that filled all the passes. While mentally noting that he was a lousy and unconvincing liar, I smilingly accepted his regrets.

The now very grubby confession was produced and I was asked to sign, Smoothy assuring me that it was for my own good. He reminded me that I had not seen my wife and son for nearly six months, adding that some members of his committee also had families and fully understood how I felt and sympathized with me. I was tempted to tell him that he was a lying, unctuous little swine, but restrained myself and replied that I liked the Tibetan climate and was in no hurry to leave.

With that I rose and asked if there was anything else they wished to discuss, as, if that exhausted the agenda, I would like to return to my cell.

'As you wish,' Smoothy said, to my surprise. 'But first we would like you to have some cigarettes.'

I replied that I did not smoke and was turning away when he cried after me, as if in panic, 'Is there anything else you would like?'

I paused and thought for a moment. We would most definitely like some sugar, for we had been drinking the insipid Chinese brick tea neat for several weeks. When I voiced my request, Smoothy further surprised me by saying, 'It shall be arranged.'

I looked around to find everyone smiling in the most friendly fashion. I had no hopes of the sugar, but walked back to my cell feeling as if a tremendous load had been lifted from my mind. I was convinced that they had been instructed to release us in the very near future and were merely playing for time in the hope that I might confess. If I failed to sign and they *had* been instructed to let us go, then we had nothing to fear. If I did sign, then our last hope of freedom would vanish and our captors would triumphantly radio to their superiors, informing them of the confession that would empower them to hold us for trial. With that thought in mind I concluded that the interrogation committee was composed of men of but feeble intelligence. Their smiles, offer of a comfortable place in the sun and cigarettes were far too transparent to deceive even a child.

Damodar was interrogated at 1 p.m., and he, too, returned to the prison with cigarettes. We discussed this new turn in events, and although we were secretly elated we took care not to show any emotion in front of the guards. Dinner proved to be a nicely cooked mutton stew with double the usual amount of meat.

When we went to the tea-urn to fill our mugs I towed Schickelgruber along with me by the lapel of his coat. There was no doubt that the attitude of our captors had changed, for Schickelgruber did not seem to mind me dragging him along. In fact, he tried to adopt an air of good-natured fun.

I stirred the tea in the urn and said '*Ta*,' the word our guards used for sugar. Schickelgruber patted me reassuringly on the back and departed for the other side of the river. Within ten minutes he was back, bearing a 10-lb. sack of sugar. The sack was of very light cotton, the poorest cloth imaginable, and we recognized it as of the same material as most of the prayer-flags that adorned the buildings at Taklakot. The sacks of white sugar had their origin in India, being transported by mule over the Lipu Lekh pass for trade at the tent bazaar in Taklakot. A couple of pounds of sugar was emptied into a bowl and the three of us enjoyed our tea for the first time in weeks. Sugar was the one thing we had craved for throughout our period of captivity.

Things were definitely on the mend and we awaited the morning with eager anticipation. To our surprise there were no interrogations that day nor on the following day. The only item of interest occurred outside the Tibetan house situated only a few yards west of our prison, the one in which I had undergone my second interrogation. As the day wore on it became evident that someone who ranked high on the Tibetan social register was in residence at this house.

A crowd of gaily dressed men and women gathered outside playing oboes and trumpets and beating drums. Three male dancers, dressed in baggy red pantaloons and black leather riding-boots, performed a dance consisting mainly of ballet-like gyrations. The dancers had long cords with a bobble at the end hanging from their waists. When they pirouetted, the decorated curtain of cord flared out from the waist like a grass skirt.

When the dancing stopped, the singing started. It was every bit as weird as that heard at Jitkot Gompa, and, like the Jitkot music, it emanated from an unseen source. The vocal effects were the same as before, the man apparently singing with two voices at one and the same time: a low bass tone accompanied by a high tenor voice. Everyone, even our guards, was silent. Fatty forgot to shut the door and the three of us stood in the middle of the lower yard looking through the doorway at this curious spectacle. The crowd around the house were looking up at the cliff face, the source of the voice. Look as we would, we could see no one. About twenty feet up the rock face was a red-painted cave shrine with a tiny verandah, and we supposed that the singing holy man was in that.

The booming base notes, changing to a sound almost soprano in quality, caused me to shiver. Occasionally there came a low moaning sound as of someone in torment. Recalling the moaning of the wind on the day of the dust storm, I presumed that the cave itself was responsible for the curious acoustic effects that we had heard before.

The singing and festivities over, a group of Tibetan boys and girls, clad in sheepskin cloaks, presented small wicker baskets full of gifts, mainly cloth, to a group of Lamas who had emerged from the house and now sat cross-legged in the forecourt. A constant stream of local villagers, intent on audience with the Bonpos,[1] kept trotting up and down the hillside. It was the largest gathering of Tibetans I had seen at Taklakot. Dusk brought their activities to an end and we retired indoors.

On the morning of December 10th I was hauled off for another interrogation. The moment I left the prison I realized that there was an unusually large number of Tibetans about. At the other side of the bridge many had gathered, some on horseback, some on foot. I crossed the bridge accompanied by two guards and passed through their midst.

The centre of attraction was a middle-aged man dressed in black from his fur hat to his leather boots. As I passed I noticed the man with the large earring who had greeted me kindly after my second interrogation. He, attracting the attention of the man clad in black, bowed in a friendly manner as I passed.

At the top of the hill the guards signalled me to halt, and I wondered why. Then all the officers came out of the red building and stood in line on the high ground that overlooked the group of Tibetans. I sat on a rock to watch the proceedings. The mounted men must have exceeded thirty in number and the retinue on foot half a hundred. Some carried modern rifles and kept close to the man in black. One of his retainers carried a large telescope; another a thermos flask of about a gallon capacity. Hardly the sort of items one associates with Tibetans. All the horses wore gaily coloured trappings and most of the saddles were decorated with silver.

At a signal from the man with the solitary earring, two men sprang forward and took hold of two strings which led from either side of

[1] Officials.

the halter of a horse ridden by the black-garbed personage. Hearing the sound of oboes and drums, I looked to the head of the caravan to see that the two leading horsemen were playing wind instruments, while a third beat rapidly on two hand drums suspended on either side of his saddle.

The cortège moved off. As they passed, the man whose horse was being led by two retainers looked quizzically up at me and smiled. I smiled back. He bowed as he passed beneath the Chinese, and the Governor acknowledged the salute with a most perfunctory wave of his hand. With that he and his colleagues went indoors. I sat for a moment or two watching the colourful cavalcade wind its way along the track that led to the north. It was intent either on Gartok or on Lhasa. I had no means of telling which. But of one thing I was sure. I had seen the Viceroy or Garpon of Gartok, and I wondered if it was the same one who had shown hospitality to Harrer and Aufschneiter when they passed through Gartok on their way to Lhasa.

The guards motioned me into the yard of the red building, where my inquisitors were seated round their table. It was a nice sunny day and I peeled off my sweater as I took the proffered tubular chair. Everyone, as I had expected, was very friendly.

Smoothy came quickly to the point.

'Hello,' he said. 'We have decided that we will order your release once you sign the confession.'

I did not believe him, and I said so.

'If you don't sign you will stay here forever.'

When he received no reply he tried another tack.

'Don't you want to see your wife and son again?'

My silence unnerved him and he launched into a long conversation with the others. I gained the impression that they were under pressure to obtain quick results or admit failure to their superiors.

I decided to test his sincerity.

'I'll make you an offer—a sort of compromise—if you like.'

He bristled with suspicion.

'What is this offer?'

'If you can prove that I was arrested in Tibet, then I will sign your confession.'

My offer was not accepted. They knew that genuine evidence to corroborate their charge could not be produced other than by such a trick as falsification of the date of our arrest.

The Governor looked as weary of the business as I, in fact, was. I had been held for nearly two months and the concrete information

Smoothy had gained in that time could be written on the back of a postage stamp. There would be no promotions for the handling of this affair.

I began to feel that the Governor was eagerly looking for a way out of his dilemma. He had to release us, of that I was sure, but he was anxious to carry out his orders with a minimum loss of face. I decided to give him an opening.

'Sooner or later,' I said, 'you will have to admit that the frontier of Nepal and Tibet is undemarcated. Because of that you have no jurisdiction over the area where we were arrested. That being the case, I am willing to sign the following statement: "If at any future date it is agreed between the Governments of Nepal and Tibet that the place where Wignall, Harrop and Suwal were arrested is inside the frontiers of Tibet, then a formal apology for an accidental incursion of the Tibetan frontier will be made to the Chinese representative in London." '

I wrote it out and handed the paper to Smoothy, who read it and shook his head.

'This is not a confession of guilt. It is a conditional statement and as such is entirely unacceptable.'

The Governor asked Smoothy for a translation, and when he heard my offer he smiled and nodded. It would be quite acceptable. Smoothy fixed me with a look of pure hatred. The tension eased and cigarettes were passed around. The Governor made a long speech, which proved to be a request that I should sign a statement saying that we had been well treated during our period as guests of the Peoples' Liberation Army.

I was assured that this was only a formality and would be used as simply part of their records. But when I refused to sign he looked embarrassed, and the matter was not referred to again.

I asked when we would be released and what food would be supplied for our journey back.

'You will be released tomorrow, and we will provide you with sixty pounds of flour.'

I decided not to pursue the matter further. We would need little in the way of food, for the Indian Government check post was only a day's ride away. I felt elated and was stupid enough to let them see it. I looked from the Governor to Ug-Lug and Smoothy. They all had the same intent, half-amused, enquiring expressions on their faces, and I began to feel suspicious. They were holding something un-pleasant in reserve, although I could not imagine what it could be.

'We are going to supply the mules and porters for your return journey,' said Smoothy. 'The Peoples' Republic will pay all the expenses.'

I replied that the Lipu Lekh pass into India was but a few hours' ride away and, being an easy one and readily negotiable by mules, we should not need porters. They grinned broadly.

'We never said that you would be allowed to return over the Lipu Lekh into Hindustan. You must return through Nepal.'

That was unwelcome information. The shortest route through Nepal would take many days longer than the way over the Lipu Lekh.

'As we have no choice in the matter, we will return over the Tinkar Lipu pass.'

Smoothy smiled again.

'No. You must go back over the Urai Lekh.'

The announcement was such a shock that I could think of nothing to say.

'The mules,' Smoothy continued, 'will take you to Kathan village. There we will hire four Tibetan porters to carry your equipment over the Urai to the nearest Nepalese village.'

'A couple of days ago you said that all the passes were snowed up.'

'The snow has now melted.'

It was a patent lie. Winter snow does not melt at such a rate, and, for that matter, I knew that none of the Chinese garrison had ever visited the Urai Lekh.

It needed little imagination to divine their purpose, and I protested strongly.

'The Urai Lekh is the farthest pass from here, and there are no Nepalese villages less than four days' march on the other side. The Urai Lekh is considered to be impassable at this time of the year. If you force us over it you will be sending us to our deaths.'

Smoothy's reply was staggering in its cold-bloodedness.

'Once you are released your lives will no longer be our responsibility.'

That ended the morning's proceedings. I walked back to our prison stunned and alarmed. At the entrance to the prison yard I turned and looked to the mountain barrier to the south. Cloud covered everything. Somewhere within that grey barrier lay the 19,500-feet Urai Lekh and it was snowing heavily.

Chapter 22

GOOD-BYE TO TAKLAKOT

I ENTERED the yard looking so troubled that Harrop thought our hopes of release had been disappointed. He was surprised when I said, 'We are going home tomorrow.'

The bombshell came a few moments later.

'They will only allow us to go back over the Urai.'

Damodar and Harrop were incredulous.

'The Urai is never crossed in December,' Harrop protested.

Damodar served to underline our anxiety when he said, 'If Berkeley Sahib had such a difficult time getting out of the Seti gorge in October, what will it be like now?'

I had to admit that the prospects of negotiating the gorge were anything but good. But they would not let us out any other way, and if we refused to go over the Urai our stay in Taklakot would be prolonged indefinitely.

'At least we'll be seeing the last of these bastards,' Harrop said.

If we had to cross the highest and most exposed pass in that part of the Himalayas to get away from the Chinese, then even the formidable Urai Lekh had its attractions.

Damodar crossed to the lavatory wall to see what was claiming the attention of all seven of our guards, who were gazing intently towards the bridge.

'The officers are coming here!'

This was a completely new departure, for not once had they visited our quarters during our stay. They filed into the yard and nodded a greeting to Schickelgruber who was running around like a scalded hen. Food was on the go in the kitchen and it was soon produced. The officers sat cross-legged in a circle and ate their food in the same unhygienic way as the soldiers, picking meat out of a common bowl and dropping it into their individual rice bowls.

When they had finished eating we tackled Smoothy about food. We could not possibly face the journey ahead of us on nothing more than a bag of flour. After a great deal of argument he consented to an allowance of 10lb. of sugar and a small piece of meat. I remarked that we would also need paraffin for our Primus stoves, but Smoothy retorted that they would be supplying us with native tsampa flour which, he claimed, we could eat mixed with cold water like the Tibetans, and the meat, too, we could eat uncooked.

I decided that we might do better with our guards and dropped the matter of the paraffin. We decided against asking for the Chinese brick tea as it took too long to infuse and was virtually tasteless. Our original stock of tea from England was now reduced to less than a couple of ounces, but with economy it might last until we reached a Nepalese village.

I broached the problem of porters for the journey, trying to explain to Smoothy that, as the population of Kathan was limited to only one family, I doubted if four porters could be obtained. But when Smoothy replied that the Kathan valley was heavily populated, I gave up in disgust.

While this argument was in progress some soldiers strange to us brought in all our kit. We were asked to examine it and sign a receipt. A farcical formality.

We had three 35m. miniature cameras, one 35m. stereo camera and a 16m. cine-camera. These, it appeared, had not been opened by the Chinese during all the weeks they had been in their hands, a fact which we never fathomed. Were they afraid that they contained booby traps?

Smoothy asked for the film from each camera, and while I ran off the 100 feet of film in the cine-camera, Harrop fiddled with his miniature and handed them the cassette. As I discovered later, he played a neat trick on our captors. While everyone was engrossed with the workings of the triple-lensed cine-camera, Harrop opened the back of his camera, cut the film with a pair of surgical scissors and handed the Chinese a cassette that contained about ten unexposed frames. He knew that much of the film left in the camera would be ruined due to exposure to the light, but his efforts were rewarded when the film was eventually processed in England. Most of the pictures were intact, though flashes of light could be seen in corners of the Kodachrome transparency. That night we extracted the film from it and carefully wrapped it up. Meanwhile a final search disclosed nothing. My diary lay undiscovered in my air mattress.

The officers departed and we were never to see them again. As they passed through the yard doorway the Governor said a few words to Smoothy. Smoothy smiled, turned towards me and said, 'I have been instructed to inform you that our intentions towards you are friendly.'

He frowned when Harrop roared after him, 'Hypocritical little bastard!'

That night was our last spent in Taklakot prison, and we celebrated in fine style. Chungnya brought in a really first-class meal
specially prepared for the occasion. Even Schickelgruber joined in
the party and insisted on shaking hands with all three of us. My two
companions were plied with cigarettes and I was given a handful of
cheap Indian sweets.

Chungnya provided about half a gallon of paraffin for our journey
from the can used for filling our tiny oil-lamps. It was one of the
happiest and most enjoyable evenings of my life. The feast was capped
with a bottle of Chang, the Tibetan rice wine, brought in by
Chungnya. The Chang was contained in a well-finished Tibetan
bottle of turned wood, bound with brass. It was thick, milky stuff,
slightly green in colour and all sorts of unidentified objects floated on
the surface. A not unpleasant drink, it reminded me of a bottle of
hock.

After two cups neither Harrop nor I was any the worse for wear,
but Damodar was decidedly merry. As Harrop remarked, Damodar
would keel over at one smell from a bottle stopper. He ended up by
climbing into his sleeping-bag, standing upright and trying to walk
round the room in it. He fell flat on his face and we had to put him to
bed. Within two minutes he was giving us the doubtful benefit of his
snoring, which sounded like a soul in torment moaning incessantly.
He kept up this performance throughout the night.

After a long sign-language conversation with two of the guards,
we finally made them understand that we travelled to India by motor-
car.

One responded with a realistic imitation of himself starting up and
driving an automobile. Then he held out the fingers of his hand until
we counted twenty-two and he pointed to his nose. That was his age.
He then held the palm of one hand about two inches above his head
and afterwards gave the sign twenty-three, repeating this again for
twenty-four. He was trying to tell us something was planned to happen
in two years' time. We were puzzled, but not after he had again demon-
strated the car-driving motions, pointed to his nose and then at the
floor, saying, 'Lhasa—Taklakot'.

And there it was! An innocent young soldier had given away the
one thing the Chinese were trying to hide from us and which their
High Command believed to be the reason for our being there. Had we
been the espionage agents the Chinese imagined us to be, then our
mission could not have been more successful.

In two years' time a strategic highway would link Lhasa and

Taklakot, an extension of the Chungking-Chamdo-Lhasa road, that would enable the Chinese to establish a huge army within 250 miles of Delhi, the capital of India and Asia's economic and intellectual centre, once called the brightest jewel in Britain's crown. Now we understood why West Tibet had been declared a security area. We understood, too, the build-up of forces, the new barracks and radio station, and the interference with the rights of Indian pilgrims travelling to Manasarowar and Kailas. If the Governor had known we possessed such information our lives would not have been worth a dud rupee.

Harrop and I discussed this choice piece of information until the early hours of the morning. Perhaps the Governor suspected that we already knew, and that explained why he was forcing us over the Urai Lekh? We would soon know the answer. To give away the identity of the guard who told us about the strategic road would, I am sure, result in his death.

On the morning of December 11th we packed our kit in the middle of the yard, making it up into four porter loads. After breakfast an officer appeared whom we had not seen before. Short, fat and jovial of countenance, we found him rather pleasant. He wore a style of padded suit obsolete in the P.L.A., and which gave him the appearance of an upholstered football. He wore a pair of Russian-style felt boots called Velinki, which lent to his feet an elephantine appearance. He was accompanied by a scraggy, spindly-legged young soldier whom we immediately christened 'Runty'.

To complete the caravan our escort included Chungnya and Schickelgruber. Chungnya and Runty carried Tommy guns and Schickelgruber and the officer each wore a small automatic pistol and a pair of binoculars. Each had a travelling valise made of canvas and leather, containing a bulky and heavy kapok-filled palliasse. Hardly the sort of bedding expected for an army which has a reputation for mobility and travelling light.

Progress was delayed when we discovered that the Chinese expected the three of us to carry not only our rucksacks, but also the four 70-lb. loads on our mounts, which was a physical impossibility. After much arguing two more mules were brought and the loads suitably distributed but very poorly tied. I was surprised at their ham-fistedness and lack of skill in adjusting loads and tying knots.

It was 11 a.m. when we mounted our mules and horses. This was my second essay on a four-legged animal, the first being when the Chinese provided saddleless ponies for the journey from Kathan to Jitkot Monastery. This time, however, the conditions were much improved. My mule had a saddle, stirrups and reins. The leather straps had seen neither polish nor dressing since the day they left the saddler's. Every strap was desiccated and the reins snapped the first time I pulled on them. After tying a knot they were rather short and I had to ride leaning forward all the time.

Harrop could make no adjustment to the stirrups of his ageing horse and had to ride with his knees up to his chin like a racing jockey. I found that I could persuade my animal to trot by jumping up and down in the saddle and yelling at the top of my voice. A pull at the reins caused him to turn to the left or the right, and I thought this wonderful. I even tried to tell Harrop, in a most blasé manner, how to ride a horse.

Not to be outdone, he asked me how I made it jump a fence. To which I replied that, if we encountered such an obstacle, then I would dismount, climb over and leave the mule to make its own terms with it.

I galloped my animal round one of the huge conglomerate boulders outside the prison yard and Chungnya joined me. We tore round and round yelling like Indians.

After two months in a cell I looked forward to the ride of about 15 miles to Kathan via Jitkot. We might even look in on the old Lama, Gin-Din-Rhou.

We passed scores of cave dwellings on our way out and the local populace turned out to bid us farewell. Young and old crowded the edge of the track and salaamed as we rode by. Many put out their tongues, a sign of great respect and good manners in Tibet. To our surprise we did not turn off up the Taklakot ridge as we had done on our way in. Now we turned left and our unwilling mounts were forced to ford the icy river, and I had to lift my feet out of the stirrups to prevent them getting wet.

There seemed little point in this divergence, for it was obvious that we should have to cross the river later in order to reach the Jitkot track.

I took a parting look at our prison, now almost hidden by a bend in the track, and glanced up to see if the new barracks was visible. It was then that the reason for the new route dawned on me. They were making sure that we did not have a good vantage point from which to see the completed building. But they were unable to disguise the fact that it was there, nor could they alter the fact that we had seen it on the way in and that we knew that it was also a radio station. The Chinese mind works in a way that is peculiarly its own.

As the distance increased, so the previously foreshortened summit of Gurla Mandhata appeared to rise out of the plain. It now assumed a majesty that superseded everything else in sight. No longer a snow mountain, the whole of the summit pyramid was bare bleak rock, swept clean by the bitter winds from the northern plateau. Winter snow may fall on the Nepal peaks twenty miles to the south, but the arid, windy Tibetan winter would ensure that the Gurla Mandhata remained clear of snow until the monsoon of next year.

After recrossing the Karnali our mules and ponies scrambled over broken, decrepit mud and stone walls that divided the fields from the river's edge. Soon we reached the track proper, and there our fore-bodings regarding the loads were realized. Runty, who carried a riding-crop, ruthlessly struck at the two pack animals in an effort to speed their progress. The poor beasts broke into a gallop, but they had barely covered fifty yards when our precious equipment burst from its moorings and was scattered all over the ground. We were particularly worried about our two-gallon paraffin can, which would stand little of such treatment, for without the paraffin we were doomed.

We became involved in an argument with the fat officer and Runty. They were unable to see that the few minutes gained by whipping up the horses to a gallop resulted in a loss of twenty minutes while the loads were retied. Before we had journeyed another mile the same thing happened again and we ended up roundly cursing the Chinese.

We realized now that Runty was a trouble-maker. With a Tommy gun in his hands he was all-powerful, but lacking the protection of a weapon he was a coward. He whipped Harrop's mount once and that proved his undoing. Harrop grabbed at Runty, who jumped from his animal, cocked his gun and hid behind the animal's flank. We decided to go on strike and sat down on some flat resting-stones on the outskirts of the village of Marsha Kalya. Chungnya had a long talk with the fat officer and Schickelgruber with the result that Runty was reprimanded and refrained thereafter from whipping the animals. It was obvious that our speed would be reduced to that of the slowest members of the convoy—the pack animals.

Damodar had the liveliest mount of all and he took advantage of this to gallop off ahead along the track. I whipped my mount with the riding-crop Gin-Din-Rhou had given to me, jumped up and down in the saddle and screamed like a banshee, but Damodar easily retained his lead.

Shortly after midday we passed under the great monastery of

Jitkot, its towering walls silhouetted against a bright blue sky. Our track now ran close to the river bank and the monastery stood on top of the hill. Damodar reined back his horse to tell me that he thought that Gin-Din-Rhou might be compromised with the Chinese if we carried out our promise to visit him on leaving Tibet. Damodar was right. As much as I would have liked to see the old Lama again I decided against doing so.

Kojarnath came into sight by the middle of the afternoon. The village was situated on the opposite bank of the Karnali. With its three huge red monasteries it made a wonderful picture, the cluster of snow peaks that make up the Nalkankar range providing a perfect backcloth.

The track now turned west, steeply uphill and away from the river. The gradient was such that we were forced to dismount and lead the animals by the reins.

We passed a small village of about a dozen houses, which we had failed to notice on our way to Jitkot on the day of our arrest. We must have passed within yards of the houses, then concealed from us by the darkness. Chungnya stayed behind at the village, though at the time we had no idea why.

We toiled up the ridge, the going terrible. The ground was covered with rubble and the small round stones kept slipping from under our feet. Being in very poor condition after our weeks in prison, we gasped and panted like three old men. Halfway up the ridge we had further trouble with Runty. He tried to retie one of the pack loads and our only billycan went tumbling down a steep ravine. Runty walked over to me and rudely waved me down the hillside to retrieve the can. I refused to go and started an argument with him. He backed away from me and I followed him across the ridge. He displayed no courage until Schickelgruber came on the scene, when he squared up and prodded me in the chest with his gun.

I lost my temper, grabbed hold of the barrel of the gun and tried to hit him. In his efforts to avoid my blows he stepped back and fell. When I followed him up, Schickelgruber jumped between us and we ended up with Runty clinging to safe ground behind Schickelgruber's back and me trying to push past to get my hands on him. While this was going on Damodar had returned down the hill and now stood by his mule shouting encouragement to me. In the end, Runty handed his Tommy gun to Schickelgruber and I was forced to desist. I knew from the look in Schickelgruber's eyes that he would not hesitate to pull the trigger. I sat down on a rock and waited for the officer and

Harrop to catch up. When they did reach us another lengthy argument developed, ending, to my delight, in Runty being told to go down the ravine after the can.

He wore ordinary leather army boots without laces, and because of this his footgear slithered all over the place and he had difficulty in regaining the top of the long scree slope. I took one look at his hostile face and bulging eyes and decided that I would never under any circumstances turn my back on him. A few days later I forgot my vow, and Runty seized his opportunity to strike me in the middle of the back with the butt of his Tommy gun.

The ground levelled out into a small valley and then, after another two miles, turned uphill towards the little pass that gives access to Kathan. At the top of the pass we halted to rest our mules. Chungnya caught us up and he was accompanied by a young Tibetan boy on foot. The boy was bearing a bag containing about 15lb. of tsampa, part of our flour ration for the return trip. He also showed us our meat allocation, which amounted to only some 2lb. to last the three of us for the six- to eight-day trip to Dhuli. The food prospect was definitely discouraging.

Chapter 23

PHRUPA'S HOUSE AGAIN

OUR animals rested, we started down the steep track leading to Kathan. The ground being too precipitous for us to remain mounted, we took care of ourselves, letting the animals wander where they would.

The going was very difficult, but after some three hundred feet of sliding and slithering, mostly on our backsides, we reached easier ground again, and the Chinese mounted their mules. Harrop and I were stiff and saddle-sore after seven hours of riding, and we elected to walk the remaining half-mile to old Phrupa's house, leading our mounts by the reins.

In an effort to pass me, Schickelgruber's mule knocked me off the track and I cascaded down a steep rubble slope for about twenty feet. It was nothing more than an accident, and everybody laughed except Runty, who viewed me with naked hostility.

It was dark when we reached the village, and the male members of Phrupa's family came out to help unload our baggage animals. We entered the same dark passage and knocked our heads on the same low beam as before. We now understood why the Chinese had sent the fat officer and Runty along. Both spoke Tibetan fluently.

It was getting dark as Phrupa came to welcome us, carrying a tiny butter lamp, the light illuminating his evil-looking face. The fact that he had only one eye did not improve his looks. Harrop said that, with such a face, Phrupa could make a fortune haunting houses. But the fault was nature's, not Phrupa's. He told us that the question of porters could not be discussed until the following morning.

'And that,' he said, 'is the fault of the Chinese. They gave us no warning.'

We were shown to our room, and what a room! In England it would have passed as a disused coal cellar. The walls were only four feet six inches high, and the doorway was so low that we had to enter virtually on our hands and knees. The walls were covered with an inch-thick film of soot. This when touched accidentally favoured us with a cascade of soot that spread itself all over the room.

We blew up our air mattresses and laid out the sleeping-bags. Some young Tibetan boys carried in our kit and dumped it unceremoniously in the far corner of the room. This raised a cloud of soot that sent all three of us scrambling for the door. In our panic each one in turn banged his head on the low passage. I took a step sideways in the dark and went down a manhole in the floor. I had sorted myself out and made certain no bones were broken when Damodar shone his torch down and revealed that I was in a disused kitchen. The ladder was the usual tree-trunk with notches carved for hand- and foot-holds. I was becoming resigned to being knocked about in Tibetan houses and decided that it was all in the hands of the gods.

Damodar went in search of Phrupa and a pot of tea, while Harrop and I waited for the soot to settle, then re-entered our room. The only window in this black hole was six inches in diameter and looked out on to the courtyard. Every time we shone a torch at the opening it illuminated the face of one of the many small children that infested the house as if it were a rabbit warren. The children, who seemed to have no fixed bedtime, wandered about the place until the early hours of the morning.

We heard Damodar returning with Phrupa, who was bellowing in a rough voice. We feared that he was being queer with us until Damodar explained that Phrupa was, in fact, using his best Sunday voice.

Chungnya came in bearing two very small oil lamps. He wanted paraffin and we had to argue with him, our paraffin can being little more than half full, and the contents likely to be as precious as life itself. Grudgingly we filled his lamp, which held no more than an egg-cup full. He let us have the other lamp for ourselves, and Phrupa, taking opportunity to effect a little economy, retrieved his butter lamp. Five minutes later he too came in with a tiny paraffin lamp which we filled with but meagre grace.

He showed gratitude by sending in a large iron kettle full of tea. I don't know what was in it, but it tasted like a bad blend of garlic and blotting-paper. We protested so strongly that another kettleful was brought, this time without any additives.

We had barely drunk the tea when Phrupa asked if we would like more and, unwisely, we said yes. Phrupa then demanded paraffin for the lamps of all the twenty-two people in the house. We could not accede to his request, and a very noisy argument ensued. Tibetans never talk in normal conversational tones. They shout, and we were deafened by the noise made by Phrupa and half a dozen of his numerous relatives. We compromised by filling four more lamps, having, in all, parted with about three-quarters of a pint of paraffin.

N

Dinner consisted of some of the tsampa that had been purchased for us. We ate in Tibetan style, mixing the flour with tea until a ball of dough was formed. It made an indifferent food, and was certainly not a diet on which to cross the Himalaya. We would need much more and much better food to ensure the necessary number of calories.

We improved our tsampa balls of dough by mixing sugar with them. While mixing our tsampa we were plagued by a crowd of unwashed urchins who, coming to inspect us, found our kit far more interesting. One boy was a half-wit who aroused our sympathy. The butt of all the pranks played by the other children, he was a pathetic little figure clad in a long-sleeved cloak, just like his elders. His head was shaved and he had a more pronounced Mongoloid countenance than the others. He wore a constantly puzzled look and spent most of his time sucking his right thumb, the only clean part of his body. The dirt was caked on his hands, face and feet, but the other children were not one whit cleaner.

The average English schoolboy would view his Tibetan counter-part with envy. No set bedtime, no school, no washing. They spend most of the day chasing sheep, dogs and yaks, hurling stones at them with great force and accuracy. The Tibetan environment must be much the same as that of England before the Middle Ages. Neverthe-less, in spite of everything, and in spite of the presence of the Chinese Communists, whom they hated, the Tibetans as a race were the happiest we encountered in our travels through twelve different countries to the Himalayas.

Before we turned in for the night, Phrupa came in again bearing the disquieting news that none of his family was willing to make the winter's journey over the Urai Lekh. He would have to send a runner to the other villages in the morning, and that would mean that we should have to halt our journey for a full day. As he left us he said, 'The men you will get for such a journey will not be of the best.'

We could not decide whether he meant the men obtainable elsewhere would be poor carriers or downright villains. What we did not understand then was that Phrupa and his family were too honour-able to participate in the Chinese plot to end our lives.

Security was now rather lax and I went out on to the roof of the building to breathe some of the clear night air. I could see the faint outline of the snow-clad peaks that surround Kathan on three sides, their sharp summits silhouetted against a cloudless, star-filled sky.

Out in the open an old hag was snoring away under a pile of sheepskins, thereby unconsciously testifying to the hardiness of her race. Three little children shared her bed. They all snuggled together for warmth, their pillow a log of wood.

Smoke rose out of a hole in the floor, and I bent down and looked inside. About a dozen adult members of Phrupa's family were seated round the tea cauldron. They invited me down and I descended the tree-trunk ladder that led into the heart of the house. Squatting cross-legged in the circle I accepted a small wooden bowl of yak-butter tea.

The chattering had stopped, yielding place to a heavy silence. They all seemed to have sad expressions, and they shook their heads dolorously, tut-tutting as they did so. I had the strange feeling that something was afoot, for the Tibetans were looking at me as if I was a man already dead!

Phrupa's eldest son, very dignified looking, wore modern European shoes imported from India. He offered me more tea, saying, 'She-She,' which is pronounced 'Shay-Shay' and means, 'Please, have more.'

I replied 'Me-Me,' which is pronounced 'May-May,' conveying that I had had enough.

Their sadness was so contagious that I suddenly felt quite miserable. Then I started to shiver. I was wearing only a shirt and sweater, while they were clad in heavy sheepskins. Bidding them good night I returned to my room.

Another group of urchins was urging the little half-witted child to rummage around amongst our belongings. I admonished him roundly and bent down to push the equipment back into a kit-bag. One of the other children thrust his face against the window and shouted something to the half-wit. He, obeying instructions to the letter, promptly gave me a good clout on the ear. He could not have been more than five years old, but he packed a tidy punch. He made no attempt to run away. On the contrary, he stood right where he was, looking me straight in the eye, dispassionately awaiting further developments. I felt like boxing his ears, but was restrained by his pathetic appearance. Harrop and Damodar were already in bed. I blew out the oil-lamp and turned in.

The following day we resigned ourselves to sitting around Phrupa's house, the children pestering us endlessly. We discovered to our surprise that the baby on which I had inadvertently dropped my rucksack was still alive. Not that my light-weight sack could have injured the child. But the poor thing was still kept in a box, covered completely with old rags and skins. The temperature in the box, coupled with the fact that the child appeared to get no air, inspired the conviction that it would soon be asphyxiated, but Tibetan children, apparently, have an undefeatable determination to survive.

At midday the toothless and half-blind old hag we had seen before washed the baby. She simply filled her mouth with water from a cup and then squirted the liquid from her mouth all over the child. After some six such mouthfuls the baby, now wriggling and screaming at the top of his voice, was considered clean enough to be buried under his pile of old rags again. Tibetans evidently acquire their hostility to soap and water at a very early age. None of the grown-ups washed. The longer they lived, the dirtier they became.

One of the married daughters of the family sat with a young girl of about six years old on her knee, picking lice out of the child's hair. The woman did not kill the lice, but placed them carefully on the ground. True to her Buddhist religion she would take no life. After all, the flea hopping around under her sheepskin girdle might be the reincarnation of a by no means distant relative.

The Chinese officer had been given instructions to the effect that we must not be allowed to converse freely with the Tibetans. We observed this rule until he retired to his room for an afternoon nap, and then, with Damodar serving as interpreter, we had a long conversation with Phrupa.

An aspect of Tibetan life which puzzled me was the disposal of the dead. We had seen nothing remotely resembling a graveyard anywhere in the Karnali valley. We had a prize example of how one can be misled by faulty or lazy interpretation, for I asked Damodar to question Phrupa as to why we had seen no burial mounds.

Damodar, after listening to Phrupa's reply, said, 'They bury them like you do.'

I was far from satisfied with the answer, for it did not tally with what Harrer had said. I asked Damodar if Phrupa had actually used the word 'burial'. He hesitated for a moment and then said:

'As a matter of fact, he said that they dispose of the dead the same as you do.'

'How does he know how we dispose of them?' I asked. 'You follow the Hindu religion, Damodar. You burn the corpse at a ghat. How do you know that he didn't mean that?'

So Damodar put the question again, and he was surprised at the answer.

'Phrupa says that they just throw the bodies away and he thought you did the same. He was shocked when I said that you buried them.'

I pressed for more information, and what I got was similar to that gained by Harrer. Poor people simply throw the body into a ravine where the vultures, lammergiers and jackals eat the flesh, leaving only the bones. Those who can afford an undertaker hire one, and he cuts the flesh from the bones and then breaks the bones with an axe. Everything is then thrown into a river. They do not regard burial as a sacred rite. Once life departs, the soul flies to take up its abode in the body of some other creature—human, fish, reptile or insect. Phrupa then pointed down the valley to a limestone bluff overlooking a steep gorge. 'That,' he said, 'is where we cast away the bodies of our dead.'

During the day the Chinese helped themselves to some of our precious supplies of tea and sugar. They appeared to have made the trip to Kathan without supplies for a stay of more than twenty-four hours. The real reason was that, in keeping with Chinese army tradition, they lived entirely off the country. It was unfortunate for Phrupa and his family, who informed us that they received no payment whatsoever from the Chinese.

In the afternoon the fat officer handed over the food for our journey over the Urai Lekh—three small cotton bags of flour and the piece of meat Chungnya had bought the day before. The remainder of the 10-lb. bag of sugar that Schickelgruber had produced in prison was already in our possession. Two of the cotton bags contained white flour which, under the circumstances, was absolutely useless. The third contained the bag of tsampa the small Tibetan boy had carried from the village that we had passed on our way to Kathan. The total of white and native flour was less than 30lb. Another double cross.

Damodar sensibly suggested that we cook our small piece of meat at once, and he took over Phrupa's fireplace and proceeded to fry the meat. We were cutting the mutton from the bones when Runty came over and snatched up the largest piece. Retiring to a distant corner, he squatted, pulled out a knife, sliced up the meat and ate it raw.

Damodar experimented with a few chupatties made from the white flour. Those and the meat made up our dinner. Phrupa told us in confidence that the Chinese had demanded that he supply food for them, but he had made the excuse that trade with Nepal had been on a small scale that year due to the adverse weather and that he and his family had no reserve stock. That caused our guards no concern. They immediately commandeered our flour again. Fortunately, we had been forewarned and had hidden the bag of tsampa. The guards took one of the bags of white flour and made a batch of dough which they rolled out and cut up into squares. These were boiled in water and eaten without anything else.

I had a recurrence of dysentery and, feeling weak, I went to bed.

Early on the morning of December 13th our four Tibetan porters arrived. They were a strange, villainous-looking quartette. The leading light and spokesman was a little man wearing a red cloak and Ghurka hat. On top of the hat he had tied about half a yard of lace and a pink silk bow. Two of his partners were of average Tibetan build, but the fourth was a great hefty fellow both arrogant and impertinent.

They sat with their backs to the yard wall and Phrupa's family were forced to provide several bottles of Chang. The Chinese officer spent a few minutes giving them their instructions and then retired to his room. As the four became mellow, so they became more loose-tongued. Damodar was called over by one of them to tell them how far they were supposed to carry for us.

Damodar replied that the officers at Taklakot had stated that we would have porters to Chainpur, but we ourselves would be content if they took us only to Dhuli, the first Nepalese village. The quartette burst out laughing.

'No,' said the one with the Dior hat. 'The Chinese orders are that we drop you and your goods when we reach the entrance of the Seti gorge at Garanphu.' They had also been told that if the weather conditions deteriorated and there was a heavy fall of snow for two consecutive days, then we were to be deserted wherever we were at the time.

We exploded at this and went in to argue it out with the Chinese. All four sat round a stove made from an old ghee tin, feeding it with brushwood and dry yak dung. Phrupa acted as interpreter for Damodar and we brought matters to a head by accusing the officer of deliberately trying to encompass our deaths. He denied any such intention and said that he had instructed the porters to take us to Dhuli.

I looked at the faces of the other Chinese as the officer was speaking. Schickelgruber and Runty made no attempt to conceal their pleasure, while Chungnya looked troubled and avoided my gaze. We were leaving the room when the officer made a curious statement. He said that whatever happened, he was acting according to instructions and that orders had to be obeyed. He also admitted that his men would be remaining at Kathan for a week to ensure that we did not return in the hope of crossing either the Tinkar Lipu or Lipu Lekh pass.

As far as the Governor was concerned our fate was sealed. Damodar commented that if he died on the way back he would miss another term at college and his family would be very angry with him.

We did not know whether to believe the officer or not, and we could only wait and see. But the prospect of being deserted at the most difficult part of the return journey, several marches from the nearest Nepalese village, was a most disturbing one. The Dhuli people had no idea that we had been released, and on our way back to them we might well die of exhaustion or exposure without anyone being on hand to render assistance.

After a great deal of argument about the disposition of the loads we set off at 11 a.m. Each of the four porters dropped on his knees before the Chorten that stood a few feet from Phrupa's house. Then, shouldering their loads, they staggered off down the track towards the Kathan pass. We bade Phrupa and his family good-bye, assuring him that our impressions of Tibet and its people were good and happy. The old man, greatly touched, cried, 'Kali-Phe, Kali-Phe,' which is pronounced 'Kali Phay' and means 'Go gracefully—Go well.'

I gave a few annas to the child half-wit, and he promptly transferred them to his mouth. Whereupon he was slapped on the back by the old hag, who picked up and pocketed the money as he coughed it out.

The Chinese officer remained at Kathan and we left the village accompanied by Schicklegruber, Chungnya and Runty. Damodar, Harrop and I travelled on foot carrying our rucksacks and ice-axes. The Chinese brought their mules but, because of the slippery patches of ice that covered most of the track, had to spend most of their time on foot. We soon passed the four porters and came to the bridge where Gin-Din-Rhou and the headman of Taklakot had tethered their ponies the day we were arrested. Schickelgruber and Runty stopped to anchor their mules to a large rock, but Chungnya whipped his mount into a gallop and thundered up the track in the direction of the Kathan pass.

We soon saw what he was after. About three hundred yards away a herd of ibex had come up from the river bank and were making for the limestone cliffs flanking the lower part of the pass. When the animals saw Chungnya coming they panicked and scattered in all directions. It was only then that we realized how many there were. There must have been at least a hundred, and I counted forty in a single group which cut out from the main herd. As the ground became steeper and more difficult the mule slowed to a walk. Chungnya, Tommy gun in hand, leapt from the saddle and scrambled towards the cliff face. His efforts at hunting were in vain, for the distance between him and the agile ibex rapidly lengthened. Harrop and I were amazed at the sight of this great herd leaping about on a seemingly vertical and featureless rock face that continued its upward sweep for a couple of thousand feet.

On one occasion the rear guard caught up with the animals in front and then there was a frightful scuffle. A dozen or so were perched on a rocky pimple and, in their panic, the group behind sailed into the rear of the stationary ones. Ibex were projected everywhere. They flew from the rock point as if on wings, and I expected to see several bodies come tumbling down the face. But my expectations proved false. In that split second, as they leapt, they aimed at some small projecting piece on the cliff face and, astonishingly, found it sufficient for a hold.

The panic died down and the entire herd looked down at the mortals who had disturbed their morning stroll. I was pleased that Chungnya had failed to get near enough to use his sub-machine-gun. It lacked the range, accuracy and stopping power needed to hunt ibex, and his efforts to bring one down might have resulted in half a dozen being maimed. Chungnya glumly tied his mule to a rock and we started up the steep track that zigzagged its way towards the summit of the Kathan pass and Nepal.

Conditions had changed since the day when we had crossed the pass in the opposite direction. The lower part of the pass was covered with a great avalanche cone of hard ice. Once this had been soft snow, but constant thawing and freezing had given it the texture and surface of a skating rink. Harrop and I cut steps for the Chinese and the porters who at that time were nowhere in sight. Then, by a remarkable coincidence, I swung my axe into the ice to cut out a step and uncovered an Ovosport wrapper we had thrown away on the day that Harrop and I sat at the top of the pass waiting for Koila and Ratti to return from Kathan, the day before our arrest.

Harrop stopped for a breather and remarked that he was feeling in poor condition. I felt perfectly bloody. My knees wobbled when I walked and my boots seemed to weigh about 20lb. each. We sat on a broad flat rock and waited for the Chinese to catch us up. The Tibetan side of the pass still lay in shadow and it was bitterly cold.

Damodar voiced the thoughts of all three of us when he said, 'I don't trust those Tibetan porters.'

The big fellow, who sported a dagger with a twelve-inch blade, looked particularly suspicious and dangerous. I had the feeling that he would slit all our throats for a couple of rupees.

We had been waiting for the porters a couple of hours before we saw any sign of them, and when they came in sight they staggered along the track, hopelessly drunk, the big one in the lead. Reaching the bridge he fell flat on his face and lay there, making no attempt to rise. Their spokesman was next. He leaned his load against a rock and then slid down to a sitting position, his pack still tied to his back. The other two wandered along arm in arm, removed their packs and sat by the tall one who still lay motionless, face to the ground.

This was a discouraging start, and Harrop and I cursed the Chinese for their stupidity and incompetence. Schickelgruber swore back as if it was all our fault. There was nothing for it but to go down again. There would be no more progress that day. But what could we expect, starting on the 13th?

When we reached the Tibetans only one was conscious and he, sensibly enough, suggested that we camp right where we were and start off early the next morning.

'If we go back to Kathan,' he said, 'we will all drink Chang again.'

Schickelgruber insisted that we return to Phrupa's house, less than a couple of miles away. This time the odds were in our favour, and we told Schickelgruber that he could go to Kathan or to hell, but we were staying put. He grumbled for a few minutes and then sent Runty off to tell the sad news to the fat officer.

We pitched both our Meade tents, but the semi-conscious Tibetan said that he and his friends would rather sleep out, under their sheep-skin cloaks. We helped him drag his three unconscious companions to the shelter of a large rock and left him lighting a fire to make tea.

Chungnya borrowed the axe the Chinese had refused to return to one of our porters—Koila—when he was released from Taklakot. He proceeded to dig out tiny pieces of brushwood which grew among the stones. In five minutes the axe was ruined, the adze blade looking very much like a rake, large pieces of metal having been broken from it.

By now the sun had reached us and we sat enjoying its warmth. This would be our first night camping out and, after two months in primitive, unhygienic rooms, the prospect was, indeed, a pleasant one. To our disgust, Schickelgruber insisted on having some of our flour again. We let him have some of our white flour, our tsampa reserve being very low indeed. I doubt if we had 10lb. left.

The fat officer turned up in the middle of the afternoon and announced that he intended to discharge the four porters and send a runner for another four. But that, we feared, might take days. We decided that we preferred the devil whose acquaintance we had made rather than a complete stranger. We informed Fatty that we moved with the same porters the following morning or we all went back to Taklakot and reported his incompetence to his superiors. Not that we would have gone back to Taklakot for an Emperor's ransom. Nor would the 'Cheenee Bara Rajah Sahib' believe a word that cast doubts on the conduct and efficiency of the P.L.A.

Fatty, realizing that he could not get us back to Kathan short of carrying us bodily, conceded to our demands. To our surprise he and all the other Chinese left us at dusk. For the first time in two months we could not see a Chinese soldier in our vicinity.

We three still slept in only one of the tents in case the Tibetans decided to use the other one. They remained in the open, however, and at five the next morning we were startled by Chungnya shining a torch in our faces. He was accompanied only by Runty.

After a breakfast limited to a can of sweet tea we set off. The four Tibetans, fully recovered from their drunken orgy of the day before, carried expeditiously, and we gained the top of the pass in good time. We sat down to rest at the spot where Harrop had collected fossils two months before. To our surprise Chungnya signified that he and Runty had been instructed to accompany us to this point and no farther. Runty sat fiddling with his Tommy gun, but Chungnya, I saw, had left his behind and was wearing Schickelgruber's pistol.

It was strange, I thought, that they should not accompany us to the other side of the pass, which marked the place of our arrest.

Chapter 24

GOOD-BYE TO THE P.L.A.

PERHAPS the Chinese now realized that they had, indeed, arrested us in Nepal, and, therefore, quite illegally.

Chungnya shook hands with us and embraced us with a bear-like hug, his white teeth flashing as he grinned broadly. Runty, however, had a sickly sort of smile. In an effort to bury the hatchet, I offered him my hand and he held it limply and briefly.

We set off down the track into the Jung Jung Khola and stopped at our point of arrest. I remarked to Harrop that I would like a picture of him standing at that same point, and he obliged. Then I took one of the four porters coming down the track, turned away, and was putting the camera back in my rucksack when there was a yell from the top of the pass. Sitting on a rock ledge about 500 feet above was Runty looking at us through a pair of binoculars. Harrop looked up and saw the two Chinese disappear.

'Oh, no!' he exclaimed. 'Surely it's not a crime to take a picture here?'

The Tibetans put down their loads and said that the Chinese had shouted to them to stop. My heart sank. I had visions of a march back to Taklakot and another wearying round of explanations as to why we had committed the crime of taking a photograph in a valley consisting entirely of rock debris and limestone cliffs. Intent on saving that film, I moved behind a large stone that hid me from the track. I quickly back-wound the 35-mm. colour film from my Edixa reflex camera, removed it and replaced it with an unused black and white film. I dropped the colour cassette down the waist-band of my trousers. My trousers were tucked into puttees and the film would remain undetected provided we were not searched.

Chungnya was the first to reach us, and he looked angry, as if we had betrayed a trust. I opened the camera and handed over the unexposed film. Chungnya never doubted that I had given him the evidence that would incriminate us as spies. I tried to explain through the Tibetans, but it was useless.

I was standing there arguing when I was cut short by a vicious blow in the small of the back. Before I could move a second blow followed it, sending me sprawling on my face in the middle of the track.

Painfully turning over, I found Runty standing over me, his Tommy gun reversed. Before I could move, he swung the gun to the firing position and pulled the cocking lever back with a nervous jerk. My mouth went dry. This, I was sure, was the end. Screaming at me, he levelled the gun at my head, his bulging hate-filled eyes staring at me down the barrel.

There was a flash of khaki and Chungnya jumped in front of the gun, snatched hold of the barrel and thrust it up into the air. He waved Schickelgruber's pistol threateningly in his free hand. The argument seemed interminable, and then Runty reluctantly lowered his gun. Chungnya showed him the film and then asked us to hand over the cameras. I passed over mine and Harrop was relieved of his. Our rucksacks were searched and all the unexposed film was confiscated.

To our surprise, Chungnya told the Tibetans that we must go on and that we must not stop before nightfall. The cameras would be sent to us by runner, when we had passed a point where we could not indulge in activities harmful to the P.L.A. Damodar's rucksack was not searched, and it seemed that the Chinese did not associate him with photography.

Chungnya and Runty waved us on and we set off again. The middle of my back ached where Runty had connected with his gun-butt. I felt shaky, but was determined to put the maximum distance between myself and the Chinese before nightfall. We tried to persuade the Tibetans to hurry, but they refused to exceed their own set pace.

Losing height as we approached the river, I looked back when we reached the small bridge. Chungnya and Runty were sitting watching us through binoculars. That was an encouraging sign, for they were not rushing back to Kathan.

All three of us now voiced our fears. We did not doubt that the fat officer would either come after us or send a rider to Taklakot for instructions. Perhaps, we thought, the Chinese predilection for doing everything according to orders was now in our favour. Fatty might not dare to come after us until commanded by his superiors to do so. Time was, it seemed, the critical factor. How long would it take Chungnya and Runty if they set off right away? How long would Schickelgruber and the fat officer argue before a rider was despatched to Taklakot? How long would it take a man to ride back to H.Q., and what time would elapse before a message reached Kathan? A great deal now depended on our Tibetan porters.

To our dismay they stopped at a stream some three miles from where we had left the Chinese and announced their intention to make a brew of tea. We argued and fumed, but succeeded only in making them more obstinate. They leisurely set about collecting brushwood and yak dung and placed their pot on to boil. The thing held more than a gallon, and half an hour was lost before the water was hot enough to make the tea. The tea having been consumed, we picked up our rucksacks to leave. But their spokesman announced that they had not had sufficient tea and that they would have to make another urnful. Never in my life have I felt so helpless as I did at that moment. There was nothing at all that we could do. When more than an hour and a half had been wasted they picked up their loads and resumed the march.

At three-thirty we reached the camp site of Tharedunga, a circle of stones situated below and in full view of the track. The Tibetans informed us that they had done enough load-carrying for the day and that we would remain there for the night. Plenty of daylight remained for further advance, and we tried desperately to induce them to resume carrying, but they would have none of it. They even refused to find a less conspicuous camping site among the rocks.

Feeling thoroughly depressed, Harrop and I pitched a tent. Having no appetite, we cooked no food. Damodar suggested we ask the Tibetans for some tea to conserve our own small supply. Our request was refused, so we lit a Primus stove and made a pint of tea each, drinking it in an oppressive silence.

At dusk the Tibetans piled more wood on their fire and it snared the surrounding boulders in a weird yellow light. When we protested, they heaped more wood on the fire and produced a blaze that betrayed our exact whereabouts over a region of several miles. In the light of the fire which pierced the cotton/nylon walls of the tent I scribbled a page or two of my diary.

It was Damodar who expressed the thought which had held us silent for so long.

'I think the fat one will get troops from Taklakot and take us back.'

Regretting now that I had taken the pictures, I nodded glum agreement. Damodar asked how long it would take a Chinese escort to reach us. I said I did not think they would overtake us before early morning. Damodar shouted to the Tibetans that we wanted an early start, to which he received the surly reply that they would tell us when they considered it time to move. We lay down, but none of us could sleep. For the first time in my life I was the victim of a genuine anxiety complex.

At 10 p.m. we were startled by a shout from the track above. Looking through the tunnel entrance of the tent I saw a torch bobbing about. Harrop and Damodar were both awake, sitting bolt upright in their beds, sharing my conviction that the Chinese had arrived. The man with the torch ran past our tent into the circle of firelight. Damodar listened to the voices.

'It's a Tibetan and he has come alone.'

We leapt from the tent and joined the group sitting round the fire. Another pot of tea was on the go and the tired and thirsty runner, who had travelled from Kathan, swallowed cupful after cupful.

His thirst appeased, he handed over our two cameras, which we regarded as a good sign. He said that the Tibetans would get into serious trouble if we took any more pictures and that the cameras would have to remain in one of the kit-bags until we reached Saipal on the other side of the Urai Lekh. Whereupon the big Tibetan snatched them back and stuffed them into the bag that contained the cine-camera and the stereo camera. I noticed that a 35-mm. camera was missing.

'It's in my rucksack,' Damodar grinned, 'but I haven't any film for it.'

He questioned the runner about our film and we were surprised to learn that it had been handed over to him along with the cameras. He saw no harm in our having film if we had no camera, and he returned the film to us—three full rolls of Kodachrome, 36 frames on each.

We asked about the Chinese, and he told us that the fat officer had, as we suspected, sent a rider back to Taklakot. He would probably be along in the morning with an escort of troops to take us back. He also confirmed that the Tibetans would desert us at Garanphu, if we had the luck to get so far. Then he made a suggestion which revealed that he had little liking for the Chinese.

'I will go back now, and if they have left Kathan before I get there I will tell them that they will never overtake you because I last saw you very close to the Urai Lekh.'

When I replied that the Chinese would know how long it would take to reach the Urai Lekh, he said they could not know as they had never been there. I gave him a few rupees, thanked him for his kindness and he vanished into the darkness. The four porters urged us not to worry and assured us that their friend was very good at deceiving the Chinese.

'He will tell them that the weather is very bad here and they will go back with great speed.'

The atmosphere lost much of its tension and we sat round the fire talking through Damodar to the porters. At the best of times the Tibetan exudes no fragrance, but now, with the heat of the fire on their sheepskin clothes, our four carriers gave off the most appalling odour.

I remarked facetiously to Damodar that the big fellow sitting next to me stank like a sewer, not intending the comment to go beyond Damodar. In his innocence, however, he repeated what I had said to the Tibetan. To my surprise they all grinned broadly and the big fellow enjoyed the joke better than anyone. He said something to Damodar and they all roared with laughter. When I asked Damodar to translate he was reluctant to do so. Finally persuaded, he said:

'The big one says the Sahib himself has not the fragrance of the lotus.'

We laughed hugely at that, for it was fair comment. I had not washed at all for four days, and my most recent bath was of such distant date as to rank with history. In addition, the shirt I was wearing had not been changed for about ten weeks.

We turned in, sleeping fitfully, and waking at 6 a.m. It took considerable persuasion to get the Tibetans up and away, and they complained about the weather, for it was snowing up ahead near the Lekh. Less than an hour's walking brought us to an old moraine and we sat amongst the boulders waiting for the Tibetans.

An icy wind was springing up, and I found that the tip of my nose was frozen and lifeless. We sheltered behind a boulder regarding each other glumly, convinced that the Tibetans would not continue under such conditions. Sure enough, when they reached us they dropped their loads and said they would go no farther until the weather improved.

There was nowhere amongst the boulders where we could pitch a tent other than on the site of a snow bank that sloped away at about thirty degrees. We kept warm by levelling out a platform large enough to take the tent, while the Tibetans sat shivering in a depression behind a rock.

They then announced that they were returning to the previous night's camp, adding that, should the weather remain bad, they would be off to Kathan the following day leaving us where we were.

We took the law into our own hands, relieving them of everything save sufficient food and tea for a single meal. The rest of their food and much of their skins and spare clothing we retained as an insurance that they would return the next morning.

'That,' Harrop remarked ironically, 'was a wonderful day's march.'

We had covered a mile and a half!

If the Chinese disbelieved the runner, they were bound to be on us before nightfall.

During the afternoon it clouded right over and the wind blew hard until the evening.

The porters appeared at 9 o'clock the next morning. A glance at the head of the pass told me that it was clear. We packed in haste and were away, having breakfasted on nothing more than a tsampa sausage each and half a pint of tea. Our rucksacks on our shoulders, we moved off on the final five miles to the Urai Lekh. I had taken the spare camera from Damodar and loaded it with Kodachrome. Once the Tibetans were far enough ahead, I took a few pictures to give us a record of the lie of the country. The temperature on Harrop's thermometer registered 24 degrees below freezing, and our breath caused icicles to form on our bearded faces.

The two big lakes whose banks we had skirted in October were now frozen hard and we saved time by crossing them directly and avoiding the zigzagging, up-and-downhill track. At the end of the second lake we came to the boulder where we had cached our spring scales and enamel plates two months before. They had disappeared, taken by the wily Tibetans who had discovered them on their return from the season's trading with the Nepalese.

Damodar took advantage of the halt to wander off amongst the boulders to find a suitable place to perform what is called 'a natural function'. When I offered him some of my Chinese cotton he remarked:

'If it's the same to you, Syd Sahib, I'd rather use the Chinese flag.'

I willingly consented and performed a very dignified ceremony of handing over the pennant of the Chinese Communists to D. N. Suwal, Liaison Officer, Nepal Government; a fitting end to that trouble-making piece of bunting.

The flag episode over, we resumed our journey. It was surprising how well the four Tibetans carried their loads, moving at a much faster rate than their Nepalese counterparts. We had our work cut out to keep ahead of them.

Chapter 25

THE URAI LEKH AGAIN

AT last we reached the foot of the steep ice slope that led up to the summit of the pass. I was feeling completely spent and could hardly push one foot ahead of the other. I was revived a little when Harrop shouted back to me that he had a small flask full of cherry brandy which we had bought in Cortine D'ampezzo on our way to the Himalayas.

'We'll share it on top,' he yelled.

We wandered across the slope, taking the easiest line of approach, Harrop occasionally having to hack steps in the hard ice. I kept my eyes fixed on a point some six feet in front of me. If I looked to the top of the pass it seemed to get no nearer.

We were at approximately 19,000 feet; my nose was frozen and I only preserved circulation in my feet by waggling my toes. When it started to snow Harrop cursed audibly. It had the expected effect on the Tibetans, who shouted up that it was too late in the day to get over the Lekh and safely down the other side. When we failed to reply, they asked what the time was. My watch registered 1.15, but I told Damodar to tell them that it was only 11.45 a.m. Not believing this, they demanded to look at my 'Roleckas', and by the time they reached our level I had turned the hands back to 11.45. The Tibetans, believing the watch was bound to be right, raised no further objections.

I was so weak I even found it difficult to stay in the small steps cut by Harrop. I longed for my crampons, but they were strapped on to the back of my rucksack and I could not face the ordeal of trying to fasten them on to my boots with frozen fingers. I looked ahead. The snow, a very light fall, had stopped. The sun shone on the top of the pass and I could see the brown sentinel pillars of rock on its eastern side. I tried to cut intermediate steps to compensate for Harrop's long stride, but soon gave up.

The angle eased off suddenly, the ice slope petered out and bare patches of rock and scree were visible. Then the slope went downhill and I was looking over the other side. This was the top. It was December 16th, and the first time in history that the Urai Lekh had been crossed in winter.

The Seti valley ahead still lay under many feet of snow, but now its surface was firm and hard-frozen, offering a better proposition than the soft floury stuff that had proved so exhausting on our journey to the Urai Lekh two months before. Harrop, sitting on a rock, grinned at me and said:

'It's all downhill now.'

I nodded weary agreement. Damodar came over the top, leaned on his axe panting for breath, and said, 'Damn to the Chinese!'

Harrop produced the brandy flask from his rucksack, saying as he held it out to me, 'It's your expedition, so you have first go.'

I thanked him as graciously as I could, and proposed the toast, 'To Freedon, and damnation to the Chinese Communists.' Having emptied the flask between us, I pointed vaguely in the direction of Taklakot, saying, 'I'm sorry about all that.'

'Don't worry about a thing,' Harrop pleaded. 'The lodgings were awful, but the scenery more than made up for them.'

The Tibetans, now over the crest of the pass, were complaining bitterly about the prospects of being caught above the snowline at nightfall. As there was a chance we would not reach our old base-camp site at Saipal that night, we told them that we would stop at the first sign of running water, pitch two tents and boil their tea for them on our Primus stoves.

Damodar took a photograph of Harrop and me at the top of the pass, and I took one of the Tibetans. At first they protested and hid their faces, fearing they might suffer if the pictures were ever seen by the Chinese, but they relented after a little persuasion.

It now appeared that, once over the Urai, the Chinese were far enough away for our porters to discard their tight-lipped silence about Tibet and Chinese rule. The little red-coated Tibetan did most of the talking, the others nodding assent. He lent credence to the reports of political unrest in Tibet by claiming that while the Chinese control the long-distance tracks by day, their powers at night are restricted to the forts and mule stations. He inferred that the Chinese baggage trains are sometimes attacked in daylight, and when asked if this was the work of Jykpas (brigands) he replied, 'No, just ordinary people.'

Spontaneously, we picked up our loads and resumed our march. The slope was icy and the little fellow went down several times. Eventually the icefield levelled out, but we found to our dismay that the hardness of the surface was no longer to our advantage. The former flat surface was now a field of swords, sharp ice blades that stretched in all directions as far as the eye could see.

Snow conditions of this kind, commonly called 'Neve Penitente', occurred to a greater extent in the great Andes of the Equator. I realized grimly that I was still learning. These ice blades varied from two to three feet in height, were six inches to a foot wide, two inches thick at the base and tapered to a sharp point at the top. They were made even more formidable because none stood upright, all leaning over at an angle as their points followed the sun's course across the sky. Two months' steady freezing at night, plus a corresponding amount of evaporation due to the hot sun during the daytime, had resulted in this vast field of ice blades.

It made dangerous and painful going. Walking on the tops caused every other blade to collapse and the leg shot down into the narrow gap between the 'swords'. When we walked in the gaps the angle of the blades kept tipping us to one side. There was no easy way. We did the best we could and were extremely fortunate to escape injury. For even a minor injury at that stage must have had fatal results. We had no medical kit, and the nearest village was more than four days' march away.

Several hours on this field of blades took us no more than halfway to our old base-camp site at Saipal, and we found ourselves stumbling along in the dark. At last we reached the gravel bed where the other four members of the expedition had left us on October 19th. Here we should find water. Damodar's shout of '*Pani*' brought us to a halt. He had found the stream which was running too swiftly to freeze over. Harrop discovered a clear patch of gravel and we pitched the two Meade tents and lit our two Primus stoves. I boiled three pints of water for Harrop, Damodar and myself, but the Tibetans would accept nothing less than their 1½-gallon can full to the top. The heat loss on such a large container was so great that around 150 degrees F. the water reached a critical temperature above which it would not go. The Tibetans had to have it as it stood, for we had already wasted an hour's paraffin on it. Having consumed this, they returned with the can for a refill and were flatly refused.

That night was the coldest we experienced throughout our stay in the Himalaya. There was a steady down-draught of icy wind from the summit of the pass which gradually penetrated our double sleeping-bags. None of us slept. We shivered all night, our knees tucked up under our chins. In the tent next door one of the porters cried throughout the night.

At dawn we looked out of the tent to see the first light touching the summit of Kapkot, a 21,000-feet mountain that overlooked the site of our old base camp. We wriggled back into our bags, making no attempt to move until the sunlight reached our tent at 8 a.m. Ignoring breakfast, we packed everything as speedily as we could to make our way down beyond the snowline to Saipal. The way ahead lay over miles of ice blades, and I felt admiration for the Tibetans, each carrying more than 70 lb. over this awful surface.

Reaching the level plateau that marks the Saipal camp site, we sat down to break our fast—once more on tsampa flour—at midday.

It was a fine day and we sat with our backs to the stone walls of the Tibetan trade shelter which had performed the duty of expedition mess in September and October last. When we had last seen this little plateau it was hidden beneath several feet of fresh monsoon snow. Now it was completely clear. The only evidence that an expedition had been there at all were some empty jam tins.

At 1.30 p.m., the Tibetans having disposed of a gallon of tea, we set out for Garanphu, four and a half miles away. Like Saipal, Garanphu was simply a circle of stone shelters, used by the Tibetans when trading with the Nepalese. Garanphu is as far south as the Tibetans will go. The Dhuli natives make the three days' journey north to this point to trade their tsampa and atta flour for Tibetan rock salt.

The ground between Saipal and Garanphu is usually easy, but conditions had changed since we had last seen it. We were now faced with several huge avalanche cones which had consolidated into steep ice slopes, curving straight down into the Seti river. In September these avalanches had blocked the course of the river, but within a few days the water had carved a tunnel through the base of the hundred-yard-wide, sixty-feet-high wall of snow. The tunnels had since collapsed, leaving a vertical ice cliff verging on the edge of the river.

The crossing of the first avalanche proved the most difficult. Harrop, who was ahead of me, had to cut steps in the hard ice slope and then surmount a steep and slippery corner. I looked ahead apprehensively. When climbing the corner Harrop slipped and, for a tense moment, I feared that he was gone. He managed to steady himself by snatching at a sharp blade of ice, cutting his fingers badly in doing so.

The Tibetans, employing the ice-axes that had been left with us by Koila and his men, managed well on this difficult ground, being very sure-footed. The last to cross was their little spokesman. He slipped at the same place as Harrop, his load swinging perilously, almost dragging him over the drop. He was too short to reach a crucial handhold carved in the ice by Harrop, and he shouted for help. The big fellow responded by reaching down to lend a hand. As the short one made an upward jump to seize the outstretched hand, I saw our kit-bags beginning to slide from their crude carrier frame on his back. I shouted but the big fellow already had matters sized up and was now pulling his friend up by the scruff of his neck. As the little man sprawled over the top, his load left its fastenings and slid over the edge. The big fellow grabbed two kit-bags, but the third flew down the ice slope and over the edge of the sixty-feet ice cliff into the river. As luck would have it the bag contained most of our precious camera equipment. At the other side of the avalanche cone we went down to the river's edge to look for our kit. But it had gone.

Garanphu was reached without further incident, and we sorted out a comfortable stone shelter for ourselves. We were indeed lucky, for we found one that had escaped our attention when we passed through in September on our way north. This shelter was different, having a roof and being constructed rather like an Eskimo igloo. Each circle of stones overlapped the one below until one huge cap stone covered the top. We raised this stone by means of smaller stones to allow for ventilation. That allowed light to enter also, and we found to our joy that the previous tenants had left us a large pile of dead juniper wood. Using our inflator for a bellows, Damodar had a fine fire going inside ten minutes.

Dinner consisted of tea and some very unusual chupatties which Damodar made with a mixture of tsampa and white flour. That was the only time the white flour was used on the march. We made a small oil-lamp out of a circular cigarette tin, using a piece of Harrop's shirt tail as a wick. A fire, artificial lighting and chupatties! This was, indeed, luxury!

I asked Damodar for portents concerning the following day, when the Tibetans were to desert us. He replied that the portents must be good, for we had found a nice dry shelter, just large enough for three. Also, was not the free gift of a large pile of firewood a good omen? Perhaps there was something in Damodar's omens. Who can say? We saved enough wood for breakfast the following day and turned in only when the fire had burned down to a red glow of embers.

Having cause to go out in the middle of the night, I found the ground carpeted with snow and large soft flakes falling heavily. I wakened my companions to give them the news. From Kathan to Garanphu we had had very little snow, but such luck had been too good to hold.

Such a change in the weather at the entrance to the Seti gorge was the most unfortunate thing that could have happened, for we were about to enter on the most difficult part of our journey. This involved a march along a very sketchy track which, in places, skirted the rock face of the gorge at about mid-height. Part of the track was made up of stone staircases cleverly constructed by the Nepalese. Some of the staircases were flung out into space, being supported by tree branches jammed into crevices in the naked rock. If the extra heavy snowfalls of the 1955 season had wiped out part of the track, our position would be perilous in the extreme, for we had barely enough tsampa left to make the three-day journey to Dhuli. If we became trapped in the gorge we must either freeze or starve to death. A fresh fall of snow on that difficult stretch of track might well spell disaster for us.

The stone shelter had many advantages over a tent. The cracks in the walls were filled with mud and the three-feet-thick stone had high insulating properties. A comfortable fug had developed in the night and we rose early, to eat tsampa sausage and brew tea at first light. The temperature in a tent at that time of morning would have been much colder.

Breakfast was barely over when the Tibetans appeared to announce that they were returning to Kathan. They were worried about the change in the weather, and feared that a couple of days of heavy snowfall might make the Urai Lekh impassable.

I asked them if they would set aside the Chinese orders and carry for us to Dhuli. They replied that they feared to disobey the Chinese, for not only they but their families would be punished. I asked how much the Chinese were paying. They said, 'Four rupees,' and I offered them twenty rupees a day for the trip to Dhuli. They replied that they would not attempt the passage of the gorge at that time of the year for a thousand rupees a day.

With that they picked up their empty carrier frames and trotted rapidly along the track which led back to Saipal and the Urai pass. A few minutes later they vanished round a corner and we never saw them again.

There was no doubt that we must make the passage of the gorge immediately. To wait for the previous night's snow to clear might cause us to be imprisoned at Garanphu, for once the heavy snow started this part of the Seti valley would be cut of from Dhuli for nearly three months. With only enough tsampa for two or three days it was imperative to get out at once.

We ruthlessly jettisoned all the kit that had no survival value, reducing our equipment to sleeping-bags, air mattresses, spare clothing, one tent, tea-can, the tsampa and a little white flour, plus some

6 lb. of sugar. To save on weight we discarded the two Primus stoves and the can of paraffin. Everything would now be decided by a single throw of the dice. We must get through the gorge and down to the tree line that same night. To be caught by darkness anywhere on that track, where there was no fuel for a fire nor sufficient room to pitch a tent, would mean exposure, frostbite and certain death. As I looked down the walls of the gorge I reflected upon Sir Jacob Astly's prayer before the battle of Newbury: 'Lord, I shall be verie busie this day; I may forget thee, but do not thou forget me.'

Chapter 26

THE VALLEY OF THE SHADOW

WHEN sorting out the loads Harrop, without referring to the weight, added the 16-lb. tent to his own pack; just the sort of unselfish act I had learned to expect from him. We wasted a few minutes deliberating upon whether to take the nylon rope, but decided against it. Travelling on foot, tied together, we would be seriously handicapped and would lose a great deal of time. As a safety line it would be useless, for proper rock belays would be non-existent.

We decided that we would have to rely on our individual skill with the ice-axe. A slip by one member of the party on the difficult iced-up parts of the gorge would convert a climbing-rope into an instrument of death for all of us.

We soon spaced out along the track, Harrop leading, and Damodar behind him. I could not make as good a pace as my companions and gradually dropped behind.

The ground became steeper, the track narrower, as we gradually climbed upwards. It is a discouraging fact that in West Nepal, when following a river-course downstream, the track inexplicably nearly always climbs uphill. Naturally, it eventually goes down again, but then it also ascends again. Thus during a ten-mile march one can end up a thousand feet lower than when one started out, after having ascended and descended an extra 3,000 feet during the day.

This track was no exception. It climbed steadily away from the river level, then contoured across a steep hillside until it reached the middle of the great cliff which formed the left-hand side of the gorge.

The earlier part of the track was covered with a four-inch layer of soft wet snow which balled up on the rubber soles of our climbing-boots. I had to stop repeatedly and knock the three-inch snowball off the soles of my boots with my ice-axe. This contingency alone cost us a great deal of time. Never before had I seen rubber Vibram-type soles ball up with soft snow. The going became so bad that we had to knock the snow off every ten or twelve paces.

Our light-weight rucksacks, not meant for heavy load-carrying, swung about on our backs, frequently throwing us off balance. Once I came upon a deep scar in the snow where Harrop or Damodar had slipped off the track and braked with the axe. I wondered if I should have the strength to check myself if I slipped. I was very weary and thrust one foot in front of the other only by an effort of will.

Now and again we had to cross open gullies, and in each case the proper track had vanished into the void below. The only way across required the use of hand- and footholds, which were no more than pebbles protruding from the conglomerate surface of the gully wall. It was in one of these gullies that I overtook Harrop and Damodar. Progress was prevented by a steep ice wall on the far side of the gully, and Harrop was searching for an escape route.

He commented that he remembered this gully as one of the easier ones we had crossed in September, but it was completely unrecognizable to me. Great icicles hung overhead and a few feet below a bluish bulge of ice curved away into the void. There was no way ahead other than over the ice wall, and Harrop hacked manfully away with his ice-axe. The chips of ice, glittering in the sunlight, tinkled away down the slope to plunge over the ice bulge below. Progress was painfully slow, and I found my fingers had frozen in a set position round the head of my axe. I thawed them out in my pocket, suffering terribly as the circulation was restored.

After twenty minutes Harrop succeeded in surmounting the twenty-feet corner. We followed in his steps, moving carefully from one hold to the next, trying to maintain an upright position to prevent our feet shooting off the tiny holds. Edging round the final corner was precarious indeed, and I marvelled at Harrop's skill in cutting the steps and making the difficult moves while carrying his heavy load.

Harrop was waiting to offer assistance at the corner. Not that he could have done anything if Damodar or I had slipped. But there was worse to come. Ahead, ice sheets covered the virtually non-existent track, which sloped away at an angle of about twenty degrees, and beneath which was a drop into the river, hundreds of feet below. Occasionally we had to chip steps in the surface and move along very slowly and with infinite caution. Harrop and Damodar vanished round the next bend and I stopped to wipe the perspiration from my brow. Then I took one more step.

My right foot shot from under me and, instantly, I was flying down the slope flat on my back. I still held my ice-axe by the head in my right hand and I caught hold of the shaft with my left. The whole time I was quite unconscious of any feeling of speed or of falling through space. The load on my back impeded my efforts to turn over, but after hitting a protuberance on the ice surface I turned on to my face and was able to dig the pick into the ice. But it was no use. I was moving too quickly and ran the risk of having the axe wrenched from my grasp.

Just when I was sure that I was finished I hit soft snow. My speed diminished, and I managed to brake to a stop. I lay on my face panting for breath for several minutes before so much as attempting to move.

When I managed to stand up my legs felt like jelly. Many more minutes passed before I had sufficient confidence to move again. But maybe Damodar's omens were right after all. Another few feet and I would have plunged over the edge of a steep buttress to end my journey in the Seti river several hundred feet below.

I tried to move, only to find that I was unable to get any purchase on the hard surface beneath the snow. I would have to cut steps with the axe—the one thing I did not wish to do. But my efforts to move caused my feet to start sliding, and there was nothing for it but to begin chopping at the hard snow to form a platform on which to stand safely. This done, I looked the terrain over. The way I had come down offered no easy means of return, but over to the right the angle was less steep.

When my limbs at last stopped shaking I started to cut steps for my feet, but it was dishearteningly slow going. Inch by inch I cut those steps, only to come to a small corner where two rock walls met. I could go no farther to the right, for I was confronted by a void. I looked down. The Seti river was merely a narrow green ribbon winding its way through the gorge below. It gave me such a shock that I turned my face inwards.

Pushing my axe on to the block against which I stood I very gingerly mantelshelfed on to the top of it. Ahead, to my unspeakable relief, was a reasonable snow-slope. I picked up my axe and began the tedious, tiring task of carving out a stairway. The new snow lying on top of the old proved an unwelcome hindrance, for I had to clear it away before cutting each step.

After an unreckonable period of time, I reached the level of the track again. For the first time in my life I felt that I was on a journey that was taking me beyond the definable margin that denotes the difference between safe climbing and certain death. For the first time I experienced the melancholy feeling that this was one day's walk that I might not get through alive.

Then, suddenly, I cared no more, like a man soaked to the skin who feels happy because he cannot get any wetter. Inexplicably, I felt like that, and even more strangely I found myself uttering words that I had forgotten since childhood: 'Though I walk through the valley of the shadow of death, I will fear no evil. . . .' As I have never been of a religious turn of mind I can offer no explanation of this curious recollection.

With it, however, came the new determination, which I could not consciously summon but which had its source in some mysterious inspiration. Even if I failed to get through, I would spare nothing in my efforts to do so.

I overtook Harrop and Damodar resting at the point where the track crosses the great rock face, which posed for us the most difficult problem of the day. I made no mention of my fall, for it would have done no good. It was the way ahead which claimed all our attention, for we could see that the track had collapsed in places.

We began to inch our way forward. At one point a huge boulder barred the track we had to take, the original track having crumbled into the river. Harrop delicately edged himself past it, moving along in a sitting position, his legs dangling in space. The bulky load on his back caused him a great deal of discomfort, and for one awful moment I thought he would have to shed it to get by. Had that happened, we would have lost our tent and, worse still, Harrop would have lost his sleeping-bag.

He was safely through, however, and Damodar went next, but being smaller than Harrop he experienced less difficulty. Much less of his slender frame overhung the void. I followed, and can only describe the passage as the most difficult I had ever experienced.

Even in summer this track is not regarded as an easy one. The only animals agile enough to accompany the Dhotial natives are the load-bearing sheep. To mules, yaks or ponies the Seti gorge is impassable.

Just beyond the boulder we passed under an overhanging rock, ascended some man-made steps, and were then forced to edge along a six-inch wide, snow-covered ledge. When this terminated we found we had to leap on to the track again, some two feet beyond. The distance was not formidable, but to make the jump clad as we were and with such loads on our backs made it a terrifying task. Gradually the track petered out, and we realized that somehow or other we had taken too high a line and lost it altogether.

We were looking for a landmark, something that would pinpoint the route for us. Overhead, the face became steeper, until the perpendicular walls merged into a mass of overhanging rock. There was no exit there.

The prospect below was no more inviting. For any line of weakness leading from one ledge to another was carpeted by a winding ribbon of snow, beneath which would be a layer of ice. We edged our way down, probing with our axes. Occasionally one or the other would slip, each time managing to check his too rapid progress after a couple of feet. Suddenly Harrop let out a yell.

'There's the little col, over to the left.'

Looking in the direction he indicated, I realized that we were, at last, close to the track. But we never again discovered its true line, the snow carpet being too thick. We approached the col at too high a line and spent a very unpleasant ten minutes descending a steep snow chute. Normally cols are not found growing on a rock face. A col, of course, is a depression between two summits. The one seen by Harrop was, in fact, a depression in the top of a rock buttress projecting from the main cliff face, and which also formed one of the retaining walls of a steep wide gully which lay beyond. I remembered that on approaching the col from the other direction in September, we had to negotiate a relatively simple rock pitch of about thirty feet. What that pitch would be like now we could only guess.

We were forced to leave our snow chute at a lower level than the col, and the last thirty feet up to the little gap between the top of the buttress and the cliff face proper called for some very hard step-cutting, performed, again, by Harrop.

At the top of the col we stopped for a rest and Damodar asked the time. It was nearly 4 p.m. Hopes of getting out of the gorge in daylight were receding rapidly. We still had to cross the rock pitch, descend the gully to the river bed, and climb out of the bed across a rock face on a rock staircase that would now be plastered with ice. We then had to descend to the river bed again, reascend another rock staircase, and then cross a huge moraine before reaching a site where we could pitch a tent and where we might possibly find enough brushwood to light a fire.

Harrop volunteered to be the first to essay the rock pitch. He traversed a little ledge to a point where there were three rock steps projecting from the face, supported by branches jammed in the rocks. Here, after a slight pause, he began to chip ice from the handholds as he prepared to traverse back beneath Damodar and myself.

It was a slow business, and Harrop was forced to make several retreats to the rock steps to thaw out his frozen fingers. At one point he was spreadeagled on the holds when he shouted that he would have to let go of his axe. A moment later it dropped away into the void beneath, only to stop, standing upright, in a drift of snow about thirty feet below Harrop's feet.

Below us ran the gully which we would have to descend to reach the river level. It was a wide gully and, under normal conditions, merely a great scree chute, but now its entire surface was covered with ice. There were several hundred feet of it and it presented anything but a reassuring sight. Everything seemed to be against us. I shouted to Harrop, asking him how he was faring, and he replied that he might have to shed his rucksack to make his next move, as the weight was pulling him off backwards.

We begged him to return and let one of us have a try, but he replied that he could not. He either went on or fell off. It was as stark as that. With a desperate effort he made a swing across, his feet scrabbling against the ice-glazed rock. His foot found a tiny hold and, little by little, he transferred his weight from the ledge on which he had been standing. It was much easier for Damodar and me. Harrop had uncovered what holds there were, and our loads were not as heavy or bulky as his.

I was moving across when I heard a sharp humming sound. A patch of ice some six feet from Harrop exploded like a mortar bomb. He and Damodar moved under the shelter of the cliff face and I waited, spreadeagled on the rocks, as a barrage of fast-moving, invisible stones burst one at a time in the middle of the gully. Although we were in the shadow, the sun must still have been bathing the summits thousands of feet above, causing the discharge of mountain artillery. We waited some ten minutes, then decided that we must take our chance with the broadsides, for we could not afford to lose any more time. The passage of the thirty-feet rock pitch had cost us three-quarters of an hour.

I was now putting my feet down in the wrong places and mis-judging the distance of the handholds. That was a bad sign. Exhaustion was fast catching up on me. I took a few steps down the gully and Harrop shouted a warning. It was too late. I stepped on ice again and went sprawling on my back. This time I was saved by a patch of rough scree which projected through the ice covering. I had slithered only some twelve feet, but it was quite enough. After that I tried to exercise greater care.

I decided to let Harrop go first, for he could find a route in less time than I should find a place to stand. Damodar and I followed, slipping and sliding on our backsides, occasionally standing upright when ice was not in evidence. The angle decreased at the end of a couple of hundred feet, and we were able to walk down, picking our way amongst the huge boulders which dotted the gully bed.

Once at the river level we hurried along to the point where the flanking walls of the gorge almost join, making a narrow defile through which roars the seething waters. Here we had to follow the track across the cliff face again, using the man-made section of twisting, winding staircase. I remembered this one as having a twenty-feet rock slab in the middle which we had crossed on hand- and footholds. Fearing the worst, I was not surprised when Harrop shouted back that the slab was covered with a thin veneer of ice and was impassable.

Damodar volunteered to have a try, but we declined his offer, for a slip would result in a sixty-feet drop into the river. Even if the victim escaped drowning, he would almost certainly be injured, and if one member of the party suffered incapacitation that might spell death for all of us.

There was only one thing to do. We had to go into the river. We retraced our steps to the bank and viewed the water surging past. It looked far from inviting. In the middle it was more than waist deep and moving at a speed that would quickly render a man helpless. If we could, we had to keep in the shallows and stay close to the left-hand cliff face. Knowing it to be well past 5 p.m., I did not dare to look at my watch. It was almost dark and the steep rock walls of the gorge added a sombre atmosphere to the Stygian appearance of the river. Examination of the thermometer in the outside pocket of Harrop's rucksack showed that it registered thirty-two degrees below freezing point. It was here that Harrop made the remark mentioned in the Foreword!

I tightened my puttees around the tops of my boots and moved slowly into the water, probing with my ice-axe all the time. Before I had gone very far the icy water had worked its way through my trousers and socks and my legs and feet began to feel numb. The force of the water increased, thrusting at the backs of my legs. The walls of the gorge, acting like an echo chamber, served to greatly increase the roaring sound of the water. I tried to shout to my companions, warning them not to get too far out, but my voice was lost in the bedlam.

I was level with the left wall of the gorge now and it towered above me in a series of shadow-casting overhangs. Near the canyon walls a mass of submerged boulders made progress impossible, and I skirted them slowly, using my axe to maintain balance. The water was now up to my thighs and I feared that I might be swept off my feet or stumble on a rock at any moment. At the back of my mind lingered the anxiety that if the water became deeper and we could not get through, then we would be trapped.

Suddenly the rock walls widened and the force of the water diminished. I yelled elatedly that we had won through. Ahead I could see the river bank again, and in my excitement to reach it I almost overbalanced.

Wading out of the river I sat down on the first flat stone and removed my boots and socks. My feet were white and lifeless, without any feeling at all. Peeling off my balaclava helmet and woollen muffler, I proceeded to massage my feet vigorously with them. Harrop and Damodar joined me and did the same. I wrung out my trousers as best I could and pushed my feet into the sodden socks which had already started to freeze. A few minutes later we were on the move again, struggling along in trousers which had frozen iron stiff.

The one short cliff still to traverse gave us no difficulty at all. The only mishap occurred when I put my foot on a seemingly firm snow-covered stone only to have it overturn and plunge into the river below. After that I tested every step with the greatest care.

Soon after 6 p.m. we reached the great moraine through which the track ran. Having no chance of finding the track through such a wilderness in the dark, we contented ourselves with climbing over a succession of boulders. It was the most impressive rubbish-heap of stone I have ever seen and, in the main, it was covered with a layer of snow. We kept sliding down into shoulder-high drifts, repeatedly having to pull each other out. By the time we reached the far side we were all utterly exhausted and ready to give in. I thought it a strange stroke of fate that we should get so close to safety only to be cheated at the last moment, and I went on a little farther.

The track was narrow, steep and snow-covered, and we dare not chance being benighted on another difficult section. We looked around for a place to bivouac for the night. Harrop remarked that, with a little help, he might clear a platform big enough for our tent. I lent a hand, and we managed a space that allowed us sufficient room to rig up the tent in such a way that we had shelter for the night. We were all worried about our feet, being anxious to get them thawed out in our sleeping-bags as soon as possible.

Damodar had disappeared, and we were reminded of his existence when he shouted that he had stumbled on the remains of a long-extinct fire. That was heartening news, for it meant that wood must be available in the vicinity. A little later Damodar called that he had found a tree growing out of the cliff face and that he would try and break off some branches with his axe. In a few minutes he appeared with an armful of green wood and a broken ice-axe. This was one of half a dozen such axes we had purchased in Austria for the porters. We had resolved that Damodar should keep all his kit, including boots, windproofs, trousers, woollens and everything else, and he was now heartbroken at the ruin of the only axe he had ever owned. He cheered up greatly when I told him that he could have my Swiss axe which I had brought from England. The axe had been a present from my wife several years before and I had no wish to part with it. However, I decided that Damodar had more than earned it.

Still in our wet clothes, we sat in our sleeping-bags, trying hard to make Damodar's green wood burst into flame. After about an hour's effort we managed to make about half a cup of tea each. We were too tired to eat. I fell asleep sitting upright in my sleeping-bag.

Chapter 27

THE LAND OF THE LIVING

THAT night we slept for fourteen hours, waking on the morning of December 19th when the sun was already high in the sky.

Our trousers were still damp, but had we left them off for the night they would have frozen board hard. Breakfast consisted of tsampa and tea, well laced with sugar. The sugar must have provided the greater part of the calories we had consumed on our trip from Taklakot. It is doubtful if we ever exceeded 1,000 calories per day at any time, and it is likely that our intake on some days was as little as 800. We were using up our reserves so rapidly that we could not possibly last out much longer. Harrop announced that we had enough tsampa for one more meal, after which we would have to start eating each other.

As we packed up the tent I remarked how my longing for food had progressively become less ambitious. In Taklakot I had dreamed of roast beef. At Kathan I would have settled for a poached egg on toast, while now I would be happy to make a meal of a round of good English bread, untoasted and minus butter. Harrop said that persistent hunger had had a similar effect on him, and Damodar, who had relished our English food at base camp, now decided that he missed his native diet of rice, dhal and chupatties.

We shouldered our rucksacks, which appeared to have doubled in weight since the previous day, and set off up a steep, slippery, snow-covered track which, to our relief, eased in angle after about fifty yards. Turning the corner, we found ourselves standing on the threshold of a magnificent forest of conifers. The treeline at last! I sat down on a sweet-smelling, springy patch of pine needles and was joined by my companions. We sat in silence, no words being necessary. Overhead, small birds chirped happily in the sunshine. We were once again in the land of the living.

But our troubles were by no means over. We were much happier, but we were very weary as we resumed our march. To our relief we found the snowline was now behind us and that the track was firm and easy. At midday we stopped at a point by the river bank in the shade of a huge boulder, there making an extra large brew of what was perforce very weak tea, for there was so little left.

That day's march was a long one and, in our weary state, the weight of the loads told on us heavily. There were more stone staircases to negotiate, but these were better constructed than the ones in the upper reaches of the gorge. In the early afternoon we passed a Hindu shrine, set on a ledge in the middle of a great cliff face. Having a few annas in silver coins, I left them in the recess as an offering to the gods whose duty it is to protect travellers on this ancient route. Nightfall found us in another great forest, and we pitched our tent and camped for the night. Harrop and Damodar discovered a log of tremendous proportions, which was virtually a tree.

Damodar lit a fire, gradually heaping larger and larger logs upon it. Eventually, the big tree-trunk was alight and, soon, the intensity of the heat drove us farther and farther from the blaze. Long after we had turned in the fire burned merrily, and I remarked that, with luck, it should dry out the socks and trousers which we had left hanging on some sticks. That proved to be an error of judgment. In the morning the fire was still burning, and burning, too, were our socks. I rescued the two pairs that were mine, only to find that most of the feet had been burned away. I now had two pairs of woollen spats.

We swore and then the sight of each other's feet poking through the footless socks reduced us to laughter. Sadder but wiser, we breakfasted on a pint of tea each. The tsampa had all gone. I had eaten my share mixed as a paste with tea and sugar the night before. Dhuli was still a good day's march away and we decided to make an all-out effort to reach it before nightfall. Failing that, we should be hungry to the point of starvation.

We passed through what we called 'The Fairy Meadow', a stretch of flat terrain used by traders as camping ground. There we discovered signs of the camp site used by the other members of our expedition on their return more than two months before. A plank bridge across the Niuno Khola, a tributary of the Seti, led us on to our final stretch, the steep uphill climb of some 1,500 feet to Dhuli. We stopped repeatedly to rest, never covering more than a couple of hundred yards between halts.

The effect of the gradient on our speed was striking. On the flat we had covered a good three miles an hour. Now, the slightest incline reduced our speed to a tortoise-like pace. It was out of all proportion to the steepness of the ground and was due solely to our spent condition. I eventually reached the stage where I knew that if I sat down again I should not be able to get up. So I plodded wearily on, ignoring

Harrop's and Damodar's entreaties to stop. They rested whenever they wished, and always caught me up.

Just after midday we heard sounds of voices on the track ahead. Very soon we came upon two Dhotials, a man of middle age and a young boy of about ten years. Regardless of our ragged clothes and bearded faces, they immediately recognized us and salaamed. The man said that the people of Dhuli had prayed for us daily since hearing that we had been arrested. He was pleased indeed that we were alive, but could not understand how we had managed to cross the Urai and force the gorge at this time of the year. Nothing would persuade him or his friends to attempt a journey to Saipal until the spring.

Our chances of seeing our equipment again were nil, for the Urai Lekh would be navigable long before the gorge and the Tibetans, being first on the scene next spring, would regard what we had left behind as treasure trove.

The old man showed us the little snares he and his grandson were setting to catch the tiny deer, no bigger than a terrier, which frequent these forests. They were arranged on deer runs which, though apparent to their trained eyes, were invisible to ours.

Like a true Dhotial, the old man shouted after us as we left that the village was only just round the corner and about half a mile away. The distance, in fact, proved to be more than three miles, and we reached the outskirts three hours later. The track contoured the hillside, always rising, and running downhill on the odd occasion. I cursed these downhill stretches, knowing they would have to be paid for later on.

Just after 3 p.m. Harrop and Damodar stopped on the edge of a forest to sample some clear spring water that was cascading down the mountainside, but I, not daring to stop, went on. For what seemed an age we had been expecting that every rise would be the last one and that the next corner would bring Dhuli into view. But no, the track seemed to stretch ahead interminably. Now, however, looking down the hillside, I saw that it was terraced and cultivated. Then three women turned the corner of the track, each one carrying a brass water urn. They were on their way to the spring where Harrop and Damodar were sitting, but now they gathered round me like a trio of hens, fussing and tut-tutting. It was apparent that they knew who I was.

I could not converse with them, and, after begging to be excused, left them talking to Damodar. One more corner and I was there. A couple of houses came in sight, and a small child, seeing me, ran yelling indoors. In a matter of seconds I was surrounded by the sympathetic populace and was escorted to a plot of flat ground in front of the headman's house.

The headman appeared bearing a large hubble-bubble pipe and I was requested to help myself. I declined, signifying that all I wanted in the world was food. A straw mat, of the type on which vegetables or tobacco leaves are dried in the sun, was produced, and I was invited to sit down. Nearby, a young man, whom I recognized as one of our original expedition porters, was weaving baskets, and he offered me a cigarette. A pan was brought and I drank great draughts of the sweet-tasting mountain water.

The headman's wife went off to find some 'alu' (potatoes), the mere thought of which made my mouth water. A few moments later Harrop and Damodar arrived and we were able to converse with the villagers again. While we sat in the sun, food was prepared, and soon we were enjoying a meal of potatoes, boiled in their jackets, chupatties, wild honey and boiled eggs. It was the finest meal of my life. When it was ended we asked how much we owed and were informed that under no circumstances could they accept any reward from us.

'We have prayed for your safety and deliverance,' said the headman. 'It is sufficient reward that you are back with us, alive and well.'

The concern of these simple hill folk for our welfare was profoundly moving. I wondered if the inhabitants of the so-called civilization which we had left months before would show such concern for the safety and well-being of comparative strangers.

We were surprised to learn that a Government check post had been set up in the village since we had passed through in September, staffed with Ghurka soldiers and Indian Army officers. They were encamped about a mile from the headman's house, and the old man sent his son off to notify the officers of our presence.

Meanwhile we were shown to an upstairs room and told we could stay as long as we wished without payment. Like most top storeys in West Nepal village houses, this one had one open side, giving a commanding view of the mountain ranges to the north of the village.

We sat there waiting for the arrival of someone from the check post, and soon one of the officers appeared. Clad in a sports coat and an old pair of flannels, he was greatly surprised to see us in Dhuli. Like everyone else he thought, on our release, that we would be able to choose our return route and that we would naturally elect to cross the easier and lower Lipu Lekh into India.

Shortly afterwards the C.O. arrived, also in mufti. A most charming person named R. M. Dass, his first questions were about the alleged improvements made by the Chinese at Taklakot, with particular reference to agriculture and tractors. Harrop informed him that there had been no such improvements. To our surprise we found that Koila had been telling stories about the benefits conferred on the Tibetans by the Chinese, when he returned with the news of our arrest. We only cleared that up when we met the officials at Chainpur five days later. Koila, in fact, had been frightened into making these statements by the Chinese, who had threatened him with dire consequences if he failed to carry out their instructions and if he ever showed his face in Tibet for trade again.

We spent the latter part of the evening at the check post, where we were entertained to dinner. Mr. Dass apologized profusely for his inability to provide suitably for the occasion, but we found no cause for complaint. Dinner consisted of boiled chicken, rice, eggs, chupatties and some very pleasing but unidentified sweetmeats, followed by native wine.

The officers had a short-wave radio transmitter, but could not send out news of our release as it had broken down and would have to be taken down to the plains to repair. They had, however, a small portable battery receiver, and we tuned in to the B.B.C. overseas programme and heard a Pablo Casals recital. We then listened to the news from Radio Delhi, which made no reference to us.

'The Chinese have not yet seen fit to announce your release,' Mr. Dass said. 'Had they done so we would certainly have made some effort to reach you.'

When they asked us about the prospect of the Chinese building a strategic highway from Lhasa to Taklakot, our hosts were visibly shaken on learning that not only had the road been started, but it would be completed in less than two years. The officers escorted us back to our quarters and we promised to look in on them on our way out the following morning.

Getting started the next day was no easy task. We had the usual haggling match over wages for the two porters who were now to carry our food and equipment, and we did not get away until 2 p.m.

We called in to say farewell to the Indian officers at the check post. The C.O. asked Damodar to write out a report in Nepali for Khatmandu, and while Damodar complied Harrop and I questioned Mr. Dass about the national boundary in that area. His reply confirmed our belief that our arrest by the Chinese was illegal and irregular. Mr. Dass said:

'The frontier between Nepal and Tibet is as yet undemarcated, but I would point out that my instructions state specifically that the Jung Jung Khola is in my patrol area.'

With that we set off for Chainpur. The route we had taken on our way into the Himalayas was now blocked by heavy snowfall of September and October. Our two porters pointed up to the snow-covered 12,000-feet ridge which provides the shortest route to Chainpur, shaking their heads.

'No, sahib,' they said. 'We will have to follow the Seti river, which will take perhaps a day longer.'

They reduced our disappointment with the news that we would be able to stay in a village every night and that a wonderful variety of food would be available. That cheered us considerably and, as Harrop pointed out, another day or two was neither here nor there. One thing was now certain: we were not to celebrate Christmas at home.

As sugar and tea had not been available at Dhuli, we still had to conserve our supplies. Tsampa, too, was out of stock, and we had settled for atta, the native flour, using it to make porridge for breakfast and for dinner every day. Most of the Dhuli potato crop had been either sold or eaten, but we succeeded in buying sufficient for one meal. As a special treat, we had two very tiny, hard-boiled eggs apiece to eat on the march. We ate them as we went, trying to force the pace with our two porters in an attempt to compensate for the fact that most of daylight had gone before we left Dhuli.

Our two porters told us that they had no intention of spending a night in the open. A large and very rapacious tiger had been active between the villages of Dhuli and Kando, and although it had as yet evinced no taste for human flesh, it had killed and eaten six water-buffalo. Harrop, Damodar and I travelled very light, carrying nothing more than a spare sweater or a windproof jacket in our sacks. The effect on our performance was startling. I felt feather light and was able to keep up a faster pace than on the way into the hills several months earlier. I had not had a bout of dysentery for several days and found that, although I was lean and hungry-looking, I was, relatively speaking, in good condition for hill walking.

By dark we realized that we could not reach the village of Kando that night and our porters begged us to stop at a disused hut perched high on the mountainside. The younger of our two men, Arunya, was a born comedian and the village idiot. He was terrified of the dark and was excessively superstitious. Try as we would, we could not persuade him to go alone for water. He insisted on a companion, being afraid of the 'spirit of the stream' which had strangled a man at the same spot two years before.

I tried to find out more about this spirit, but all the porters could tell me was that a man from Kando had been found strangled with the Thuggee type 'runnel', and that it must have been the work of evil spirits. When I suggested the possibility of murder these simple hill-men were both shocked and affronted.

'No one would want to take the life of anyone else, would they, sahib?' they protested.

Murder was little known in the hill villages of West Nepal, and when the infrequent incident did occur the people could not recognize it for what it was. It was much easier to ascribe such a terrible act to 'demons'.

Our shed, for that was all it was, boasted an upper floor free of sheep droppings, so we sheltered there for the night. A stone fireplace occupied the middle of the room, and we lit a fire and cooked our potatoes. Arunya and his friend dined off half a dozen chupatties each. I asked them if they ever ate anything else, and they admitted that, although they grew potatoes, onions and other vegetables, they rarely ate them. They ate chupatties, sometimes with ghee and sometimes with honey, but generally dry. When I asked if they ever tired of chupatties, they did not understand me. Arunya thought that I was asking if illness ever caused him to refuse chupatties, and he replied that when he was ill he ate more of them than usual and was soon well again. While talking to me he was stuffing these half-cooked mon-strosities into his mouth with obvious relish. Chupatties were good, and to him each succeeding one tasted better than its predecessor.

We turned in at 8 p.m.; we into our sleeping-bags, Arunya's friend into his blanket and Arunya into a small basket he had found in the hut. The basket was only three feet square, and he curled up inside it like a dog. In the morning he was still snoring lustily under a blanket and looking very much like a basket of washing. When we told him to get up, he asked, without so much as lifting a corner of his blanket:

'Is it still dark?'

'No,' we assured him.

'Are you quite sure?'

'Quite sure.'

With that he peeped from under his cover and, having assured himself demons were nowhere in evidence, he unwound himself.

We decided against cooking breakfast and carried on to the village of Kando, where we received a warm welcome, though none of the villagers had set eyes on us before. News travels fast in the hills, and soon the entire population of Kando had turned out to see the two sahibs who had been prisoners of the 'Cheenee'. They had no potatoes, but offered to sell us atta or rice. We already had atta and we had seen enough rice to last us a lifetime. Someone made us a few chupatties for one anna (1*d.*) each, and the headman produced eight annas' worth of wild honey. Our hunger satisfied, we set out on an arduous day's march, first losing height to cross the Gad Khola, a tributary of the Seti, and then climbing some 3,000 feet out of the other side of the valley.

We reached the village of Dhalaun at 3 p.m., too spent to go farther. There we put up in a loft. During our dinner of chupatties, Damodar remarked on how the attitude of Harrop and I had changed towards the natives during our stay in Tibet and Nepal. On the way in we had been besieged by the usual crowds of villagers, at times losing our tempers when we found that we could not cook or eat a meal without a large audience. Now we accepted the scheme of things as if we had lived in the hills all our lives. The natives sat with us, handled our kit, passed around the hubble-bubble pipe—which we declined—and talked until, as if by some prearranged signal, they drifted away to their homes.

After the usual breakfast of a bowl of porridge we departed on the morning of December 23rd for Lokondo village. Arunya described the trip as 'a rather flat walk'. Surprised at this, I asked if we would be doing any uphill work.

'A little,' he replied.

'Do we go down again?'

'Just a little.' As an afterthought he added, 'Then we go up again.'

'Much?'

'Just a little.'

I now expected the worst, and was not disappointed. We had to climb something like 1,000 feet to gain the top of a ridge. We were rewarded with a splendid view of the 23,000-feet summit of Mount Saipal. The name Saipal on the map meant nothing to the local villagers, who called the mountain 'Zema'. Arunya pointed out the route taken by local trappers and hunters when skirting the great rock faces that separate Dhuli from the distant massif of Saipal (Zema). In the centre of a great rock amphitheatre was a small green meadow, described by Arunya as 'Pharali Ket', an abode of spirits and demons. We looked at this truly beautiful spot through our binoculars. A small, well-watered, lush oasis, it lay in the middle of a ten-mile-long 20,000-feet rock barrier.

Arunya remarked that the locals, when hunting, avoided the place like a plague. There were, he said, fine bears and other creatures.

'What other creatures?' I asked.

'The wild creatures of the snows.'

The word 'yeti' was unknown to him and he admitted that he had never seen one of these strange animals, nor did he wish to do so.

Seated at the top of the rise was a goatherd with his flock of load-carrying animals bound for Talkot and Chainpur. On and off we enjoyed his company for the rest of the trip. He was accompanied by a cheerful young fellow whose right leg was set in a permanently straight position, due, as he said, to poisoning caused by a thorn a few years before. He was on his way to see a herb doctor at Chainpur who would, for a fee in rupees, ease the pain a little. It was a pity that the services of a properly qualified doctor were not available anywhere in the mountains of West Nepal. This cheerful lad would have his affliction until the day he died, but he was resigned to the fact, regarding life with the buoyant philosophy of Dr. Pangloss, believing that everything was for the best.

We made up a curious cavalcade. Two unkempt, bearded Englishmen, a young Nepalese in European clothing, and the lame lad, bearing a load of cheap tobacco he had grown himself and which he hoped to sell for enough to pay for his 'treatment'. Behind us straggled the herd of goats, their little bells tinkling as they wandered along through the forests, the old goatherd striking his charges with a stick in an effort to increase the speed.

After reaching the top of the ridge the track zigzagged steeply down the other side for about 1,500 feet. Looking across the valley I could see that we faced another uphill trek of at least a couple of thousand feet before we reached our destination.

Another herd of goats approached us from below and the two men in charge announced themselves as natives of Dhuli. They were returning from a successful trading trip to Chainpur and the saddle-bags of their goats were empty. The men carried the usual wicker baskets supported by a head-band and these contained the bargains they had bought. One carried two new hubble-bubble pipes and a dozen spare bamboo stems. The other was loaded with an assortment of brass cooking-pots and a few rolls of brightly coloured Indian cotton cloth.

They were joined by a companion who came up the path leading a tiny pony by a halter. In answer to our question about using a horse in such difficult country, we were told that they had paid 250 rupees for the pony and that it was bought as an offering to the gods. The sacrifice, apparently, was inspired by the menace of the local tiger and the poor crops of the previous year.

When our porters caught us up, Arunya introduced the man carrying the hubble-bubble pipes as his father. This was followed by a family get-together and we were made the handsome offer of a goat to eat and at a very cheap price. Pleased at the old man's generosity, we asked which goat it would be.

'It isn't one of these,' he replied. 'It's dying lower down the hillside after eating a poisonous herb.'

Having thanked him for his dubious offer, we went to inspect the goat. A descent of some three hundred feet brought us to the poor creature, which was very pretty, having a long black shaggy coat reaching down to its ankles. Harrop and I watched its efforts to stand and its curious twitching fits with some misgivings.

'Ten rupees, sahib,' Arunya said.

'Three,' I replied.

'*Acha.*' And with that he cut off the goat's head with a deft stroke of his knife.

He skinned the carcase and cleaned out the offal. The young lad with the stiff leg, whom we had christened Gimpy, viewed the stomach and intestines with obvious longing, and was delighted when I said he could have them. When we added the heart, live and kidneys he was completely overwhelmed. I asked if there was any risk in eating the meat and Arunya assured me that there was not. At the worst we might have pains in the stomach and be ill for two or three days. Gimpy stuffed the bloody, dust-covered offal deep into his pile of dried tobacco leaf. Arunya added our meat to his load and we resumed our journey.

At Lokondo we were given an upstairs room and asked if any food was available. But there was only atta and rice. For some odd reason the people of Dhuli were the only ones in the upper part of the Seti valley who grew potatoes. Greatly disappointed, we settled down to cook our goat meat. No sooner had Harrop and I started to climb the mud stairs to the upper floor than we were screamed at by a woman who appeared from the room below. Three grubby little girls clung to her skirt and the woman was suckling a baby at her breast. Damodar explained that the occupants of the ground floor had got religion very bad and objected to anyone walking in or over the

kitchen with the hide of the sacred cow on their feet. I showed her
the rubber soles of our boots, but she was not to be mollified by such a
slight technicality. We took off our footwear and padded upstairs in
our almost soleless socks.

After purchasing some firewood we made a fire and most of the
juvenile population infiltrated into our loft until we were almost
squeezed out of the open side of the room, which faced west. The
main attraction was not the two Europeans, but the Li-Lo inflator.
Word had spread swiftly that the two sahibs had a new kind of rubber
bellows that brought a fire into flame as if by magic. I think a smart
salesman could do a roaring trade in India, Nepal and Tibet selling
air-mattress inflators. They were a source of wonder wherever we
went. Damodar borrowed a cooking vessel and we boiled the hind
legs of the goat. It proved insipid stuff, nothing like as tasty as
mutton.

In the morning we had to scour the village for Arunya and his
companion. Then the truth came out. They were very tired, they said,
having been up half the night skinning goats to sell to the villagers.
Arunya grinned and patted his purse. Our goat was not the only one
that had succumbed to the poisonous herbage. All told the old man
had lost half a dozen goats. Arunya knew that, had he told us this the
day before, the resultant glut on the market would have ruined his
chances of gaining as much as three rupees for the one he had sold us.

Our loads packed, we looked around for the old goatherd and
Gimpy. When these had been located we set out for Talkot.[1] We had
been wandering about half an hour over terraced fields when Damodar
asked if today was not a Christian holiday.

'What holiday?' I asked.

Then it dawned on me that it was Christmas Eve. I asked Harrop
what he wanted in his stocking and he replied: 'A grand piano. Anything smaller will fall through the holes in my socks.'

Chainpur being only one more day's march from Talkot, we
rejoiced that we would be spending Christmas Day in a reasonably
civilized place, where some of the people spoke English and where
decent food might be had.

The day's journey to Talkot was a long one but not as tiring as
the others, as there was much less uphill and a great deal of downhill
walking. The most prominent feature of the village was a very fine
white house standing on top of a spur that ran down the mountainside
towards the Seti river. We resolved that, if the house belonged to the

---

[1] Talkot is a Nepalese village—not to be confused with Taklakot in Tibet.

Rajah's family, then we should indeed enjoy a welcome. But our luck was not in, although we were not aware of it at the time.

The head people of Talkot were in the middle of a very involved dispute with the young Rajah of Bajang. It seems that, several generations ago, the ancestors of the present Rajah conquered this region of Nepal and also the greater part of Taklakot. Since that day the local people and Tibetans have regarded the rajahs as hereditary kings and paid annual tribute. Unknown to the Chinese, many of the Tibetan inhabitants of Jitkot and Taklakot still regard themselves as subjects of the Rajah and pay him collectively a tribute of thirty maunds, about 2,400 lb., of rock salt a year. This salt is transported over the Urai Lekh on sheep and yaks. At Garanphu it is transferred to the backs of Dhuli natives who carry it down to Chainpur by the same route we ourselves had taken. For the past two years the people of Talkot had seized this salt, without offering any explanation. Oom Jung, the twenty-four-year-old Rajah, who had the right to try the case and pass judgment himself, had waived this right to show the people of Talkot that judgment should not be biased against them. He had transferred the case to the court at the State capitol, Siligari Dhoti, where it would be tried by the local Governor.

The people of Talkot warned us that the big house was bursting with people. Harrop had a look inside and remarked that the attractive, white-painted exterior did indeed belie what lay inside. The place was crammed with people and was filthy.

We retired to the public guest-house, a plain stone-built structure, with open windows and doorway. The floor was deep in dust, reminding us of our cell in Taklakot. The old goatherd departed for another village and we never saw him again. Gimpy announced that he had eaten all the offal from the goat and that it tasted bitter, gave him stomach pains and made him feel sick. Apart from that, however, it was all right. As a special treat and in appreciation of our generosity, he offered to share his own meat with us.

I was surprised to learn that he had any meat, for he had previously stated that he was too poor to eat it, but he explained that he kept a little meat at home for special occasions such as this trip to the herb doctor. He produced the meat from under the pile of tobacco leaves, a filthy and disreputable piece of lamb which looked as though it had been embalmed for close on a thousand years. Gimpy said that he had had it no more than a year. But he had accepted it as payment for a small debt, and how long the previous owner had possessed it he did not know.

We declined Gimpy's offer and cooked the ribs of our goat. As they tasted 'high' we gave them to our porters, who promptly sold them to someone else. Arunya may have been the village idiot but he succeeded in selling the same piece of poisoned meat twice; initially to us and then to some other overtrusting soul.

Seeing that we did not want his meat, Gimpy returned it to its place under the tobacco leaves, as it was too valuable for him to eat. He asked what was on the menu for dinner and when he was told chupatties he beamed delightedly. He could not have been more greatly pleased had he been offered fried chicken.

Arunya soon had a pile of dough slapped into shape and Gimpy heated the thin flat cakes in the chupatty pan. Neither Harrop nor I ever quite conquered our amazement at the way these boys could put away and thoroughly enjoy one stodgy pancake after another. When we looked at them they grinned and patted their stomachs. We ate a couple of chupatties along with a small bowl of porridge, sighing for a few potatoes. As a Christmas Eve meal it was the poorest I had ever had.

Chapter 28

CHRISTMAS IN THE HIMALAYA

AT 8 a.m. on Christmas morning we emptied the last of our sugar into the porridge and drank the final cup of very weak tea, thus finishing the rations carried from Taklakot. Arunya announced that Chainpur was a very long walk, about sixteen miles away, and that we were not likely to reach it the same day. It was a cheerless possibility that on Christmas Day we might not arrive where we had friends and where good food might be available.

Gimpy bade us farewell. His herbalist lived on the other side of the river on the way to Chainpur, but on a higher level, and Gimpy was taking a different track from ours. I would have been glad to give him a few rupees to help pay for his 'treatment', but we were now reduced to a few annas and still had far to go with only atta flour to eat.

At Talkot the Seti river changes its direction from south to west, and to keep parallel with it we had to cross an unnamed tributary spanned by a well-made bridge. Arunya and his companion soon dropped behind and Harrop, seeing an easier track which, in fact, proved to be a disused leet, vanished into a forest. Damodar and I decided to face the misery of the interminable ups and downs of the track to be sure that we were travelling in the right direction. Some of the walking was pleasant, for little green meadows skirted the river, and we dawdled along, weary but happy. Chainpur lay ahead and we had visions of the wonderful dishes soon to be ours. Meanwhile, Harrop was nowhere in sight and our yells and yodels went unanswered.

Passing through a tiny village we stopped to enquire about the food prospects, Damodar addressing a young woman who was throwing hay down from the top of a haystack. A Nepalese haystack is usually in the form of a tree with the hay jammed expertly between the branches. They present a weird sight to the traveller, a ball of hay some ten or twelve feet wide perched about fifteen feet above the ground on top of a slender sapling. The answer to the food question was the same as before. If it wasn't atta and rice, it was rice and atta—a maddeningly monotonous diet.

Toiling up the hill beyond the village we looked back to see

Harrop crossing a small clearing. He waved and then was lost to sight amongst the houses. Damodar and I reached the top of our hill and sat down for a breather. A few feet away a young girl was perched on top of a twenty-feet-high tree hacking away with a sickle. Below on the ground a pile of leaves was being scattered by the faint breeze. She was cutting down fodder for the cattle. Never once did I see men doing this type of work. It was always left to the women.

From our high viewpoint we looked back towards the mountains we had left a week before. Their tops were hidden in heavy cloud, and they had only been clear for two mornings since we left Dhuli, and then by midday a thick mist had settled over them. Thank heaven, I thought, that we were not doing the trip now. Another week must have resulted in disaster.

We waited in vain for Harrop, who had taken the wrong track out of the village and was lost again. We wandered along, shouting from time to time, but our cries were muffled and lost in the dense forests through which we passed. Every time we turned a corner I saw a patch of flat ground ahead on the other side of the river, and I would shout to Damodar, 'There's Chainpur.' Always I was wrong and, after five hours, I no longer looked ahead. I simply placed one foot in front of the other, wondering wearily if I should ever arrive at Chainpur.

I cursed the map, which shows a straight track from Talkot to Chainpur, the real track being nothing like it. In places we had to cross small tributaries which meant traversing the hillside and moving ever farther from the river. Then, when a small bridge was reached, we crossed to the other side of the narrow valley and retraced our steps until we reached the banks of the Seti again. I thought this the most annoying part of the march.

Reaching the river bank we looked back upstream and could see the track turning the corner of the subsidiary valley only a few hundred yards away. Yet to get from that point to this we had been forced to make a detour of about a mile. At one point the whole mountainside for several thousand feet had collapsed, leaving a great grey scar on the steep hillside. Amongst the greenery of the forests and terraced fields these landslides leave scars which look for all the world like quarry faces, with the remaining surface covered with a cement-like dust. The track ran across this and the drop below was far from pleasant.

Although I did not know it at the time, Berkeley, one of the other four members of our expedition, had slipped on one of these landslides when returning to Chainpur. In addition to damage to his camera, he had suffered a nasty cut on his face, resulting in a scar he will bear for the rest of his life. Using his ice-axe he had managed to stop after a relatively short distance and was lucky to have escaped serious injury. The local natives think nothing of this sort of terrain and trot across the exposed places like professional tightrope walkers.

We were back on level ground when my legs began to feel like lead and I had great difficulty in keeping going at all. Then I had spells of dizziness and perspired profusely. I asked Damodar to sit down for a breather, and while we rested Harrop caught us up. He had had enough of exploration for one day, and, having covered a much greater distance than Damodar and I, resolved in future to be content with the dubious benefits of the recognized route.

I began to feel that we would never reach Chainpur, and was greatly relieved when Damodar said, 'Isn't that the school on the other side of the river?'

I looked across. It was, indeed, the school. A group of women passed us returning from work in the fields, and we asked if the bridge across the Seti was very far away. They replied that it was two miles away and that, having crossed it, we would have to walk almost that distance back to reach the school. I sighed for a boat to take us that short distance across the river, for it was impossible to ford the water.

Having wandered along the edge of a thirty-feet-high cliff for about a mile, we dropped down to the river bank where the track rambled, seemingly aimlessly, amongst tiny fields, each divided from its neighbour by a leet. The walking itself was tormenting, but the hopping from one place to another was purgatory. Every time I jumped across a small stream my legs buckled under me and I was forced to sit down. Harrop and Damodar forged ahead, but waited for me at the bridge that we might cross to Chainpur together.

'Do you remember the little shop where we bought native pipes?' Harrop said. 'Didn't they sell tea by the cup?'

That was enough. We resolved that our route to the school must be via the shop, and we wandered around the fields looking for the 'main road', a mule track from which we quickly came upon the tea-shop.

Recognizing us at once, the shopkeeper brought out all his relations to greet us. When we asked for tea, we were told, 'In just a few minutes.' At the end of a quarter of an hour the tea-making members of the family were still in the room either asking questions or sitting listening. I cried halt, saying we would answer no more questions until the tea was brought. Remembering the last cup of tea we had had in that shop, Harrop sought confirmation that the tea would not be spiced with pepper, ginger and salt. The assurance was given and, within minutes, the tea was served in a broad shallow brass bowl. It was ladled into metal cups without handles and I wrapped my once red, but now very black, handkerchief around the outside to prevent my hands from being burned.

As for food, there was only brown sugar, in the form of a cake the shape of a pudding-basin, and coconut. The native coconut grows only to the size of an apple, contains no nectar and is sold without the outer shell. One coconut was very expensive at twelve annas and a block of brown sugar also cost twelve annas. Having divided the whole into three equal portions, we sat down on a very ancient and mangy leopard skin and ate our Christmas dinner. The tea tasted wonderful, for it contained both sugar and milk. We asked if our credit still remained good and were assured that we could have whatever we liked, paying at our convenience. With that we had another round of tea, and then, prompted by a whisper from Damodar, Harrop asked if he could indent for ten cigarettes.

Being a non-smoker it had not occurred to me that my two companions were watching in torment as the shopkeeper puffed away at a cigarette. The shopkeeper produced a packet of native Bidis, at twenty-five for 2d. Both Harrop and Damodar moaned, for Bidis are made of a dried, rolled leaf, filled with a throat-searing fumigant. When they declined the shopkeeper produced another make in a gaudy packet with a picture of a railway engine on the cover. The man was smoking one of these himself and offered Harrop one as a sample. Harrop took two puffs, coughed violently and returned the sample to its owner, complaining that it tasted like 'Tibetan underwear'.

With that a superior brand of English cigarettes was produced and my companions were content.

The shopkeeper said that there was a big celebration under way at the school and that if we were not too late we might share in all the good things that the young Rajah had provided for the feast. We set off at once. The entrance to the school was a low staircase of stone leading up one side of the wall and down the other, and was flanked by two poles decorated with garlands of coloured cloth and paper flags. Almost the entire population was there, the compound in front of the school building being thronged with people. A platform had been erected in the centre of the ground and on this sat the headmaster,

Q

Mr. Ram-Watt-Awhasti, and the young Rajah, Oom Jung, wearing a neat brown suit.

It turned out that we had arrived on the annual prize day and had made our appearance in the middle of the prize-giving ceremony. One of the teachers, an Indian national named Mohan Chandra Pant, spoke perfect English. He took us in hand and we were found seats on a verandah overlooking the proceedings. The majority of the prizes consisted of reams of blotting-paper given to our expedition by the British Museum and intended for a botanical collection that never came into existence. We were glad that the other members of the expedition had put our surplus materials to good use and had not paid porters to carry back some 50 lb. of paper.

When the official proceedings ended we were surrounded by dozens of small boys, all of whom spoke good English, all asking questions about Taklakot and our treatment by the Chinese.

We asked about the other members of our expedition, and were glad to learn that everything had gone according to plan and that they had managed to get out of the Seti gorge with about twenty porter-loads of equipment. Berkeley was the first to reach Chainpur, having left Saipal a few days before Harrop, Damodar and I had started on our journey over the Urai Lekh. At Chainpur he had engaged porters and sent them back to base camp to carry everything out. Then he had continued his lone journey to Pithoragarh and later Tanakpur, where he had to arrange for the main party to be met by Indian Customs officials. When Harrop and I did not return to base camp at the appointed time, Roberts undertook to shepherd the porters back to Chainpur. He set off, leaving the two mountaineering guides, Dwyer and Henson, to wait for us. Two days later Koila and Ratti and the other two Dhotials staggered into camp after making a very hungry and exhausting journey over the Urai. Koila handed Henson my brief note and the news of our arrest was out.

A runner was sent off to Roberts to inform him of what had happened and Henson and Dwyer packed up their camp and departed when they realized that there was little likelihood of our being released for some time. Henson also said later that he presumed that, on our release, we would return to India over the simpler and much safer Lipu Lekh pass.

As Koila later confessed, his story about Chinese improvements in Tibet had been forced on him by the Chinese, of whom Koila went in mortal fear.

When tea was served the young Rajah joined us on the verandah.

The headmaster brought a brazier of charcoal from indoors and we sat and talked into the night. Both the teacher and the Rajah expressed the view that the Chinese had no territorial rights in the area where we had been arrested, and that we had been taken only because of the intensive military activity in progress in the Taklakot region.

The number of pilgrims journeying to Lake Manasarowar and to Kailas had dwindled to negligible proportions because of the Chinese interference. The Chinese had not banned Indian and Nepalese pilgrims, but had gained their end simply by making conditions impossible. One man, searched, questioned and imprisoned for a few days, frightened other prospective travellers from making the journey to what were to them the holiest places in the world.

That evening an arrangement was made whereby we were able to borrow sufficient money to buy food for our journey and hire porters for the march to Pithoragarh, ten days away. The money came from the Rajah's treasury, a tin trunk in the keeping of the headmaster. Mr. Ram-Watt-Awhasti explained to us how he came to act as the local Chancellor of the Exchequer.

The young Rajah's total income from taxation was equivalent to about £3,000 per annum, from which he paid taxes to Khatmandu, to the Central Government. He was also obliged by custom to support all his relatives, and there must have been scores of them living in the Seti valley. The residue, some £1,800, was his own. Unlike the rajahs of international fame, however, who grace the race-courses and gambling-houses of Europe, Oom Jung kept himself on something like £6 a week, donating the rest of his money to education. Thus the local school, founded by his father, receives the greater part of the income of the Kingdom of West Nepal.

Refused the State aid that all other schools in West Nepal receive, this school boasts the most comprehensive curriculum in the State. In addition to mathematics, geography and social sciences, the pupils are taught Nepali, Hindi, English and Sanskrit. Compulsory education is forbidden. Consequently the hill people have little understanding of the obvious benefits that education can bring to their children. The Rajah, faced with the problem of securing enough pupils for his school, decided on the revolutionary step of forming his own police force of two men whose duty it is to pressgang children from distant villages. The parents, if they are poor, are told that the Rajah will bear the entire cost of educating their children.

Some very tasty sweetmeats, imported from Pithoragarh by the Rajah, had been left over from the day's festivities, and these we consumed eagerly. One of the downstairs classrooms was placed at our disposal and we pitched our bedding on rush mats placed on the dried-mud floor by the children. Other than the odd chair or two, furniture was non-existent, the pupils sitting on the ground cross-legged in front of their teachers. The classrooms were used only on wet days; classes being held outside in fine weather. Of the 200 children, about a third are resident pupils who come from villages many days distant. They live on the upper floor and all cook for themselves. Owing to the caste system, central cooking is impossible. Some of the pupils were high-caste Brahmins, others Chetri caste, being sons of small landowners and men of similar position. The low-caste children, surprisingly, are the offspring of such artisans as gold- and silversmiths, shoemakers and carpenters.

Some day, with universal education, the caste system will vanish. Until it does, India and Nepal will suffer great difficulties in their political life and respective economics. We witnessed some of the errors and indignities of the caste system before we left Chainpur. A story circulating in Delhi claims that Indian chauffeurs have introduced a caste system of their own. In it there are two castes, the upper and the lower. The lower castes drive anything in the size range between an eight-horse-power family car and a Chevrolet. The higher caste drive anything bigger than a Chevrolet. Thus a chauffeur may refuse to drive your twenty-horse-power saloon, and I reflected that it was a good thing that the native porters in the hills were not like that. One look at our ragged condition and they would have disdained us.

I went to bed that night feeling all in, and on waking on Boxing Day I found I was running a high temperature and was in a feverish condition. It was dysentery again, and the worst dose I had experienced since I first contracted it in Persia. I was immensely grateful that I had suffered no such relapse on the journey from Taklakot to Dhuli. The local sanitary arrangements came under the heading of 'As you like it and wherever you can find it', and, against my will, I had to rise and begin a series of journeys to and from a field at the back of the school.

While making a sortie in the afternoon, I saw countless little spirals of smoke curling up from behind walls, from hollows in the ground and from amongst the nearby trees. Harrop informed me, in amazement, that these were from fires of boys of five to ten years of age making chupatties or boiling little bowls of rice, each group being composed of the members of a caste. We were further surprised to learn that the teachers and pupils rose at 4 a.m. and that classes started at 6 a.m. At six that morning we had heard boys singing, and Damodar explained that it was a hymn dedicated to the gods Ram and Krishna. The words started like this: 'Harri Ram, Harri Ram, Ram Ram, Harri Krishna,' 'Harri' being a form of exclamation. It had a catchy tune and by the time we left Chainpur we were able to sing it right through.

I had forgone the morning porridge, but in the afternoon I rallied when Mr. Pant, the assistant to the head, brought in a dish of boiled chicken which had been arranged by the Rajah. This was followed by chupatties, which, much to my disgust, were eaten by Harrop and Damodar.

We borrowed money to pay off our two porters from Dhuli and they left in the early afternoon. At dusk we were visited by R. M. Dass, the C.O. of the Dhuli check post. He was going to Siligari Dhoti, and from there to his home in India for a month's leave with his family. Our constant calls for tea brought the chef down from his kitchen on the top floor and kept him on the go all day. He was a pathetic figure, only nine years old, barefooted and sad and wistful, his head being tilted to one side. He never walked, performing all his duties at the double. There was no Catering Act to protect him. He was up at 4 a.m., not retiring until between eight and nine at night. He would have loved to attend the school, but his widowed mother needed the wages he earned—about ten shillings a month.

The 27th was another day of rest for me, and I was thankful indeed that we were amongst friends all of whom were greatly concerned about our safety and health. In the afternoon the students introduced Harrop and Damodar to volley ball, the games master being Chandra Pant, whose side severely trounced anyone who had the temerity to oppose them.

Early on the morning of the 28th the Rajah, along with his retinue of servants and porters, set off for Siligari Dhoti to have his case against the head people of Talkot tried by the State Governor. Harrop and Damodar went into Chainpur to visit the tea-shop to buy cigarettes for the homeward trip. They returned with 10 lb. of white sugar and a tin of Nestlé's milk. We whistled for the little cook and were soon enjoying tea with milk again. There is little fresh milk in the hill areas although the farmers all keep water-buffalo for ploughing their fields. The amount of milk they give is incredibly small. Being always in short supply, milk fetches as much as 1s. 6d. for less than half a pint, and that in a land where the average native can live comfortably on some 3s. a week. Consequently, once a child is weaned, milk no longer forms a part of its diet. The milk is sold to the middle classes who are prepared to pay the price.

When I asked if a child received milk when it was sick, I was told that it was possible, but the safest cure was for the father to kill a chicken as a sacrifice to the gods.

We found to our horror that potatoes were non-existent in Chainpur. We also tried for fish, which we knew inhabited the local streams and rivers, but none was forthcoming. We could buy only atta and rice. God preserve us, we were back on that awful diet again! I make no pretence of my dislike for that part of the native diet. Varied to some extent with concentrated European food, native diet can be interesting and very sustaining, but by itself it merely provides the means of keeping alive. Eating becomes a necessary function only and no longer a pleasure. Our porters remarked that we ate too many different things and that we ate too much. But I doubt that they found the same interest or enjoyment in their food that we did. The chupatty is the oldest form of cooked food known to man, for it dates back to the Stone Age and is the forerunner of our modern loaf.

On my third rest day I was feeling much better. By late afternoon I was able to walk into Chainpur and visit the shop again. I sat drinking tea until joined by Harrop and Damodar, when we bought another coconut apiece. When it became dark, the shopkeeper lit a hurricane lamp and we sat in a circle exchanging local gossip.

I had long since thrown the last of my underwear away and decided to have a couple of pairs of underpants made by a local tailor. With difficulty I selected a suitable cloth, decorated with hideous green stripes, preferring it to the only alternative—a bright red. The local tailor was called and presented himself outside the open front of the shop. He declined my invitation to enter as he was of low caste and would not be admitted by the shopkeeper. I stepped out into the dark, the shopkeeper following with his lantern.

My measurements were taken and we sat down to haggle over the price. We agreed on 1s. 6d. a yard for the cloth and to 4d. as the fee for making each pair of pants. When I said that I wanted them to fasten with buttons and not with tape, he asked for a little more money, and I agreed to give 8d. per pair. He went away delighted, having promised that the pants would be ready for the following day. The promise was kept and I became the owner of the brightest-coloured underwear ever seen in the whole of the Himalayas. I still wear it.

Deciding that I was fit enough to travel again, we made plans to start the following morning. At the school, the teachers hired two porters for the following day. We would have liked to take Koila with us, but he was not in the Chainpur area at the time. Our new men, 'Moti' and 'Nori', presented themselves for inspection that evening and promised to be ready for an early start the next day.

At 9 a.m. on the 29th we were on our way, cheered by the entire complement of teachers and pupils. The first lap ended at the shop, where we bought two 2-oz. packets of tea. The shopkeeper offered us a strange fruit from his garden which looked like an orange but tasted like lemon. I took a dozen at an anna each, to squeeze on to my porridge. We were then offered a fruit that looked like a lemon and which the seller claimed was a lemon. It certainly had the same shape, colour and texture of skin as a lemon, but it was about nine inches in diameter and a foot long. As he offered to give it to us, we accepted it and dumped it on to Moti's load.

Our two porters proved to be much better material than most of the scallywags we had been forced to employ on our journey from Pithoragarh to Chainpur in August. Both carried well and fast and surprised us when they complained if we stopped the day's march much before 5 p.m.

Our route took us along the north bank of the Seti river and was pleasantly flat. Encouraged by such going we made good time, but our fortune was not destined to last. At midday I began to feel ill and by 3 p.m. I was staggering all over the track. Harrop decreed that we stop just where we were, and our two porters, disappointed at the short march of eight miles, went off to find some wood. They returned with the news that the village of Sungala lay but a few hundred yards away and we went on to the village.

We were housed in a tiny loft and Damodar started the usual business of trying to buy food. But there was neither milk not potatoes, only rice and atta. But when we were asked, 'Don't the sahibs want any chickens?' I nearly dropped dead. Harrop let out a whoop and we asked how long the haggling would take. We had found that even after the price has been agreed, the locals still like to sit around and discuss the matter, being a friendly people and having nothing better to do. In this instance all the usual rules were discarded. Our offer of six rupees for a big bird was accepted instantly, and it was plucked, cleaned and delivered inside half an hour.

The fireplace in our room consisted of a circle of stones round which we and almost the entire population of the village gathered. Unlike our previous village quarters, this room lacked the usual open end, and in a very short time the atmosphere reeked of wood-smoke and sweating humanity. Everyone had a go at blowing up the fire with the Li-Lo inflator until there was grave danger of the low thatch roof catching fire.

An old woman kept screaming at us from below, though why at us I did not know. She was cooking downstairs, and every time any-one banged on the loft floor or moved his position a load of dried mud detached itself from the ceiling below and fell into her cooking-vessels. The more she screamed the more the villagers bumped the floor, until we could not hear ourselves speak above the bawling and laughter. When the chicken was cooked everyone, save half a dozen children, took their cue and said good night. I crushed some rock salt in the bottom of my cup and was soon enjoying a magnificent chicken leg. In ten minutes the entire chicken, except for the bones, had gone.

The next morning, having breakfasted on porridge with sour orange juice poured over it, we departed on the next stage of our journey. This time I carried not so much as a rucksack, Moti adding it to his load. The flat track was easy and we made good time until 3 p.m. when I again had to stop on account of general weakness and dizzy spells. The weather being pleasant, we camped on the bank of the Seti about a hundred feet below the village of Suni Khola. While our porters were collecting wood, a small boy shouted down from the village, 'Do the sahibs want to buy some tomatoes?'

The thought of tomatoes caused us to forget chupatties. The boy came down bearing twenty tiny tomatoes, each the size of a marble and less than an inch in diameter, in a palm leaf. He also had three cauliflowers with heads no bigger than golf balls. He agreed to our offer of one rupee for the lot. We were eating the tomatoes when the boy returned with a present of nine potatoes, all that the village could provide. He had no wish to accept any money, but we pressed a few annas on him. The potatoes and cauliflowers made a small but very tasty meal.

Afterwards Moti and Nori prepared to cook rice. Moti washed the rice and then left it to stand in about an inch of water in a small brass dish. While Nori lit a very tiny fire with about four sticks, Moti un-dressed completely, and while he put the pot on the fire and blew into the embers, Nori also undressed. It was now getting dark, the sun having long since disappeared behind the western hills. Damodar explained that both our porters were of the Chetri caste and that it was part of their religion that they should always be completely naked whenever they cooked rice. For nearly half an hour they sat shivering by the rice pot. It looked a very poor meal and they added nothing to it. Afterwards they dressed and curled up for the night under their blankets. We made a late-night brew of tea and used up the last of our precious condensed milk.

Curious about the football-sized lemon, Damodar cut it open right down the middle. It was filled with a layer of white pith which had a definite lemon flavour. In the centre was the replica of a normal-size juicy lemon, which proved to be quite tasteless. All the taste was in the pith. Damodar and I ate a piece each and gave the rest to the porters, who willingly accepted it, Moti hiding it beneath his blanket.

The night being clear and cool, we pitched our sleeping-bags and slept under the stars.

In the morning the same small boy came down from the village and offered us six small eggs, which we readily accepted for one rupee. These we boiled and ate spread on chupatties, the nearest thing we could get to egg on toast. I seemed to have recovered from my sickness and we put in a good day's march, following the course of the Seti for part of the day, and then turning up the banks of the Kali Gad which feeds into the Seti from the north. We had ample evidence that this was a trade route. All day long we encountered scores of people carrying loads of cloth or tins of ghee from Pithoragarh or Tanakpur, all bound for Chainpur.

We were passing a group resting at the side of the track when a man dressed in an old pair of khaki shorts and almost soleless boots sprang to his feet and ran over to us. Saluting smartly, he said, 'I am proud, sir, to make your acquaintance.' He had been in the British Army in the Ghurkas and had not seen a European for many years. We had a long chat with him before continuing on our way.

At midday Harrop said that he would wash in the river, and produced a piece of soap, bought at the Chainpur shop. We went down to the bank, stripped, and roared with laughter at each other's filthy appearance. Much scrubbing was needed to remove the hard-caked layers of dirt which we had carried on our bodies all the way from Tibet. When, at last, we had done, I felt happier, fitter and about a couple of pounds lighter. We could do nothing about our beards, although I hated every minute that I wore mine. I would have given anything for a shave at that moment.

At 5 p.m. we camped on the banks of the Kali Gad, and dined on porridge and chupatties. I sighed for a nice thick juicy steak. It was

New Year's Eve, and tomorrow we should become the Welsh Himalayan Expedition 1956 instead of 1955. The sadness of the occasion
and the lack of festivities was offset by Moti and Nori cooking rice
again. This time the temperature was well below freezing and they
must have suffered considerably.

'Tell the sahibs,' said Moti, 'that it is very cold work cooking
rice.' I looked at their shivering nakedness and told Damodar that I
knew just how cold it was and that I thought they must be barmy.
Harrop remarked that it was perhaps no more unusual than the
European habit of dressing for dinner. We laughed at the prospect
of reversed circumstances, imagining a lot of stuffed shirts sitting down
to dinner at the Savoy and then having to strip to their suspenders
before they could touch the rice pudding. That is, of course, if they
eat rice pudding at the Savoy. I would not know.

Chapter 29

THE LAST LAP

It froze hard in the night and when we woke on January 1st our sleeping-bags were covered with a stiff coating of ice caused by condensation. After porridge we started out, intent on moving north along the banks of the Kali Gad until we found a bridge that would give us access to the west bank.

No sooner had we started than we heard a loud wailing from high on the pine-covered ridge at the other side of the river. Moti and Nori wandered off ahead and Harrop, Damodar and I waited to discover the cause of the lamentations. Eventually, a long cortège wound its way down the hillside consisting of some fifty people. Four walked in front holding sticks above their heads from which were suspended a plain banner of white cloth about twenty feet in length.

Behind the banner-carriers came a group of pall-bearers carrying a human body swathed in white cotton and suspended on a stout pole carried by four men. Then came a crowd of wailing relatives. Damodar said that there must be a burning ghat somewhere on the opposite bank of the river and that we might have the good fortune to witness a Nepalese funeral. We were anxious to see this strange sight, provided of course that our curiosity did not offend the mourners. We sat down on some large flat stones and waited.

The leading figures were within twenty yards of the bank when one of them gave a signal. Every man not gainfully employed in banner- or pall-bearing dashed off into the woods in search of dry timber. We were surprised at the amount of wood they produced within a few minutes. Everything from a twig to a ten-foot tree-trunk was tossed over the edge of a small cliff on to a pebble-covered beach at the side of the river, where the pall-bearers had now gathered.

The party now divided into three groups. One lighting a fire on the river bank, the second fetching wood and the third building the burial platform at the river's edge. First, long logs were placed over the space between the boulders which were about six feet apart. Smaller branches were laid on top of the logs and an intricate platform was carefully constructed until the piled-up brushwood was about three feet in height, the base being about a foot above water level.

While this was going on, one man stood resting the pole, to which the body was tied, against his shoulder, the other end of the pole resting on a stone. Damodar said that the body must on no account touch the ground. Occasionally the fellow changed the end of the pole from one shoulder to the other, but no one offered to give him any respite.

The pyre complete, the men who had built it stripped to a tiny loin cloth and all six plunged into the icy water up to their thighs to help the pall-bearer place the body on the pyre. The swaths were cut and the pole removed. Then a man opened the side of the coverings, bared a human arm and from it pulled bangles and trinkets, handing them to a relative on the bank. Ghee was then poured over the wood to make it burn well, and the wood piling was resumed until very little of the white-shrouded body could be seen.

The half-naked men waded back on to the bank and approached the group sitting around the fire. Bundles of specially prepared faggots of pine were produced and handed over to the pyre-builders who ignited them one by one. Returning to the ghat, they entered the water, made two circuits of the body and then, standing at prearranged points around the corpse, they held the lighted bundles of wood in their right hands while, with their left hands, they splashed the icy water over their shoulders. Having done this three times, they thrust the burning pine sticks into the pyre and, inside a few minutes, the entire thing was a mass of flames.

Satisfied that their task was well done, the fire-lighters retired to the bank and resumed their clothing. Damodar said that they could not leave until the last vestige of the corpse had burned away, which sometimes required them to be on hand for a couple of days. The ceremony completed, the ashes of the deceased one would fall into the Kali Gad, to be transported by the waters through the mountains of Nepal until the river reached the plains and joined the sacred Ganges.

The people on the other bank, too busy to notice our presence earlier, were now looking at us. We salaamed, our heads bowed low, the palms of our hands together. They returned our greeting, and we departed, moving upstream.

We crossed the Kali Gad and, after a stiff climb, reached a village called 'Cheer'. Moti and Nori lost us in the ascent of the steep hillside covered with terraced fields and, thinking we intended a much longer day's march, skirted the village and passed on. We lost a good hour in finding them and persuading them to return to the village. Cheer is marked on the map as Saukatia, a name, of course, which the locals had never heard before. We found that sixty per cent of the village names shown on the $\frac{1}{4}$-inch Indian survey sheets are incorrect, bearing no relation whatever to the names used by the villagers.

We were sitting watching five men operating a sugar-cane mill when a small boy came up to say that his father would sell us some oranges. Damodar hustled off and brought back the entire village stock of 18 oranges at 2 annas apiece. We ate the lot there and then, watching the working of the primitive mill. The machinery consisted of two iron rollers geared together by a cog. The whole thing rotated by a windlass, around which four men ran, as if winding up a ship's anchor. In the middle sat the man tending the machine who was pushing long stalks of sugar cane into the mill. The resulting liquid ran down into a wide bowl placed below.

The day's work completed, the liquid was evaporated and the residue of brown sugar run into a basin-shaped mould, to be sold at 1s. for a 2-lb. block. We used it in our porridge and found that, when the hot porridge melted the brown sugar, all the dead flies and other insects that the sugar contained floated to the top, enabling us to scoop them off with a spoon. We also ate the brown sugar whole, in lumps just like treacle toffee, complete with all its dead insects. This might have been the prime cause of the hill diarrhoea to which Harrop and Damodar became addicted. Their symptoms differed from mine, but their suffering was no less acute.

We put up at a native house for the night and, for once, were left entirely to ourselves.

Our route across West Nepal the previous August had been different from the one we were now taking and none of the ground we had covered since leaving Chainpur had been familiar to us. During the next day we hoped to pass the village of Lima, which was known to us, for we had passed close to it several months before. Our route from Chainpur to Cheer had been much shorter and less exhausting than the one taken when walking into the Himalaya. All told the journey back to Pithoragarh should take only ten days as against the thirteen days it had taken in the other direction.

At 8 a.m. we set off for Lima and after an arduous climb up a steep terraced hillside reached a wide level track which, after a couple of hours' walking, brought us to a depression in a ridge that ran at right angles to our route.

Once over the other side, Lima came quickly into view and in half an hour we were sitting talking to some of the natives who had carried for us in August. Amongst these I recognized Virjeet Singh, an eleven-year-old boy who had carried an 80-lb. load. We had been ignorant of his age until the day he left us, otherwise he would have been packed off much earlier.

Food was unobtainable and once more we resumed our weary way. It was a long day's march. After Lima we contoured around a hillside for about five miles and then crossed a high col. Turning right, we followed the hillside for another mile or so and camped at 5 p.m. in a woodcutter's hut. There were some half-dozen other houses in the vicinity and the place was called Bitar, again unmarked on the map. We would have slept out of doors, but the terraced fields were thickly covered with a new layer of dung. So we savoured the doubtful benefits of the hut which had almost as much dung indoors as there was outside.

On the morning of January 3rd we started on the long journey over ridges and cols at high level to the head of the Skait river. By midday we had reached river level. After a refreshing wash we walked downstream hopping from bank to bank as the track zigzagged from one side of the river to the other. In August we had been forced to ford this river several times with the aid of fixed ropes. But now, in January, it was merely a thin stream. We were making good time and during our long march we passed two of our previous camp sites.

We tried to buy food from the villages en route, but our paper money was not acceptable. This was the first time in our travels through West Nepal that the local populace insisted on silver coinage. The last of our loose annas were gone and we had only two Nepalese rupees left. These were refused by the villagers, although the silver content of the old Nepal rupee is much greater than that of its modern Indian counterpart. Only Indian rupees would be accepted, a sure sign that India was not far away.

We camped a mile short of Bangsala, again in a woodcutter's hut. Harrop and I slept out of doors for a couple of hours and then it started to rain. Disgusted, we carried our sleeping-bags indoors and slept on a floor that seemed to be composed entirely of sharp-pointed stones.

My diary for Wednesday, January 4th, records that it rained all day. Even so we covered a record stretch of ground, doing in one day what had taken us a day and a half on our monsoon journey into Nepal in the summer. We asked some natives if it always rained at this time of the year, and they replied that they had never before known it rain in January.

Inside half an hour we were wet through, the water running down inside our trousers and into our boots. My almost sockless feet squelched about in boots that now seemed to be about two sizes too big. In the middle of nowhere we came upon a small shop that boasted a covered porch. About thirty load-carrying natives crowded into the little shelter there was and we pushed our way through. The shop was closed, the owner being asleep upstairs. We roused him by shouting and beating on the door with our ice-axes, and he came down wrapped in nothing but an old shirt, grumbling every inch of the way. He had nothing to offer except brown sugar and coconut. We bought some cheap cigarettes for Moti and Nori, adding a lump of brown sugar which they regarded as a luxury.

We were on the point of leaving when the shopkeeper said, 'Would the sahibs like some potatoes?'

We were lucky, for he had enough to last us to Baitadi, the State capital. We bought the lot and succeeded in getting a ten-rupee note changed. Then we pressed on in rain which now seemed to be falling right out of one huge bucket. I could no longer distinguish the droplets. At 5 p.m., bedraggled and thoroughly miserable, we reached Liskita, not marked on the map.

A small, very wet little boy showed us to a padlocked loft. The owner being out of town, we levered the hasp from the door frame, to which it was secured by nothing but a few nails, and went inside. We wandered about half naked and tried to dry our clothes in front of a fire, while Damodar cooked a large pot full of potatoes. At bedtime a small boy brought to the hut a kettle of tea flavoured with some kind of herbs that proved delightfully refreshing. He had been sent by a schoolmaster who lived some distance away and who had heard of our presence. A suitable note of thanks was given to the boy for delivery to our schoolmaster patron.

In the morning our clothes were still wet but we put them on, hoping they would dry on the march, which, in fact, they did. Urged on by the hope that Baitadi would provide good food, we put on a fast pace in an effort to do a march of a day and a half before nightfall. We were not clear of the village when we were accosted by a small boy who asked if we would like to buy some oranges. When we said yes he took us up a short track to his home, and wakened a skinny wizened little old man who, clad only in a loincloth, sat sleeping on the front doorstep. The old man proudly showed us his tree. It was covered with oranges ranging from the size of a pigeon's egg to some as big as tangerines. We offered to buy eight annas' worth and nearly fainted from shock when the old man said we could have five big ones for one anna.

He climbed nimbly up the slender branches and proceeded to shake down the oranges while we shouted to him where the biggest ones were. We had gained forty oranges when I asked the old man if he could change a rupee, and he said that he could not. He then said that we had better have another eight annas' worth, making it one rupee in all. With that he started shaking oranges down again and we piled them into Damodar's rucksack which, unfortunately for him, was the only one at hand.

Damodar struggled to pick up his sack which looked quite weighty. He asked if we would draw the line and let the old man have the change as *baksheesh*, to which we readily agreed. In addition to the succulent samples we were eating at the time, there were forty-eight oranges in Damodar's sack. With those we set off for Baitadi and we had consumed the lot before we had gone halfway.

At midday we passed Guru Khola, one of our camp sites of several months before. At a shop we managed to buy a very rusty-looking tin of condensed milk for the extortionate price of two rupees eight annas. Tea-shops not being in evidence, we continued until we came upon a pleasant-looking group of shops on the edge of a broad green. Tea was served without milk, and we opened our own tin. But we had been done, for it was dark brown in colour and stank to high heaven. The shopkeeper consoled us with the offer of a couple of pounds of ground (monkey) nuts, and we spent a good half-hour taking the shells off and looking for the almost non-existent kernels.

In the late afternoon we reached Baitadi to the accompaniment of cheers from the villagers who had seen us pass through four and a half months before. We reached the Governor's residence and the new Governor, Mr. Kirti-Bahadur-Bhista, came to the door to welcome us. Unlike his predecessor, Narayan Prasad, whom we had met in August, Mr. Bhista spoke perfect English.

Seated in comfortable upholstered chairs, we gave the Governor a full account of our experiences and he promised to radio the news to Khatmandu the following morning. We had seen the radio transmitter when passing through in August, but at that time there had been no operator available. Now a fully trained Ghurka from Darjeeling had been sent by the Central Government and he promised that a separate message would be transmitted for Harrop and me for the British Embassy in Khatmandu. We were thrilled at the prospect of getting news home to our families and quickly prepared a report for Colonel Proud of the Embassy. Strange to say, although the operator sent both messages to the Nepal Government the following morning, they did not release news of our arrival nor did they pass, on the message to the British Embassy, with the result that the outside world did not know that we were safe until the news spread from Pithoragarh several days later.

A young woman, whom the Governor introduced as his daughter brought in a tray loaded with sweets and biscuits. A servant woman followed bearing a beautiful tea service which, Harrop remarked, could not have been made in India. He confirmed this by looking for the maker's name on the underside of a cup. It had, in fact, been manufactured in his native Stoke-on-Trent. Tea was followed by a magnificent dinner of chicken, potatoes, dhal and rice. I begged to be excused the rice.

His Excellency was greatly disturbed at the treatment Indian and Nepalese traders were receiving at the hands of the Chinese, and he described a recent incident he had investigated. A group of traders had agreed to supply a large quantity of Indian cloth to the Chinese authorities at Taklakot against a firm contract. The order was so large that about a dozen traders had to participate to finance the deal. The cloth, made in the mills at Kanpur, was sent by rail and bus to Pithoragarh, being transported from there to Taklakot by pony.

When delivered, the Chinese refused to recognize the contract price, offering an alternative that left no margin of profit. The traders replied that they would rather take the cloth back to India than sell it at a loss. But they reckoned without the cunning of the Communists. The Chinese then informed them that it was illegal to export cloth from Tibet without written authority from their Headquarters. The permit was applied for and was, of course, refused. The matter ended with the traders selling the cloth to the Chinese for half the original purchase cost in India.

The Governor had kept press cuttings concerning our arrest and regarding the efforts made by the Indian, Nepalese and British Governments to secure our release. High-level representations in Peking at regular intervals during our captivity culminated in the events which must have convinced Peking that it was not in her interests to hold two mountaineers and a Nepalese student prisoner any longer.

Peking announced that the two foreign climbers had been released after 'admitting their guilt'. That was a good one. Any such admission would have seen us on our way to Lhasa and Chungking. The fact that the Chinese had not informed the British Government of our release until December 27th served to confirm what Harrop and I had believed all along. The Chinese had deliberately planned that we

R

should not survive to make known the truth. Final proof was provided by the Peking announcement which stated that we had been released at the Tinkar Lipu pass. All the pieces fitted most exactly. Refused exit over the Lipu or Tinkar passes, we were forced against our will over the Urai. Then the porters had been commanded to desert us. Finally the Chinese had delayed sixteen days before announcing that we had been released to guard against the possibility of anyone trying to help us. Further action had been taken to prevent assistance reaching us by the announcement that we had crossed the Tinkar pass. We had learnt a most revealing lesson concerning the duplicity and cunning of the Chinese Communists. There was mockery in Smoothy's claim: 'We are not Fascists. We are very democratic.' Perhaps they are in one respect, for death is indeed the most democratic of all human experiences.

The Governor's home being full of relatives, we were shown to a house in the main street and given an upstairs room. We retired very thankful and altogether happy. On the morrow we would be across the sacred Kali river and in the British Commonwealth again. That night we slept the sleep of the just.

Early on January 6th we bade the Governor farewell and walked down the hillside to the banks of the Kali, about 2,700 feet below. At the bridge we paused for one last look at the ancient kingdom of Nepal. A few strides carried us across the frontier into India.

At the other side of the bridge we were met by two officials in civilian dress who asked for our passports. They knew who we were, and, like everyone else, could not understand why we had made the dangerous trip through Nepal when the Indian border was so near to Taklakot. One, looking at me, said, with a fine absence of tact, 'I am sorry, sir, to witness your miserable condition.'

We wandered through the village of Julaghat in search of a tea-shop. Damodar pointed to a stall selling sweets and we purchased a large quanitty of sticky caramels which the shopkeeper called 'chocolate'. We were sitting there when two Tibetans passed, one about thirty years old, the other a lad of not more than fifteen. They were very ragged and their feet showed through their worn-out felt boots.

I called them over and asked what they were doing in India. The older one said that they had entered India to get away from the Chinese Communists. When asked if he liked the Chinese he replied, 'Two Maunds'. As this means twice 80 lb., its significance eluded me, but we all had a good laugh.

We gave them a few annas and some sweets, but when we offered a cigarette, the older one replied that he would rather have another anna. He got both. We learned from him that there were several encampments of Tibetans at Pithoragarh, and we passed more than one group before we reached our final destination.

Fortified by a couple of pints of tea at a local tea-shop, we wandered uphill through the village and camped about four miles out on the road to Pithoragarh. At 7 a.m. on January 7th we were off on the last lap, reaching Pithoragarh at three in the afternoon. Our first call was on Miss Shelby, an American missionary, who had allowed us to store equipment while in the hills and to whom we owed a great deal for hospitality shown to us early in August. Unfortunately she was away and so for that matter was the missionary, Benson Greenwold.

When we went to see Laurie Baker, an architect who lived with his wife, an Indian doctor, in the hospital and dispensary they themselves had built outside Pithoragarh, we found that Baker also was away for a few days. Mrs. Baker, however, made us very welcome, but we returned to Pithoragarh feeling frustrated because everyone we expected to see was away.

We had turned off the main highway in search of the Post Office when a gentleman in a very smart suit and bearing a silver-nobbed cane accosted us.

'Gentlemen,' he said gravely, 'I thought you were dead.'

He then introduced himself as Mr. Ghanshyam Pande, assistant magistrate for that part of Kumaon. In a matter of minutes, arrangements had been made to advance us any sum of money we cared to name. I was taken to the local hospital for treatment, and meals were ordered to be delivered to the Dak bungalow, where we were given quarters. Instructions had been sent from Delhi to Mr. Pande to render whatever aid we needed the moment he learnt that we had crossed from Tibet into India.

On hearing of our supposed release over the Tinkar pass, he had sent agents to Garbyang, the nearest Indian town to the Tinkar valley, with instructions to provide clothing, food and money, and anything else that we might need. Mr. Pande's representatives waited in vain, of course, and Mr. Pande, learning that we had been released a month before, had presumed us to be dead, as did the Chinese, no doubt.

We then received some very interesting information. About a fortnight before, an Indian trader who did a great deal of business with the Chinese passed through Pithoragarh on his way to, of all places, Lhasa. When I expressed curiosity about this incident, Mr. Pande said that this trader had explained that it was much quicker to travel across India by rail to Darjeeling, and then by pony north through Sikkim to Lhasa, than it would be to travel direct to Lhasa from Taklakot by horse, a journey which normally took several weeks.

That made sense until Mr. Pande said that this trader, who was well known to the Chinese, was a very close friend of the other Indian trader who had been arrested and held by the Communists for nine months in a cell at Taklakot. That sounded peculiar, and I asked Mr. Pande to describe this Indian who was so much a favourite of the Chinese. Mr. Pande's description served to confirm my suspicions. This Indian, dressed in good-quality gaberdine trousers and coat, wore a fine pair of black riding-boots that laced up the back of the calf, and, even more important, he had two gold teeth. It was none other than the spy who had searched us on the day that we arrived at Taklakot.

We explained to Mr. Pande the real purpose of this Indian, and he expressed the opinion that his Government would like to have a long chat with that fellow the next time he showed his face in the country. The reasons for his journeys through India became more and more obvious. Travelling down through the Kali valley from Taklakot he would be able to observe the full strength of the Indian check posts and note the progress the Indians were making on their new road that is to link Delhi to the frontier at Garbyang.

At the other end of his journey across India he could make similar observations on his way to the Sikkim-Tibet frontier. If he wished to reach Lhasa in a hurry, he could travel by horse from Taklakot until he reached the most western point of the new highway, journeying from there to Lhasa by truck. Harrop and I marvelled at the impertinence of the man, stalking through India wearing a pair of Chinese officer's riding-boots.

The dates mentioned by Mr. Pande suggested that this spy left Taklakot several days after Harrop and I had been released. Yet when Mr. Pande questioned him about us he denied any knowledge of our arrest and whereabouts. He might have said that we had been released and been forced over the Urai Lekh into the West Nepal Himalaya, but, being a loyal Communist stooge, he kept silent. As for his claim that he was a friend of the Indian who had been arrested and held for nine months at Taklakot, it was obvious that he had befriended the man on instructions from the Chinese and had later produced the trumped-up evidence that had resulted in the victim's detention.

We commented on the number of impoverished-looking Tibetans we had seen, remarking that there appeared to be no restrictions on their movements, such as the ones the Chinese imposed on travellers in Tibet. We learned that the Indian Government, being sympathetic to the plight of the Tibetan people, allowed them to travel wherever they wished, without hindrance, provided they returned to Tibet after six months. The Tibetans, on crossing into India, were given a chit stating that they must recross the frontier on a certain date. The Tibetans proceeded to beg their way across the United Provinces, making a better living than was possible under the harsh rule and heavy taxation of the Chinese. The six months up, they walked back over the border, stayed a day in Tibet and then returned to present themselves at an Indian check post for another 'six months' chitty'.

Leaving Mr. Pande, we headed for the Treasury, bearing a note that entitled us to draw the amount of rupees we needed. On the way we came upon a group of very ragged and poverty-stricken Tibetans, bearing their belongings on little wooden frames on their backs. We stopped to have a chat with them. Their ancestors had lived for generations near Kailas and had farmed and grazed their own land until the Chinese came. Resenting the new taxation and Chinese methods, they had resisted forcibly. The Chinese had reacted by confiscating their family lands and seizing their yaks and sheep to feed the P.L.A. They and their children were left on the desolate plain with nothing save the clothes they were wearing.

Forsaking the land and a way of life that had been theirs for countless centuries, they made the march to the Indian border, being fed on the way by sympathetic villagers. They were quite happy working or begging in India, and none desired to return to Tibet while the Chinese were in occupation. We received a graphic description of a Chinese soldier bullying Tibetan people, and we heard again the same shouts and oaths we had come to recognize during our stay at Taklakot. When offered a packet of cigarettes, they said they preferred money, so we gave them both.

Thanks to Mr. Pande, we were able to repay the loan from the Rajah and were also able to purchase a shirt apiece and some socks. I could not remember when I had last worn a clean shirt.

We wired Delhi and the news was out. Our friend Alex Campbell came out to meet us in his car, bringing sufficient funds for us to discharge our debt to the Treasury. We journeyed by bus to Loharghat where we picked up Campbell's car. Two days later we arrived in Delhi.

We spent the next two days trying to adapt ourselves to a normal routine again. Comfortable chairs seemed to be an extravagant luxury and every time anyone said 'Hello' I expected it to be followed by the phrase, 'Now answer more honestly.' Good food gave me severe indigestion and spirits were definitely taboo. We reported to the U.K. High Commission and the Nepalese Embassy, and it was there that we said good-bye to Damodar.

As in all Embassies, the atmosphere was awfully nice and just a little stuffy. Now and again somebody said something just to break the awkward silence. I went to the door with Alex Campbell, and Damodar followed us out. I tried to think of something fitting to say. Then Damodar said: 'The Chinese. We gave 'em hell, didn't we?' He grinned all over his lovable friendly face.

'Yes, Damodar, we gave 'em hell. What's more we got through and that's something Smoothy and the old Governor won't like.' As we drove out of the grounds I looked back. Damodar stood, a small, lonely figure; he was waving something. It was my ice-axe.

EPILOGUE

SINCE this book was written, news of open revolt against Chinese Communist rule has leaked from Tibet. In one area a Chinese garrison of 850 troops was wiped out to a man. Before a support force of 30,000 men could be brought up to pacify the area, the Chinese had to withdraw from eight provincial regions in Eastern Tibet.

Characteristically, the Communists have retaliated with harsh and brutal repressive measures. Whole villages and monasteries have been destroyed by aerial bombing, artillery and mortar fire and the survivors have been subjected to severe reprisals. It is also known that the strategic highway which runs from Chungking to Lhasa via Chamdo has been cut in several places and rendered temporarily useless. This by simple peasants and nomad herdsmen armed only with swords and primitive muzzle-loading rifles.

It says much for the steadfast courage of the Tibetan people that they have rejected thought reform and political indoctrination and retained their independence of thought and action. The reader will also recall that during my interrogations the Chinese claimed territorial rights over land where people of remote Tibetan extraction lived. This is further reflected in the news item from Burma that Chinese Communist troops had invaded Northern Burma on a 150-mile front to a depth of 60 miles and had distributed leaflets to the native population informing them that they were really citizens of Tibet and were now to consider themselves to be under the suzerainty of Communist China.

With reference to Chinese Communist justice, or those aspects of it that were revealed to Harrop and me at Taklakot, a remarkable pamphlet on the subject has recently been published by the International Court of Jurists at The Hague. Excerpts from this are quoted in the *Journal of the Royal Central Asian Society*, April, 1956, in the article 'Law in Communist China'. The author of this pamphlet, Father Bonnichon, formerly Dean of the Faculty of Laws at University Aurore, Shanghai, was imprisoned by the Chinese Communists. He quotes a statement made by the judge at his trial which is singularly revealing: 'If you have been arrested, it is not without reason, for the Government acts always in the right. It is therefore certain that you are guilty.'

One of the principles used at the political trials in China today, and which is even put down in writing, is, '*Defence amounts to revolt*'.

Some interesting news from Tibet is also contained in the *Himalayan Journal*, 1955–56, in the article 'Three Months in Upper Garhwal and Adjacent Tibet', by Gurdial Singh. This article is an account of a pilgrimage which Gurdial Singh and an Indian friend made to Manasarowar and Kailas in 1954. Singh states that he and his friend were stopped near Manasarowar by two Chinese soldiers and were asked if they were carrying cameras. On the advice of the Indian Government cameras and maps (both of which are illegal in Tibet) had been left at the Indian check post at Hoti, in Garwhal. Singh also states that all Indian pilgrims and traders entering the Taklakot area have their persons and their baggage searched by the Chinese. A nation which carries out such stringent security measures in a remote mountain area *must have something to hide*.

In the same issue of the *Himalayan Journal*, Ian Davidson gives a brief but very interesting account of the Oxford University Expedition to West Nepal, 1954. They visited the same area as our party and used the same base camp at Saipal trading ground in the upper reaches of the Seti valley. Davidson finishes his story by stating that when his party was breaking camp for the return march through Nepal to India, Nepalese traders coming over the Urai Lekh pass told him that the Chinese garrison at Taklakot knew of the existence and whereabouts of the expedition and were sending over a party of soldiers to arrest them.

It is, then, perhaps as well that, due to the difficulty of travel caused by deep snow prevailing at the time, only Harrop and I fell into Chinese Communist hands. Given fine weather all the time, we might have been rewarded with the spectacle of a whole company of Chinese soldiers descending on our base camp in West Nepal.

What the build-up of forces, the strategic highway and the resulting security curtain portend for the future of India and Nepal remains a subject for speculation. But it is false to regard the Himalaya as an invincible protection against a Chinese Communist invasion of Nepal, India and Pakistan. Before the days of the five-ton truck, trench mortars and Tommy guns, these regions were invaded in force by the Chinese armies. The past may not point the future, but it should not be ignored.

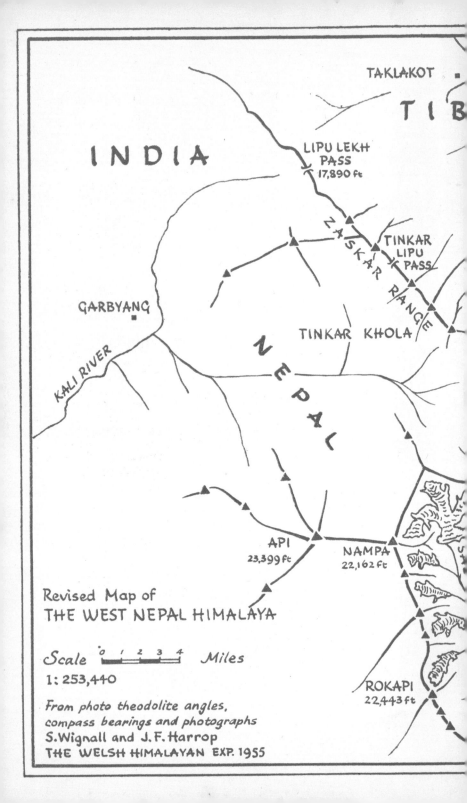